THE SALTY SHORE

Also by John Leather

The Northseamen
Gaff Rig
Clinker Boatbuilding
Barges
Spritsails and Lugsails
Sail and Oar
World Warships in Review 1860 – 1906
The Sailor's Coast
A Panorama of Gaff Rig
Colin Archer and the Seaworthy Double-Ender
Modern Development in Yacht Design (joint author)
Smacks and Bawleys
Albert Strange – Yacht Designer and Artist
The Gaff Rig Handbook

THE SALTY SHORE

The Story of the River Blackwater

by

JOHN LEATHER

Seafarer Books

2003

First published in 1979
Terence Dalton Limited

Reprinted in this edition by:
Seafarer Books
102 Redwald Road
Rendlesham
Woodbridge
Suffolk IP12 2TE

ISBN 0 9542750 1 2

British Library Cataloguing in Publication Data
Leather, John
  The salty shore
  1.Shipping – England – Blackwater Estuary – History
  I.Title
  387 .5 ' 09426756

  ISBN 0954275012

Text photoset in 11/12 pt Garamond

Cover design by Louis Mackay

Printed in Great Britain at
The Lavenham Press Limited
Lavenham, Suffolk

Contents

Index of Illustrations

Acknowledgements

THIS book owes much to Hervey Benham of West Mersea, an old friend whose splendid *Last Stronghold of Sail*, published thirty years ago and too long out of print, inspired a youthful exploration of the Blackwater under sail, the first of many happy times spent on its waters in my own and other craft. Besides, Hervey has always been generous with information and has provided several illustrations. Frequent invitations over the years to sail or fish from West Mersea on board his yachts and small craft have always proved a delight and his knowledge of the Blackwater and its history is unparalleled.

Jack Mole of West Mersea has contributed his lifetime's experience of oyster cultivation and memories of his days spent yachting led me to meet his old friend Jim Mussett, who has sailed in smacks and large yachts and can tell from experience what it was to be one of the crew of a first class racing yacht. John Frost has given the views of one of the present generation of progressive Mersea fishermen and Tony Purnell, who has joined that fortunate community who live and sail at West Mersea, has helped in several ways.

Mersea men Peter French, Harold Cutts, Ken Gowen, John Milgate, Ruben Pullen, Ernie Ponder, Lewis Hewes, Ben Clark and his brother Albert, Jack Owen and others have, over the years, added enlightenment on many aspects of the Blackwater, about whose marine life few know so much as Michael Frost of Colchester, owner of the river's oldest smack, the *Boadicea*, which he rebuilt a few years ago with his own hands.

Also at West Mersea Donald Rainbird, Paddy Hare and Donald Pye have helped by providing information and photographs. Fid Harnack's paintings have been a constant source of inspiration and pleasure as have the drawings of the late Archie White, another gifted Mersea artist.

Bygone Tollesbury came to life from the recollections of the late A. E. South who served in smacks and large yachts and raced in an America's Cup challenge while modern sailmaker Gayle Heard has contributed to my understanding of the village's continuing determination to keep ahead in sailing.

At Maldon Fred Taylor, Cliff Cook, Ted Pitt and Alf Last added many recollections while Sam Poulton, Tom Hedgecock and Gerald Denis assisted with photographs and reminiscence.

ACKNOWLEDGEMENTS

Tom Cardnell helped with references to Lawley and with illustrations. Arthur Bennett provided photographs and tales of his days sailing these waters in his yacht barges *June* and *Henry* and at Heybridge Basin Mr Clarke, the lock master, was able to answer several queries.

The splendid photography of the late Douglas Went of Brightlingsea has brought life to many chapters and Mrs A. E. French of West Mersea kindly loaned the painting of the smack *Daisy Belle* for use as the dust jacket.

Author's acknowledgements tend to overlook their publishers. With mine I share a common interest in endeavouring to produce a good book and their patience and skill in achievement results from friendly co-operation, which has added considerably to the pleasure of its writing.

John Leather
Cowes, Isle of Wight
1979

Author's note to second edition

Since this book was written a quarter-century ago, some of those mentioned have passed on, but their friendship and contributions to my understanding of the river are gratefully remembered.

Fortunately the Blackwater remains little changed and still offers the delights which inspired these writings and almost sixty years continuing enjoyment of its waters and watersides.

John Leather
Fringringhoe, Essex
2003

Introduction

IT WAS an east coast morning to make your heart glad. A spring day of
lightness and bold cloud. I sat with Tony Purnell, an old sailing friend,
breakfasting at his home, looking out from Maldon's little hill, down the
winding course of the Blackwater River. A light breeze set moored dinghies
dancing on the high water and stirred the bowed topmasts and canted sprits of
sailing barges by the town quay, where masts of sailing smacks showed above the
red tiled roofs of Cook's bargeyard, below the tree-bowered church. Small
fishing boats throbbed downstream, round Herring Point, past tree-crowded
Northey Island and the cluster of masts that was Heybridge Basin, swinging
through Colliers Reach towards the mass of Osea Island, which held the mid-
ground of our view, silhouetted by the river broadening beyond. A slick of golden
glitter spread there from rays striking down from the sun lipping a cloud, until
the estuary ran golden with light, eastward towards the distant North Sea. ''The
Incomparable Blackwater'' Arnold Bennett called it, and he was right. It has not
the dramatic charm of some rivers but the subtle appeal of its estuary, a finger of
the North Sea, the wide skies and salting bounded shores backed by undulating
fields, wooded Essex countryside and old traditions make it fascinating and
timeless. I have always regarded it as the salty shore, correctly as the Blackwater
is the saltiest river in England, rivalled only by the Cheshire Dee.

We ate and watched the play of light and shade on river panorama and I
knew I would write this book to express something of the story of the Blackwater;
its seafarers, fishermen, yachtsmen, boatbuilders, sailmakers, wildfowlers and
others of varied occupations whose lives were linked to the pulse of the tides,
strengths of winds and changing seasons rather than time tables and production
schedules.

The Blackwater shares a common, shoal-studded estuary with the River Colne
and is entered between Sales Point to the south and Mersea Island to the north.
The approach may be from the Wallet, a deep water channel following the Essex
coast from the Naze to Colne Point, or from the river Colne itself, where to save
time rounding the southern extremity of the Bench Head shoal, small craft
drawing a maximum of 4 feet can use a swatchway across the Cocum Hills flats.
But sizeable craft should pass close to the south of the Bench Head buoy from

which the Blackwater stretches 14½ miles to the town of Maldon, at its navigable head. The tides are reasonable in strength and range, running at about one and a half knots on the flood and two knots at ebb, the stream turning at about high and low water.

"Maldon River" some call it, though Mersea and Tollesbury men stoutly resist the name. It runs generally in a west, south-west direction from its mouth for a distance of six and a half miles to Osea Island. The width between shores at the mouth is about one and a half miles but the extensive flats on each side narrow the navigable channel to about half a mile at low water. However, this width is maintained until Mill Point, about four miles upstream, where the river trends more southerly to skirt Osea Island and the channel narrows to about 400 yards. From the mouth to Osea Island, a least depth of about 12 feet can be found and there are some deep holes in the channel where, since the 1920s, large merchant ships have been laid up at various times because of the river's moderate dues.

Unlike the Colne, the Blackwater's size dominates its shipping. A score of 12,000 tonners can, and sometimes do, lay-up between Stone and Bradwell Point without putting the river out of scale. From the Bench Head buoy the Blackwater spreads to the west, wide, often windswept and if the wind is strong and is over the tide, raising a short, breaking sea to greet an incomer with wavetop spray and force him to tack. The low profile of Mersea Island lies to the north and the shallow flats off East Mersea run well out to pick up the keels of the unwary and although accidents are fortunately few, some craft have been damaged and occasionally wrecked on that shore in strong south or south-east winds. One way to avoid them is to keep the black shed on Packing Shed island, at the entrance to the West Mersea creeks, clear of West Mersea church tower and the few trees remaining around it.

St Peter's Flats extend seaward a considerable distance from Sales Point and are unmarked, though the shallower water can generally be quickly spotted in daylight by its brown colour, from the mud and sand washing off or stirred by a brisk wind and chop. The south shore of the lower Blackwater is low, flat and marshy but behind its sea-wall face the land rises and has many trees. On the opposite shore the long shape of Mersea Island has trees along much of its length, marking hedgerows and roads, with a few plantations.

Man has known and used the river for centuries. Ancient British settled by its shores; Romans created ports, fortifications and villas, and relished its oysters; Saxons and other Europeans invaded and colonised, Norsemen raided and plundered and subsequent generations of English history have sailed from it and lived by it. Yet the Blackwater remains largely unspoiled. The winds can blow unhindered across its lower waters and best of all it has a spaciousness denied to many east coast rivers. Broad mudflats stretch to the tidelines, glittering in the sun at low water, reaching to the cant of saltings hazy with sea lavender and bordered by green sea walls behind which cart tracks once cut rutted brown ways to tiny barge quays built out from the walls, the foreshore mud then carefully kept clear of big stones, soggy timber and other refuse likely to damage a barge's vulnerable flat bottom. Local farms are extensive but are withdrawn from the river, flanked by red tiled or thatched barns and often shaded by tall elms reaching away down the field boundaries like hedgerow sentinels, towards the river walls. This is a river where perhaps plough and sail have met and mingled more than elsewhere in Britain.

The Blackwater compares well with the Solent in size and appearance, fostering almost as many (we think better) yachtsmen on its broad waters and narrow creeks; boatbuilders and sailmakers flourish along its shores; oyster, trawl and other fisheries survive and a strong sense of tradition runs through all these activities though, as many are, the participants are youthful and use the most modern craft, methods and materials. The Blackwater, and indeed all north-east Essex, has the East Anglian atmosphere of long tradition buttressing present actions and thoughts for the future. The Blackwater communities had slightly different values and opportunities than their contemporaries elsewhere. Theirs was a generally quieter way of life. Here were few heroics, few dramatic traditions, but a quiet tale of waterside communities and a subtly salty way of life; unostentatious, continuing, unconciously felt and relished by its participants, transmitted through succeeding generations and regarded as worth savouring by growing numbers of amateur sailing people during this century. West Mersea and Maldon are now its principal centres but Tollesbury was always a vigorous fishing village and for the first forty years of this century became a rising centre of professional yachting.

Bradwell, Tollesbury, Salcott, the Stumble, Thirslet Creek, Goldhanger, Steeple Stone, Lawling Creek, Osea Island, Northey, Herring Point . . . what lovely names they are, spoken with a fine, round sea flavour. These creeks and islands and the little communities have been the homes of generations of smacksmen, bargemen and wildfowlers. They are rich in memories and abounding in local lore. The Colne men were, generally, more thrusting and competitive; always building bigger smacks, faster yachts, larger ships; restlessly seeking advancement in general seafaring and particularly rising to international fame in yacht racing. In contrast, the Blackwater's maritime population were more content and generally preferred a quieter life; barging, oyster dredging, trawling, often within the river and its estuary; usually content with smaller smacks and returns, entering professional yachting much later than their neighbours in the Colne and then principally from Tollesbury, with some West Mersea men joining in. There was an air of kindliness about many of them, often lacking in their Colne contemporaries; almost a deceptive atmosphere of gentle seafaring, if one did not know that any maritime living in the days of sail was hard and precarious.

Happily the Blackwater's past does not overshadow its future. Although the oyster fisheries have declined there are more young men fishing from West Mersea now than for many years, using gear and boats their fathers could not imagine a quarter-century ago. They work as far afield as Whitby, on the Yorkshire coast and the Solent. A busy sail loft sends its sails all over the world, two yachtyards build and repair yachts and boats and the village yacht designers produce craft whose elegance is admired throughout the sailing world. Three yacht and sailing clubs flourish, catering for the landsman's apparently insatiable appetite for maritime activities.

Across the river, Bradwell Creek is overshadowed by a bulky nuclear power station and is crowded in summer with craft which cannot squeeze into the deep-dug marina above the old barge quay. The creek resounds with voices and energetic activities from the sailing centre and the *Green Man* continues to attract mariners from Mersea and elsewhere.

Tollesbury, at the head of its winding creek, has revived with a crowded yacht harbour, wood and plastic boatbuilding, a sailmaking business and a flourishing sailing club. Upstream, hundreds of dinghies throng Steeple Stone and yacht moorings fill Lawling Creek. Heybridge and its Basin is also crowded and wooden yachts are built on its foreshore. Spritsail barges line Maldon quay under the low hill with its distinctive church and the *Jolly Sailor* pub at its foot, but they are pleasure craft now and the timber cargoes entering this ancient port arrive in motor coasters which have to pick their way through the scores of yacht moorings lining the narrow channel. Maldon still has fishermen, a barge yard, yachtyards and a busy sail loft. It is the limit of navigation, though the river continues inland.

This watery heritage of the Blackwater should be protected against un-desirable change. The movement of population into north-east Essex and consequent need for leisure facilities has brought pressure on the Blackwater. Its waters and shores should be developed to a plan for the positive conservation of the oyster and other fisheries and for recreational use to the exclusion of most commercial development.

It is a river of enjoyable and ever-changing moods; incredibly blue under a summer sun, particularly with the south-easter of afternoon blowing fresh, bringing the smoky haze of fine weather to the coast and sending yachts, smacks and barges bowling along, crunching over the short seas outward bound or rolling home into the afternoon sunshine. Misty horizons of spring and autumn contrast with the stark clarity of atmosphere presaging a summer blow, bringing the steep, tumbling waves of a "wind over tide" beat upriver and the always surprising rough and tumble of the narrows between Osea Island and the Stansgate shore. There are the quiet times; washing down after anchoring in Thirslet Creek on a summer night of phosphorescence, when the deck ran with the liquid fire of those strange marine organisms, whose remnants were traceable next morning on the varnished covering boards.

The dinghy sailor can spend a pleasant day in the creeks in wind and sun, alive to the pull of sheet and tremble of the tiller. There is never much sea and the banks do not withold wind, except at low water. At high water he might sail miles inland and find wind sighing over the marsh grass and spiralling larks singing above saltings dusted with purple sea lavender. There are evocative sounds. The chirrup of patent blocks as a little fleet of smacks prepares to get under way in the Deeps and Thornfleet; voices echoing across the creeks in friendly banter before the annual town regatta smack race; big jibs being roused along bowsprits, old hands at the tillers and young ones at the sheets.

Clammy dawns, creeping, under oars, through misty curtains rolling over creeks whose muddy waters gurgle grey between the boundary muds; the grey sea walls unseen above and moored yachts looming like supertankers. A fleet of racing dinghies running hard, strung down the Nass towards the Seaview mark, sails sunlit brilliant white against the black north-westerly clouds before they gybe with a wham, in turn around the bobbing, glistening yellow buoy.

Winter fishing. Blackwater herrings shining dim white as the drift net is hauled over the boat's gunwale. Then the stove-crackling warmth of the cabin, with scaly oilskins swinging slow arcs on the bulkhead as she rolls to the anchor. The rich smell of fried herring. Mugs of scalding tea and then delicious sleep. Finger tingling wildfowling. The discomfort of cold, damp, saturated clothing. Ears and eyes straining towards the gabble of wildfowl on a tideline invisible in the freezing blackness of a winter morning, before the dawn flight.

Wind on the marshes. The call of the curlew and the chuckle of the tide at the forefoot of a dinghy stemming down a brim full creek; this magic is still there on the Blackwater for those who seek it. May it always be so.

CHAPTER ONE

The Island Which Is Too Good To Leave

THIRTY years ago I first sailed into the River Blackwater, bound on a cruise in a small cutter loaned to myself and two other shipyard apprentices by Bob Sainty, a fellow shipyard worker whose generosity and trust have never been forgotten. Our fancy was drawn to the river after reading Hervey Benham's then just published book, *Last Stronghold of Sail*, in which he caught the full flavour of the Blackwater seafarers and their craft in a manner which compelled us to seek out those salty creeks and quiet watersides for ourselves, becoming acquainted with the river and its mariners from the deck of a small yacht rather than our bicycles. In those days, not so very long ago, the brown-sailed barges and little cutter smacks were still working from the river. The yachts there were mostly not those we knew, there were strange one-design classes and we knew that the girls of Mersea were remarkably attractive.

We were a merry crew and the *Girl Pat* was well laden; the forepeak stuffed with seabags, oilskins, guernseys and waterboots. The cabin full of blankets, food, gramophone, records, hoopnets, fishing lines, air gun, sailing books and charts; Uffa Fox and Joshua Slocum mixed up with tins of jam, records, parcels from Woolworths and cameras. The lockers stuffed with food for at least a week and all the excitement of a great adventure.

As we reached the Bench Head buoy, taking the responsibility of our three foot draught as seriously as the master of one of the 10,000 ton ships then laid up in the Blackwater ahead, we took the first of the flood into the river, which spreads west, wide and windswept with wind over the tide forcing us to tack and raising a short breaking sea, greeting us with salt spray. The low profile of Mersea Island lay to the north and the shallow flats of the quaintly named Cocum Hills, to which we sometimes rowed to rake cockles, run well out to pick up the keels of the unwary.

We were bound for Mersea but as the cutter beat upriver the Bradwell shore became clearer as our tacks took us south to the unmarked edge of St Peter's Flats, spreading eastward from Sales Point and defined by the brown coloured water from the mud and sand washing up in the chop.

Most yachtsmen entering the Blackwater are bound for or are attracted to the anchorage at West Mersea; a village now grown to small-town size at the

The spirit of the Blackwater. A smack yacht chases a sailing smack in West Mersea Town Regatta, 1938, with the south shore of Mersea Island in the background.   *Douglas Went*

western end of Mersea Island. Mersea is an oval shaped, agricultural island five miles long and two wide, with a low ridge running lengthways down it. It is divided from the mainland by the salting-edged channels of Pyefleet Creek which leads off the River Colne, opposite Brightlingsea and at the western end by the Strood Channel; a creek merging with Mersea Fleet off the village hard and flowing into the Deeps, which is the approach channel to West Mersea and its anchorage for deep draught craft. Nowadays this is the only swinging anchorage remaining, since the Thornfleet, the other principal creek and the Ray, which continues its course towards Peldon, along with Mersea Fleet, the Strood Channel and Buzzon Creek are all filled with moorings or piles for yachts and boats, giving the place an air of activity, with comings and goings at all hours. Other creeks lead off from the Deeps and Quarters; to Tollesbury and Salcott and Virley, villages across the marshes to the west, nestling against the low rise of the hinterland. But it is the masts of Mersea which attract the eye and the wooded atmosphere of its lanes and roads, where houses settle back amongst the trees or peer boldly over the saltings along the Coast Road.

Arriving at Mersea by water is a delight but somehow I always think of coming to it from the land. For me West Mersea holds some of the happiest memories of childhood. My earliest recollections of it are set in the mid-1930s when our approach was by the black tarmac road to the island causeway over the Strood, joining Mersea to ''England'' as some islanders liked to put it.

The ''Old City'', West Mersea, 1907. William Wyatt's small boatbuilding shed at left, the site of the present Dabchicks Sailing Club. The carriers to Colchester started from here, often with the day's oysters despatched in barrels for the railway station.   *from a drawing by E. H. Oliver*

From our home in the rural village of Fingringhoe, not far from the River Colne and the maritime village of Rowhedge, I, my parents and friends often cycled to West Mersea at week-ends or holidays. If we were late starting in the morning or were too early in the afternoon at spring tides, we arrived at the Strood before the lapping tide had ebbed from covering the roadway on the Strood causeway so, with bikes laid in the spiky marsh grass, we sat and waited the waters dropping and gleefully anticipated the splash when Berry's bus drove boldly through with a bow wave like a destroyer. Afterwards we resumed our pedalling over the wet tarmac, covered with newly stranded driftwood, marsh litter and small crabs, towards that magic island. I can recall my first view of the Blackwater from the Coast Road near the church and the thrilling dash down "Monkey House steps" to the crisp, shingly beach where little high water waves were tumbled in by a brisk westerly wind which set the whole estuary dancing with sun sparkle. There were tantalising views of garden slopes of the houses clustered beyond the church, some with fascinating little private doors and gateways opening on to the beach; what possibilities of pleasure unfolded—if only one's parents lived there! I remember leaving Mersea with regret. I still do, for it has most of the magical attractions of youth; it is an island, an anchorage, has boatyards and sailmakers, yachts, boats and fishing vessels in profusion, quiet lanes, snug homes and not too many inhabitants, besides all the splendid sailing waters of the Blackwater and Colne estuary on its doorstep.

West Mersea stands on a low hill with the church and centre of the village on the south-facing, sunny slope, overlooking the Blackwater and the creeks. This is the village of the Hewes, Mussetts, De Witts, Frenches, Pullens, Rudlins, Cudmores, Carters, Brands, Howards and others whose descendants still live there; oystermen, winklers, yacht hands, good boat sailers, boatbuilders, sailmakers and bargemen. There, houses nestle amongst the trees at odd angles and winding lanes run to the waterside. Here is an almost rural quiet and, more important to many, a sense of tranquillity now unfortunately rare in most communities. Perhaps this had something to do with the apparent reluctance of West Mersea men, good seamen though they are, to stray far away from the Blackwater in the days of working sail. While Colnesiders fished their bold cutters and ketches all over the North Sea, down Channel and often far beyond, the Mersea men usually preferred to dredge and trawl in the Blackwater or the Wallet; rarely venturing into the Swin. Who can blame them? As Hervey Benham has written, "Mersea is all too good to leave."

The threadbare, tide-washed hulks of two large old smacks lay on the hard at the foot of Firs Chase and in childhood provided many a happy hour of playing during these all too short visits to the Coast Road and hard and the little wooden cottages of the "Old City"; the quaint and ancient name of the part of the village where the Coast Road ends. Here was a world of tarry boatbuilding sheds, a sail loft and boats and yachts of many shapes and sizes lying at

3

intriguing angles in the mud berths. One could paddle and splash around the strange floating oyster shed called ''The Legend'' and by the yachts hauled up on the cradles of Clarke and Carter's adjacent slipways. Or enjoy windy high waters with white sails and the creek lap-lapping at the bows and lands of scores of dinghies moored off the hard. There was cheerful laughter from the Yacht Club lawn, where finishing guns boomed and members and their friends took afternoon tea in those last years of the 'thirties, which retained an almost Edwardian calm under the recurring threat of war.

The hard was greatest fun on a sunny, spring tide high water, with boats sailing up to the road and a cluster of dinghies, rowing and sailing, alongside the wooden causeway which runs down to the low water mark. One summer afternoon my father and I stood on the causeway admiring yachts in the anchorage and watching the small boats come and go. A lugsail dinghy rushed towards the clutter of boats bobbing alongside, sailed by a boy of my age. She flew in before the smart south-westerly breeze and shot head to wind, lugsail aflutter, by our feet as the boy reached out to catch a nonchalant turn through a ringbolt with his painter. She was honey-coloured with golden varnish, from her spruce planking to the yards of her lug with its racing number, for she was one of the West Mersea Yacht Club 10-foot class; a beautiful piece of island boatbuilding by Mr Clarke. My father said, ''When you can sail a boat like that I will try to buy you one.'' I never forgot my envy of that boy's ability or of his bright-varnished, immaculate dinghy. Thirty years later we bought two of that class of boat for our then young son David and daughter Susan, who have both sailed them as well as the boy of long ago and both boats are treasured by their owners.

The Mersea anchorage and its associated creeks are a dinghy sailor's paradise, broad and windswept at high water, narrow, secretive and intriguing at low tide, when the brown muds uncover and the yachts' hulls sink down out of sight behind Cobmarsh, Packing Marsh, the Middle Ooze and the Ray Mud. Nowadays they stretch the moorings up the Strood channel, down the top of Deeps and into the entrance of Salcott Creek; that charmingly unspoiled waterway probing deep towards the marsh farms of Wigborough and Salcott, where the high waters of summer afternoons seem timeless and a 10 foot dinghy seems a craft sufficient for anyone, her active turning and reaching to the very cant of the saltings mocking the inactivity of expensive cruisers and offshore racers swinging to moorings lower down. I am convinced that besides the waters of the Colne, I most enjoy sailing at West Mersea where the magic of childhood seems to linger for many besides myself. Truly, happiness afloat is a 10 foot dinghy!

*   *   *

The Romans appreciated Mersea and Counts of the Saxon shore reputedly lived near the temple which stood on the site of West Mersea Hall, near the church. Their men watched the Blackwater against raiders and obtained native oysters from the river and its creeks. All of them forded across the strood, where the present causeway carries the road from Colchester. There are few early records of Mersea's maritime interests but around 1300 A.D. now unlikely places such as East Mersea and Salcott owned coastal shipping and were the homes of hardy seamen. Although agricultural East Mersea has bred few mariners during recent centuries, in 1547 fishing boats from there were, amongst others from Maldon, Colchester, Fingringhoe and St Osyth, landing sprats near the Tower of London.

The face of the oysterman; George Stoker of West Mersea in 1944 (left).
Charlie Hewes, foreman of the Tollesbury and Mersea Oyster Fishery Company, 1938 (right).

Hervey Benham

5

But oysters were the backbone of Mersea's fisheries. In 1770 the 25-ton smack *Neptune* was built at Rowhedge for a West Mersea oysterman who paid £120 for her. By then the village had a fleet of smacks, some of which ventured in the North Sea fisheries, though most worked at oyster dredging in the Blackwater.

On 2nd September 1789 an oyster fishery protection association was formed on the Blackwater and Colne Rivers by thirteen West Mersea oyster merchants, with eleven from Brightlingsea, three from Wivenhoe and three from Tollesbury. Meetings were held in Colchester and members paid a half-yearly subscription of two shillings in the pound of their annual rents for the layings, plus four shillings for each boat. The first year's income was £33. 4s. This association was dissolved in 1790 but was reformed with all West Mersea members, who held their meetings at the *White Hart*, the village pub where so much local oyster and regatta business has been transacted.

There were then layings in Salcott Fleet, Salcott Creek above the sluice, Tollesbury Fleet, Dyche, the fleet below the causeway, and elsewhere.

One entry in the association accounts was:

"May 7th 1802. Jonathan Cadman having run up Salcoat Fleet at an improper time of tide—came ashore on Mrs. Elizabeth Overall's laying but in consideration of the said Jon Cadman paying 10s 6d for expenses and 4s for advertisement in the Chelmsford Chronicle acknowleding his fault, no prosecution was instituted against him."

The principal object of the association appears to have been the apprehending of thieves. Oyster poaching was then frequent but detection less so, despite the rewards which were offered. In the harsh social conditions and poverty of the times the temptation to steal oysters from the extensive layings must have been immense. If caught thieves faced severe penalties. At the Easter sessions in 1811:

"Jas. Cook for dredging and carrying away a quantity of oysters. The chairman told the prisoner he was found guilty of felony which subjected him to transportation for seven years but the court in mercy to him only sentenced him to twelve months imprisonment and hard labour in the county goal."

At times, oyster merchants from Rowhedge, Brightlingsea, Burnham and Tollesbury subscribed to the association funds, presumably to assist in proceedings against thieves who obviously operated throughout the area. The association built a watch house which was manned by one employee and by members. Its situation is unknown. In 1818 Jack Hubbard was appointed watchman at ten shillings per week. By 1824 the watchman went afloat when the boat *Sarah* was purchased at a cost of six shillings and his wages had risen to

Mersea oysterman, Bob South, and the Woolf Brothers floating oyster shed, known as "The Legend". Mersea hard, 1945.

sixteen shillings weekly. Much of this time appears to have been spent in warning-off smacks anchoring over or likely to ground on the oyster layings. The association appears to have ended in 1830, but some expenditure continued for three further years.

Thomas Brand, grandfather of Miss Sybil Brand who has recorded so much of Mersea's social history, was an oyster merchant, following the business of his father William Brand. Oystermen then usually had several apprentices to help work the layings and assist on board their smacks. Thomas Brand had several from the workhouse indentured to him, as did many other oyster merchants and fishermen around the coasts. In the manner of the times, these boys from poverty-stricken homes or orphaned or abandoned children were indentured at an early age and boarded at their "master's" house, where they slept in wooden bunks and fed with the family.

Early in the nineteenth century some Mersea smacks joined many from the Colne villages in dredging sea oysters and scallops "down Channel" in early summer, catches being sent to the London market. The Essex smacks sailed for Jersey and Falmouth in February or March and were away for about three months. In January 1831 the Mersea smack *Mayflower* sank off the Isle of Wight with the loss of her crew of five, described as the worst misfortune to a Mersea smack in thirty years.

Some Mersea smacks voyaged to Norway, perhaps in the lobster carrying trade from there to Harwich and the Thames in which smacks from Harwich and the Colne participated. In 1839 the Mersea smack *Essex* unloaded a total of 41 Norwegian ponies at Brightlingsea. She probably carried them six or eight at a time in stalls in the hold.

During the 1860s, West Mersea was described as a "Pleasant fishing and bathing village" with a population of about 930. Amongst the waterside community were several who described themselves as "Oyster Merchant and fowler", including Arnold Freshwater, James Hempstead, John Innes, John May, John and William Mussett, James Mussett and his son, James junior. James Mussett also supplied marine stores, including rope and paints, blocks and gear of all kinds. William Rudlin, one of Mersea's three carriers, took quantities of fish, winkles and oysters to Colchester in his horse van, starting off from the small quay where the Dabchicks Sailing Club now stands, then known as the No'the. He brought back many kinds of goods including twist tobacco for the fishermen. His service was rivalled by the Cudmore family.

Oyster pits at West Mersea in the evening sunlight of a winter's day. The Packing Shed island in the middle distance, across Mersea Fleet.

West Mersea smacks in light airs, 1935. *Douglas Went*

Bathing machines were then kept on the shingle beach below the church and James Mussett junior was also described as a "fish and coal merchant and bathing machine owner". High above, on the coast road lookout, John Underwood the coastguard officer and his ten men kept watch over the lower Blackwater and along the road at the old city, Thomas Wyatt was the village shipwright and boatbuilder, with a young son, William, beginning to toddle about the yard.

9

Besides the local craft, the Mersea creeks were visited by many other vessels; barges, ketches and brigs came to lay on the hard and discharge coal into a yard where part of Clarke and Carter's laying-up premises are now. Occasionally French long lining luggers called to buy herring for bait and a few cockney peter boats visited when their crews came to stop the creeks for flounders. During the 1870s several Mersea smacks, including the quaintly named *Palestine* owned by the George Brands, father and son, sailed to the French coast for the scallop dredging season out of Étaples and also dredged sea oysters in the English Channel, on the Varne and the Royal Sovereign grounds in company with smacks from the Colne, Emsworth and Bosham in Sussex.

Few great events have affected Mersea's peace. It was "Shook up considerable" by the Essex earthquake of 1884 when both East and West Mersea churches were damaged and houses at the Strood and the *Peldon Rose* were cracked. The chimneys of West Mersea school crashed through its roof and the bell turret collapsed but the 130 children escaped unhurt. Up on "the hill" near the church, fissures 150 yards long appeared, but closed in a few days.

West Mersea coast road from the south end of the hard, 1908. *from a drawing by E. H. Oliver*

Ashore, Mersea was divided into the "Uplanders" and the "Downlanders", or the landworkers who lived north and east of the *Fountain* public house and the seafaring community at the south west point. Their smouldering rivalry burst out in an occasional fight, perhaps outside the *Ship Inn*, which then stood in The Lane, running down into the Old City.

Adult amusements were few. There was much boat sailing for pleasure as well as work. Cricket was played on the Hove Marsh, west of Fisherman's Hard.

There were few excitements except the annual regatta or the flower show, or perhaps a parade by the coastguards, smart in bluejacket uniforms, with white gaiters and rifles, swinging out from their yard and quarters on Churchfields, where they frequently practiced with semaphore flags. There were occasional family outings to Colchester or a country picnic or Sunday School treat, clopping along in Rudling's yellow brake and at the end of each day, Cudmore's red mail cart set off at a spanking pace with the post for Colchester.

In the 1880s West Mersea's land and shoreside business was dominated by Mrs Round, "Lady of the Manor" and by Alexander Bean, who dabbled in everything from agriculture to oyster layings. The island population then numbered 1,360, most of whom lived in the village of West Mersea, where oyster dredging and cultivation were the principal employments. The village oyster merchants included Elijah Cook, Adam Howard and John May. George Brand combined that trade with keeping the *Victory* pub and James Hempstead also owned a grocer's shop. Thomas Wyatt, the shipwright, continued to repair the village's fleet of forty or so small cutter smacks, many of them old, leaky craft then being replaced by new carvel-planked cutters built at Brightlingsea by Aldous. By then, few large smacks were owned by Mersea fishermen, whose interests were chiefly centred on the Blackwater oyster fisheries, and none sailed from there in the later days of sail.

The plankton-rich waters of the Blackwater and many of its creeks have been noted for sustaining "Native" oysters since Roman times. Oysters are shellfish and each produces large numbers of "spat", at first invisible, then appearing as a white milky cloud in the water. This discharge needs a clean surface on which to cling and continue growth and in natural conditions the minute oyster clings to a clean shell or stone on the river bed. "Spat fall" usually occurs during May in these waters and on the oyster layings, cultivated in creeks and shallows, oystermen prepare for it by laying clean old shell which has been dumped on hards and saltings to bleach in sun and wind for a year or so. This is carried out by the ton, to be broadcast in the creek or part of the shallows where a spat fall is likely to be received.

Before 1914 the creeks at West Mersea were anchorage for fifty to sixty small cutter smacks manned by over 150 villagers, with other men working oyster layings in the creeks with skiffs and others winkling with bumkins (now called winkle brigs by many) and rowing boats. A yachtsman described them under sail in the early morning:

"At five o'clock the smacks got under weigh in the grey mists of early dawn in a light air, working through the narrow channels without mishap or foul. About thirty smacks came gliding out from each of the three creeks, (Thornfleet, Buzzun and Tollesbury) those from Tollesbury Creek all having topsails set, the others being under lower sails only."

11

These little West Mersea smacks, with others from Tollesbury and Maldon, regularly dredged oysters in the river and were comparatively shallow draught and manoeuverable. They could be sailed by two men or be worked with three or four on deck for handling dredges. The crew could live on board for short periods but most were used as day boats, as these craft did not stray far from home after the mid-nineteenth century, mixing dredging with fish trawling, especially for spring soles on the Bench Head, a shoal at the mouth of the Blackwater.

Dredging under sail was often more like being hove-to rather than sailing and the tide was used to assist the work. But if there was any breeze the smacks were things of life and in stronger winds the problem was to maintain a desired, even speed to tow the dredges along the bottom correctly, hoeing the oysters into the chain mesh bottom and fibre net-backed dredges, streaming astern on bass warps.

Working in the river on an ebb tide running eastward to the sea in a moderate south-westerly wind was a typical situation. The smack commenced dredging across the ground, upwind, from its northern side, following the tide eastward with her bow headed approximately south and the breeze over the starboard side. Each smack had her own idiosyncrasies of handling in differing conditions of wind and water but usually, to slow forward movement, the mainsheet was slacked away and probably the gaff might be "rucked down" by easing the peak halyard, but the sail still kept the bow up to windward. The jib would be partly run in on its traveller along the bowsprit to balance the mainsail's drive and was trimmed just short of luffing, sometimes aback. The staysail might be backed over to windward or be stowed. The sheets of all the sails were adjusted to suit wind strength, to control speed and balance. In this subtle equilibrium between wind, tide, sails and the dragging effect of the dredges on the bottom, the skipper allowed the smack to drive across the tide in a desired path, almost hove-to.

The length and scope of a dredge warp varied with the depth of water but in the river, in water varying from perhaps 10-30 feet in depth, a warp of 8-12 fathoms might be used. This was made fast to the ring at the head of the dredge with a fishermen's bend and when working, led to the smack's rail, where it was made fast to a thole pin set in a hole in the bulwark rail with a single round turn having the end backed over. A dredge which "came fast" on an obstruction then jerked out the rope, which could be slipped off the pin in a trice and be let go with the white painted wooden buoy which was made fast to the ends of the warps, to be worried free when they sailed back up-tide. In confined waters and creeks, each man worked one dredge for quickness in the short hauls. In open water two dredges might be worked per man and sometimes three or four, depending on the amount of "soil" on the bottom and strength of wind. The dredges were cast on the windward side, usually aft one first by the skipper, the others following, casting from the deck so each dredge fell face down in the water to reach bottom in a working position rather than "on its back"; a disgrace to a fisherman. The oystermen knew by the feel of the warp if the dredge was working properly. They also knew the bottom of the ground like their own garden. Every hump and gully, "fast" and change of ground was noted in their minds and favourite dredging areas were found repeatedly by noting marks ashore; keeping a certain big tree clear of a house or a beacon "on" with a clump of trees, and so on. Marks were used when entering an oyster ground and when leaving it and as transits to find a desired spot. The length of haul depended on the quantities of oysters on the ground and the speed of the smack with her dredges hoeing paths along the bottom.

Despite a smack's slow speed, hauling was hard work and the bass rope picked up tiny pieces of shell to cut the hands. With the dredge awash alongside, its frame was brought across the rail, with a couple of shakes to clear some of the weed and water, then the wooden stick which extended the after end of the net was lifted and its contents were shot out on deck. The dredge was cast again and sorting began. Any oysters were flipped into a tub or basket but the mud and rubbish went overboard, except for enemies of the oyster such as whelks, tingle, limpets and starfish, which were kept back to be put ashore later. Crabs were squashed underfoot. So it went on, perhaps with some adjustment of

Mersea smacks reach out of the Deeps on a summer morning in the 1930s: *Boadicea* (C.K. 213) in the lead. The handy rig and shapely hulls of these little cutters emphasises their work in dredging oysters and beam trawling for flatfish in the River Blackwater and its approaches.   *Douglas Went*

thole pins forward or aft to suit the balance and direction across the ground. Haul and sort, haul and sort; on good ground this was constant. When it was time to haul in strong winds the jib might be let fly to ease the labour.

A number of smacks dredging under sail made an animated scene; men chaffing each other and hauling dredges, culling the catch on deck and throwing the "culch" overboard with "sheards"; two pieces of board held in the hands to gather the rubbish from the culling. Smacks were sailing or dredging in apparent confusion. Those sailing back up-tide to recommence dredging just slipping past the sterns of others dredging down-tide; but every smack was under complete control and though each was in a varying part of the fleet's dredging cycle, all dredged parallel courses, sheering about, hove-to across the tide, dredge warps straining, keeping proper speeds and avoiding collisions. A smack's correct relative position within the fleet was vital to the smooth working of the group on the ground and no one consciously violated this principle without expecting reproach.

At the end of the ground being dredged, all dredges were hauled, the jib sheets and the staysail were trimmed in, the peak halyards were swigged up, the mainsheet got in and the smack gathered way, to stay round with the surging sureness of "wending" in smooth water; a clatter of slatting sails, creaking blocks and pattering reef points. The sails filled again on the other tack and she settled to the new course, heeling slightly, to make a tack or two back up river, to recommence her dredging. Then the crew had a spell and the skipper or a hand perhaps, enjoyed the short beat over the tide. Maybe the boy was allowed to steer for this short interval, while the men culled the catch on deck and checked the dredges. He would enjoy the feel of the trembling tiller and wind on his face, oblivious of an aching back and tired arms, sore hands and perhaps a pinching sea boot in early endeavour at the old Essex art of going to windward under sail, though the skipper would keep a wary eye on him, remembering beneath a gruff exterior his own youthful pleasure at the tiller.

Many older smacks had apple-cheek bows but most later craft had a lean entrance, hollow at the forefoot, swelling to a pronounced shoulder by the mast and fining away abaft it to a long clean run, ending in a shallow counter stern. The sheer fell in a graceful sweep from the comparatively high stem to only about 15 inches freeboard aft; useful for handling dredges or a trawl but making them wet in a seaway. Most were arranged with a long, low fo'c'sle cabin entered by a deck sliding hatch abaft the mast. The after hull space was a hold for fish and gear. Construction was strong, with carvel planking, often a mixture of woods which at best might be pitch pine in the bottom and fir sides on oak-sawn frames. The hull was lined inside with a pine or fir ceiling. Ballast was scrap iron and cement set in the bilge. The cutter rig usually had provision for a topmast, though many smacks left it ashore much of the year and during the present century most Mersea smacks set only three lower sails for working.

The West Mersea smack *Mayflower*. Rebuilt, owned and sailed by Donald Rainbird.

They were not all fast and a few were slow to windward but all were certain, stable and for their work, sea kindly; the result of evolution for the needs of their owners and the knowledge and skill of their builders. The *Mayflower* is typical with dimensions of 36 feet 7 inches overall, 31 feet 4 inches water line, 9 feet 10¾ inches beam with 4 feet 10 inches draught aft and 3 feet 5½ inches draught forward. She has been rebuilt and restored to her working condition by Donald Rainbird of West Mersea who has a fund of knowledge of smack sailing and she is a frequent prizewinner in the several smack races now held annually on the Blackwater and the Colne.

These small smacks were built for £10 per registered ton, hull spars and ballast. Many were constructed for a deposit, typically £50, the remainder being paid off in instalments of perhaps £25 annually; a form of hire purchase. The 11-ton *Evergreen* was built by Aldous in 1887 and was paid for in this way. She cost £109. 6s. 8d. Aldous provided a bible in a box for the cabin of each craft he built and a silver shilling was placed under the mast when it was stepped, for good luck. Many of Aldous craft were designed by Mr Polley, the yard's loftsman.

The *Peace* was built at Brightlingsea by Douglas Stone and Sons in 1909, to the design of Robert Stone and proved a fast and weatherly smack. She is one of the few for which detailed plans and design calculations were prepared. These little cutters spent most of their existence working no further than the Wallet or the Whittaker but a few owners were more adventurous. At one time half a dozen Mersea smacks sailed down Channel in autumn to dredge at Falmouth for the winter. Others were fitted out in autumn for fish trawling on the flats and as the season progressed, in deeper water. Many were laid up for a time. In spring, some trawled for soles, then it was back to oyster dredging, working in the Blackwater on ''common ground'' or ''Company ground'', some in the narrow creeks on various layings.

Imported oysters were laid to fatten at West Mersea around the end of the nineteenth century and shipments came in from the London docks, often carried by the large Rowhedge smacks *Aquiline* and *Qui Vive*, which loaded them from the steamer at Rotherhithe and sailed round to Mersea to discharge by hand over the layings then worked by the Heath family of Wivenhoe. Each could carry 22 tons and it was hard work shovelling out the load of Tagus, Brittany or Chesapeake oysters. In 1913 local landowner Bean became bankrupt and many layings were sold, which allowed the purchase of them by fishermen, who usually worked them with tow-haul skiffs. Some families had extensive oyster interests: the Cook family of oystermen worked most of Salcott Creek and also had oyster ground in the Orwell and off Shotley, in the Suffolk Stour. The tradition of importing oysters continues and since 1945 millions of Portuguese oysters have been brought in to fatten in the nourishing waters. Some Mersea smacks trawled eels on the Mersea Flats, on the south shore of the island where the soft mud then supported a good crop of eel grass *(Zostera Marina)*; a plant distinct from seaweed, which grows in salt water, waving long leaves when waterborne or lying like a squelchy green lawn at low water. Brent geese feed on it and it supported millions of eels which were reputedly first trawled there by a Tollesbury fisherman. Smacks from there, and later a number from Maldon, worked the flats at high water until a change in tidal scour and a few harsh winters killed the eel grass. Half a dozen Mersea smacks worked there during the summer of 1907, catching about 50 pounds weight of eels each hour. In winter the fishermen sometimes speared the eels from their holes at low water, walking the muds with a trident-like eel spear called a "shear", or a "pritch" by some. The eel trawls had a fine, fish-sized mesh except for the close-meshed cod end. Several Mersea smacks were fitted with wet wells for the trade and the *Sarah* carried cargoes of eels from Mersea to London. Sometimes the *Waterlily* went away trawling eels in the Suffolk rivers Deben and the Ore.

Winkling provided something of a living for the owners of the little gaff rigged open boats or bumkins from West Mersea and the small smacks from Maldon and Mersea which lay in the outfalls along the Dengie Flats. Before rubber boots became available their crews walked the soft mud in "splatchers" as the boards strapped to their feet were called, gathering the catch. The Mersea smack *Brothers* carried cargoes of winkles to market at Norwich.

There were other odd catches. The Harwich bawley *Prima Donna* sailed to West Mersea in summer to catch green crabs in the creeks. These were carried back in sacks and lived until the winter when they were used as bait for whelks, the catching of which as bait for the local cod lining smacks was a winter staple of the Harwich bawleys.

Two West Mersea winklers with children and their boat *Black Duck*, May 1914. She is an old rowboat, probably from a yacht, rigged with a standing lugsail. The men wear the typical thigh boots and guernseys. One has a "cheese-cutter" cap, the other a linen racing hat.

By courtesy of Hervey Benham.

About 15 Mersea smacks drifted for herring in winter, usually in the Blackwater, sometimes in the approaches to the Crouch. The train of herring nets, often 200 yards long, was set across the tide with the smacks' boat at its leeward end with a lamp and a man and boy in it. They drifted for the tide, hauling at low water. After the 1870s a few Mersea smacks joined the many others from Harwich, the Colne and Leigh trawling shrimps from Harwich. Some also worked in the Wallet, landing the catch at Brightlingsea or Mersea. A few smacks dredged mussels using oyster dredges moused with yarn on the hoe to prevent them digging into the bottom. The long nosed gorbills, or guardfish, were caught in season with a form of seine having an exaggerated cod in its middle and seines and peter nets were used to catch mullet on the Dengie shore by the little, transom-sterned Maldon smacks.

The Mersea and Maldon fishermen had little interest in spratting, unlike the large numbers from the Colne and some from Tollesbury engaging in this arduous winter fishery. However, the Mersea *Priscilla* and the *George and Alice* were cut in half and lengthened to increase capacity and seaworthiness for stowboating and joined in for a time as the only Mersea smacks to use the net in living memory.

The little 35-foot river oyster dredgers in the Blackwater remained sailing craft into the 1930s because of the restricted nature of their work and the cost of installing an engine. The Blackwater and Colne oyster fisheries were worked principally under sail until 1939. During the 1939-1945 war a very few oyster layings were cultivated by old men and boys, but most were temporarily ruined. Forty years later a flavour of old ways was retained, but cultivation of the extensive layings in these waters is now totally by motor craft.

The origins and owner-builder relationship of many small smacks are fascinating examples of local lore. The little *Deerhound* was built for a West Mersea fisherman/yacht hand in 1889. Her owner was serving in the crew of the 40-rater racer of that name, under Rowhedge skipper Captain Tom Jay. While the yacht was on passage down the Irish Sea at night in heavy weather, the skipper was swept overboard but was saved by the quick-witted Mersea man grabbing him by the head and dragging him back on board. In thanks the skipper is said to have presented him with £100, which he promptly decided to invest in a new smack from Aldous of Brightlingsea, for his winter trade of winkling on the Dengie Flats. Having written to his family to ask them to order a new smack from Aldous for his return from the racing season, they sailed round to Brightlingsea, the quickest way of getting there then, and duly placed the order. Aldous bore in mind that the owner was a racing man and built a dainty and sharp bottomed little cutter which, though a joy to sail was practically useless for the frequent grounding of the winkling trade and was eventually sold by her despairing owner!

The *Daisy* is a far travelled Mersea smack. She was built by Aldous at Brightlingsea in 1884 as an oyster dredger for a West Mersea owner and after fifty years spent mainly inside the Bar buoy, was bought by Douglas Dixon as a cruising yacht. He renamed her *Dusmarie* and she cruised the North Sea and to the Baltic, where she became headquarters ship for his pre-war Manno* schoolboy adventure expeditions. Caught laid up in Lapland by the 1939-45 war, she weathered ice and snow until peace came and her owner returned to find her still serviceable but needing repairs. During these the Baltic shipwrights superimposed the flaring topsides of their native craft on to her low-sheered Essex hull with startling though pleasing effect. No Blackwater or Colne mariner would now readily recognise *Daisy* the dredgerman in the high sided yawl, which nevertheless returned to win the Mersea smack race in 1954 before leaving to continue her wanderings in the Mediterranean and European waters. She still competes in local smack races. The *Unity* was reckoned the fastest Mersea smack of her times, with the *Peace* running her close. *Skylark* and the ex-Mersea *Fashion* and *Gracie* were Maldon's champions.

The now traditional race for smacks and ex-smacks under 15 tons measurement, forming part of West Mersea Town Regatta, was established in 1928 when Lieutenant Mulhauser R.N., a member of the Blackwater Sailing Club at Heybridge and a circumnavigator in his yawl *Amaryllis*, made a bequest in his will of a ''Challenge cup to West Mersea to be sailed for by the smacks of the Blackwater to be known as the Mulhauser Cup''. By 1929 there were few fully rigged smacks at Tollesbury and as Colne smacks, which were by then as scantily rigged, were debarred, the cup became a symbol of challenge between West Mersea and Maldon fishermen. It was first raced for in 1929 when the Maldon *Lizzie Annie* owned by A. R. Wright won. The race revived in 1947 with the first post-war West Mersea Town Regatta, when Peter Pullen's *Mary* was the first non-working smack to win. L. French with the *Hyacynth* was the last working sailing smack to win the cup, in 1948 and 1949. It has since been sailed for by ex-smacks sailed for pleasure.

Like all the Blackwater communities, West Mersea men were involved in smuggling. The extensive creeks and saltings of the Blackwater were ideal for landing goods and were the despair of revenue men. There seems to have been little of the swaggering brutality which characterised contemporary south coast smugglers and most runs were stealthy and, one suspects, were made by craft from elsewhere bringing contraband to be landed in the river. ''Free trade'' as it was known, was certainly old-established in these waters. In December 1745 customs officers were alerted because of the anticipated flight of the Pretender from the Essex coast ''to keep watch on or near the Island of Mersea and the rivers and waters of Colne and Maldon to hinder such persons as may attempt to embark on board the fishing boats thereabouts and to search fishing boats for any such persons''.

*In the Gulf of Bothnia: expeditions were made here in the 1930s by parties of English public school boys.

The preventive officers of that time were poorly paid and were not entitled to a pension if disabled, so sometimes they preferred to look the other way.

There is the tradition of the boat's crew of revenue men who were found drifting by the Sunken Island with their throats cut, apparently surprised by night, but there is no evidence to support this story which has persisted in local lore for a century and a half. Another tale is of the ghost which haunts a cottage which was once the *Old Ship* inn. After a successful smuggling run in the mid-eighteenth century a girl who worked there betrayed the smugglers and was subsequently murdered. She is reputed occasionally to return in remorse.

Though many have read Baring Gould's *Mehalah*, few know his other novel, *Richard Cable*, much of which was set at West Mersea. It is also rich in local colour but is wildly melodramatic. The early setting is at Orleans, the large house which stood near the church until it was demolished in 1959 to allow the building of flats.

Mersea has always had its usual local share of nicknames to distinguish between the many sons of branches of families sometimes having the same Christian name and surname, which led to nicknames sometimes being used in school for distinction between pupils. The origins of most are now obscure, others originated from incidents. Oystermen Fred and Herbert Mussett, with Isaac Pullen, left Mersea about 1905 to work for a few years on oyster layings in the Swale, the channel between the Isle of Thanet and mainland Kent. All married girls from Queenborough before returning to life at Mersea. Afterwards Fred Musset was known as "Foreigner". Others of his family were "Curlew" Mussett, so called because as a boy he disturbed a shooting party by lifelike bird calls and Alfred "Swan" Mussett whose nickname arose when his nephew shot him one night in mistake for a wild swan.

Mersea's dry humour is delightful. Mr Clark Mussett, fisherman and yacht sailor, dignified in blue guernsey and cheesecutter cap, his kindly face bronzed and lined by the suns and winds of a lifetime took in the return of some spray-soaked young yachtsmen and remarked: "Ah, if I was a gentleman, out for pleasure, I wouldn't never turn to windward!"

Merseamen are keen wildfowlers and until the 1930s several punt gunners spent the winter nights seeking fowl for market. Many punts were built by their owners, as they are still, others were by local boatbuilders such as Bill Wyatt at West Mersea and John Howard of Maldon, who was reckoned to build the best. Traditionally the Blackwater and Colne punts were open, varying between 16-18 feet length and from 2 feet 6 inches to 3 ft beam, pointed at each end. These were usually planked in English elm, two strakes on each side on oak frames. Local tradition decreed that if the punt leaked on launching day the builder stood the owner as much beer as she took in. This led to considerable care in construction.

20

A West Mersea wildfowler with punt and gun; "Gunner" Cook was a noted punter in the Blackwater tradition, but his punt is unusual in being decked. The rowlock chocks for the short oars, called "paddles", are well aft and the low coaming is cut down in way of the punter's arms to allow the use of hand paddles or setting sticks in shoal or confined waters.   *Douglas Went*

Some punt guns are breech loaders but those favoured by the fishermen—fowlers were muzzle loaders about 8-9 feet long and about 1¼ inch bore, firing about three-quarters of a pound of shot. The barrel of the gun rests in a score in the stem head and its stock on the gunbeam or a thwart, to which it is made fast with a rope breeching. Punts are rowed, are poled or move with hand paddles or setting sticks. The punter tries to get within 60-70 yards of the fowl before firing and it takes considerable skill and fortitude in a winter's dawn or sunset to manoeuvre in range and fire at these wily birds. Punting is a lonely and eclectic sport which retains a following on the Blackwater but has almost died out in the Colne. Sometimes a small spritsail or a "leg of mutton" is set on a short mast stepped through the thwart and steering is by a paddle held under the lee quarter. Centreboards were not used in working punts, though some large "sportsmen's" punts had them, usually for sailing down "on the Main". Races for gun punts were held at West Mersea and Maldon regattas but have long been discontinued, but punts still sail on the Stour at Manningtree and Mistley.

The late "Gunner" Cook was amongst the most noted West Mersea wildfowlers; wise in the ways of and wiles of birds and the difficulties confronting those trying to outwit them. He had a wonderful fund of knowledge and on weekdays was usually to be met with a bag of cartridges across his back, a bag of provisions, a gun over his shoulder, blue guernsey and leather thigh boots. He returned with widgeon, teal and plover to be sent to markets and hotels, or for local sale. Sometimes he was away wildfowling for up to six days at a time, living on board a small smack which carried punt and gear and could be sailed to the likeliest places in the Blackwater or down along the Main. Yet on Sundays he appeared smartly dressed; brown felt hat, bright tie, tan shoes and carrying instead of a 12-bore a silver headed cane in the then fashionable manner, to mark his day of rest. On winter nights Mr Cook set off from Fisherman's Hard, down Buzzon Creek and along the Blackwater shore of the island to the Mersea Flats, a favourite feeding ground for black geese but dangerous in east or southerly winds. He was one of the most noted Mersea wildfowlers and continued to get large bags until 1939, shortly before his death.

Amongst his contemporaries was "Sooty" Mussett, a skilled wildfowler and a noted spinner of outrageous yarns. His favourite concerned a day's shore shooting with local Doctor Salter. They were walking back through a copse when the Doctor stopped and said: "Good gracious, Soot, look at all those 'dows' (wood pigeons) in that tree." Sooty said: "I ups with me gun, but we aint got a cartridge between us. Then I finds a few pipefuls of powder in me pocket and a few tacks in the other. I loads her up and take aim. BANG! When the smoke cleared, what do you think, sir?" Pausing to gulp a freshly offered pint. "Well, believe me or not, all them ole dows was NAILED TO THE BRANCHES!"

Everyone thought Sooty had reached the limit with that story but one evening after he quaffed his pint at the proper pause, he concluded: "Well, believe me or not, the WHOLE BLOODY TREE GIT UP AND FLEW ORF."

West Mersea wildfowlers set off for the first shot of the new season. Professionals and amateurs in gun punts and smacks' boats leave the hard of the morning of "the 12th". The gunners include from left to right—Titus Mussett, "Sooty" Mussett (in sou'wester), Douglas Mussett, Charles Prigg, and on extreme right, Harry Banks.   *Douglas Went*

Once, challenged by a keeper on the sea wall with a brace of rabbits, Sooty said with a smile: "Copped 'em a swimmin' the creek, mate, wunnerful clever them ole web footed rabbits."

Wildfowling often contributed something to a fisherman's living on the Blackwater and at least one Mersea smack, the *Phantom*, is reputed to have been built mainly for gunning. The opening of the wildfowling season was traditionally on the last night in September. Bulkily clad, thigh booted figures tramped down to the hards after the pubs closed and rowed, poled and sculled off to favourite creeks to await midnight, when a heavy salvo was discharged to greet the new season. Then, having alarmed every bird for miles, they continued to use all their considerable skill and guile to "set to fowl" and really blazed away at the dawn flight, after which they returned to Mersea, bleary-eyed and with several hours to wait before consolation could be found in the warmth of the *Victory* or the *White Hart*.

In 1898 a visiting yachtsman described the *Victory's* interior as "A long, low old fashioned room full of fishermen, farmers, coastguards and pilots. An ancient boatman, clad in old guernsey and cord breeches, broad in the beam, was badly beating a farmer at bagatelle on a prehistoric table. The bar parlour afforded more space and a long argument was in progress covering all disputed subjects from barge yachts to oyster culture." When I was last in the *Victory*, cruising in a friend's yacht in June 1977, almost the same atmosphere prevailed at a mid-week lunchtime.

Amateur wildfowlers come ashore with their bag on West Mersea Causeway. Double-barrelled 12 bores glint in the sunshine of an early autumn morning and one gunner, third from right, carries an automatic shotgun of American pattern. "Sooty" Mussett in the *Migrant* yacht guernsey was the sole professional at this gathering.   *Douglas Went*

CHAPTER TWO

More Mersea

THE old waterside world of fishermen and fowlers was soon to be invaded by yachtsmen; cruising men in small craft at first, enjoying the Blackwater for its unpretentiousness. Their numbers grew and the West Mersea Yacht Club was established in 1899. Its clubhouse, overlooking the hard, is one of the most charming anywhere. It was rebuilt after a fire in 1933.

Soon after 1900 there were rumours of a railway coming to West Mersea. In June 1902 the Light Railway Commissioners granted powers for the construction of a proposed new railway from Southend to Colchester, which was to cost £500,000, then a huge sum. The line was to cross the River Crouch by a steam ferry at Creeksea and the trains were then to steam across the Dengie Hundred farmlands to Bradwell Quay where another steam ferry would carry them across the Blackwater to West Mersea, from where the line would continue along the waterside and up the side of the Strood Channel, across the causeway and on to Colchester.

Yachting magazines hailed the project as making the Blackwater easy of access for yachtsmen from London and prophesied that West Mersea would quickly become a favoured yachting centre, also that many yachts would migrate there from the Crouch and relieve congestion at Burnham. Fortunately this ill-conceived scheme was never constructed and saved its backers from certain financial disaster, besides considerable trouble in attempting to get a train ferry to berth in Bradwell Creek at low water.

At that time the West Mersea Sailing Club were a buoyant group, much interested in sailing ex-smacks converted to yachts. R. Frost Smith was club captain, owning the ex-smack *Clara*. An annual cup was given for a race amongst these craft, to qualify for which craft must have been used for "fishing, piloting or trading purposes" and "subsequently converted into yachts and since used only as yachts". The first race in 1901 was won by the *Clara*. The 30-ton *Queen of Sussex* won in 1902, *Glance* in 1903, *Rustler* 1904, *Clara* again in 1905 and in 1906 only the *Clara* and the *Queen of Sussex* started over the 18 mile course from West Mersea, round the Bench Head and Colne Fishery buoys and upriver to the Shingle Head, twice round. The club also held races from Burnham to West Mersea and these short passage events have always been popular on the east coast.

George Pullen of West Mersea at wheel of the yacht *Palmosa* 1929.

Although Mersea produced no skippers of large racing yachts, a number of men from the village served as hands in racing and cruising yachts after about 1890, probably introduced to it by the participation of Tollesbury men. The late Jack Owen, a West Mersea yachtsman and rigger, son of a coastguardsman stationed there, recalled how he once walked to Rowhedge seeking a berth on board a yacht, then a customary spring pilgrimage for many hands from Tollesbury and occasionally Mersea. He was referred to the yawl *Fiona*, then fitting out. He was interviewed by Captain Pearman, to be respectfully told he was too small to be of use on board that heavily rigged racer, whose strong gear and deep bulwarks matched her bronzed and bearded crew of giants, each with a wool cap and sheath knife at belt, who drove her to success in the early off-shore races of the 1890s. Undismayed, this good sailor shipped in the Scottish racing cutter *Dragon* and spent many years racing from the Clyde and sailing in many other yachts before returning to settle in his native Mersea, where he always enjoyed a sail and his trade of rigger at Gowen's sail loft.

In 1910 Mersea men were in the crew of the 15-metre *Ma'oona*, racing in a crack class. Seventeen-year-old Walter ''Navvy'' Mussett was amongst them. Racing at Cowes the topsail sheet fouled and would not render, so he was sent aloft to clear it. He was working his way along the gaff, eighty feet above the deck, holding on to the mainsail lacing as the yacht roared downwind, when she accidentally gybed. Walter was thrown clear from the gaff to swing below it, holding desperately to the lacing but unable to regain the gaff. He had to act quickly, for to fall probably meant death. He managed to crook a leg around the leach of the mainsail and gripped the sail to climb down it to the boom and safety, emerging from a near fatality without a bruise.

Several Mersea men were in the crew of Sir James Pender's 23-metre *Brynhild* under Captain Barbrook of Tollesbury, from 1908 and in 1910. In 1912 Mersea hands, with others from Tollesbury, the Colne and elsewhere were in the crew of the same owner's 130-foot schooner *Lamorna*, which had been designed and built by William Fife at Fairlie, Scotland in 1902 as the racing schooner *Cicely*, skippered when new by Captain Jesse Cranfield of Rowhedge, whose forebears were coincidentally Mersea men, not related to the many other seafarers of that name in Rowhedge. By 1912 the *Lamorna* had been re-rigged with a more modest sail area of 7,990 square feet for cruising and an auxiliary engine had been fitted. The loss of 2,000 square feet was an advantage when she raced for the King's Cup during Cowes Week, sailed in a gale, but the only concession her skipper made to the conditions was to carry jib headed instead of yard topsails for the race.

Ten great yachts started but only three finished. There was no jockeying for the start in the roaring wind, the yachts throwing spray to their crosstrees: no opportunity for finesse or the refinements of racing tactics. They sailed like demons and to steer them safely through the squalls was all that brain and muscle could accomplish. Out towards the Warner, harder squalls hit the fleet and observers wondered how long the men and craft would stand the strain. The Kaiser's *Meteor IV* lay over to her skylights, through which tons of water cascaded below. She was close to foundering, would not steer and the headsails, which could not be touched in such a weight of wind, were too much for the reefed mainsail and foresail. She could not luff and had to run back for shelter in Cowes Roads, followed by the schooners *Cetonia* and *Waterwitch*, the cutters *White Heather* and *The Lady Anne*, the sturdy ketch *Julnar* with the Prince of Wales on board, and *Corisande*. Only three survived to finish; Lord Dunraven's ketch *Cariad*, sailed by Captain Barty Smith of Rowhedge, Sir William Portal's *Valdora* and the *Lamorna* which as they rounded the Warner made one of the finest sights of yacht racing. She reached back like a train to thunder across the line, 4 minutes and 20 seconds ahead of the *Cariad*, with the *Valora* well astern, but lost the cup to the *Cariad* on handicap allowance.

Yachting in the grand manner never became established at West Mersea, which attracted small cruising yachts whose owners and friends sought quiet recreation and a snug anchorage. Few yachts were moored there before the end of the nineteenth century and some resentment was felt by oystermen towards the laying of moorings in the Deeps and the Thornfleet Creek, hindering the sailing smacks in their passing in and out from their moorings or when they dredged in the Thornfleet under sail. Handling a sailing smack in such confined waters is an art which Mersea men have to perfection. Smacks sailed in with sails well filled, keeping plenty of way on and having a hand forward to tend headsails as they hustled round in stays, for the channel at low water is often barely three smack lengths wide. There were few dramatic local incidents except of the "yachtsmen's shipwreck" variety. One yarn concerned a cruising yacht anchored in the fairway of the Thornfleet, her owner asleep in the sun on deck with one arm across the tiller. A smack beating up the creek cut things too fine and not only fouled the yacht but also hit her rudder, giving the tiller such a jerk that the sleeper was thrown overboard into the creek.

The West Mersea smack *Unity*, C.K. 197, legged up on the hard for a scrub. Standing before her is William Wyatt, the Mersea boatbuilder who sailed on board her at Mersea Regatta for many years. This shows the typical hull shape of the Colne and Blackwater sailing smacks from the mid-19th century until the end of smack construction just prior to the First World War. *Douglas Went*

As Mersea produced no skippers of major yachts, none were laid up at this now popular and delightful waterside, though over the years ever increasing numbers of small ones have been. The ritual of laying up yachts in September or October and refitting them in spring is an old tradition, seen as an accepted part of the yachting year on most parts of the British coast. The practice of laying yachts in mud berths is old. Gradually this has changed with more craft laid up ashore. West Mersea developed late as a sailing centre for smaller yachts, generally owned by less wealthy amateurs who wished to do as much work as possible themselves, to save expense. The village boatbuilders Mr Clark, William Wyatt, Hempstead and Co and later Clarke and Carter and Ben Clark, catered for this growing need and the saltings along Coast Road provided berths for many craft which, moored fore and aft against the strong winds and big tides, soon "cut a dock" or bedded their bottoms in the soft mud which cradled them until fitting out commenced in March or April. Many others wintered ashore along the waterside.

Hempstead and Co were a small yard which flourished at West Mersea after and possibly before the 1914-18 war. They built clinker dinghies, bumkins and other small craft on the site of what became Clarke and Carter's yachtyard and also laid up and refitted yachts and owned mud berths and many houseboats. Houseboats came to the West Mersea saltings along the Coast Road after about 1912 and grew in numbers until the late 1940s. Most were used as week-end or summer homes by people from elsewhere, but some were lived in all year round. Many were superannuated yachts, often racers from which the lead keel had been removed and some famous yachts are amongst them; the King of Spain's 15-metre *Hispania*, the America's Cup challenger *Genesta* and many others from 100-foot steam yachts to 35-foot smacks. Some remain thoroughly nautical, with deck fittings and paintwork making them look almost ready to fit out. Others are bizarre and a few thoroughly domestic, with porches and flower tubs.

Clarke and Carter carried on and developed to lay up and refit numbers of moderate sized yachts, besides smaller ones, their slipways bearing craft across the Coast Road to and from the creek. Occasionally they built a yacht and particularly specialised in wooden sparmaking; the fine spruce hollow spars taking shape in a special loft under the skilled hands of the boatbuilders. In recent years the yard has completed larger plastic-hulled motor yachts and continues to flourish under the brothers Griffin.

William Wyatt is perhaps the best remembered of all the West Mersea boatbuilders. I bought my first boat from him in 1947 for £25 and came back for the second two years later; his little yard had hardly changed since the early 1900s. He was then over eighty; a tall man, fairly erect despite age, with a white beard. Keen eyes were shrewd below the peak of his waterman's cap. After a lifetime as a village boatbuilder and yacht outfitter he had come to be called "Admiral" Wyatt by romantically minded yachtsmen. He always regarded himself as "Mr Wyatt" and his direct nature did not seek flattery, but he appreciated the publicity his local standing brought to the business.

William Wyatt claimed direct descent from a Hampshire family of wooden shipbuilders. He served an apprenticeship as a shipwright at the Wivenhoe yard of John Harvey Ship and Yacht Building Company on the River Colne, working on yachtbuilding and repairing and on the construction of smacks, including some large ketches for Liverpool and Lowestoft, whose keels were cut from the tree in one length by the yard sawmill, a fact which impressed him throughout life.

The young William grew up in the old Mersea traditions of rowing, sculling and sailing small boats, sailing in the smacks at regattas and participating in any form of fun afloat. He was fond of telling how he and young companions found several porpoises in the shallow water of the Ray Creek and daringly approaching, they managed to slip a bight of rope around the tail on one, then,

The boatbuilders. William Wyatt of West Mersea (left) and James Husk of Wivenhoe discuss the trade by a yacht under construction during the 1930s. *By courtesy of Harold Cutts.*

splashing and shouting they drove the terrified creatures down the creek, getting a tow from their capture until the punt capsized. Arrival of a local ''sportsman'' ended their frolic as he commenced to shoot the porpoises! Many doubted William's story but a few years ago I found an account of the incident reported by the ''sportsman'' in a contemporary yachting magazine, which tallied exactly with his memory.

Fitting out at West Mersea, 1939. William Wyatt stands, rule in hand, while the covers come off the 40-foot cutter *Florence* in the mud berths at the ''Old City'' end of the waterside. The bermudian ketch, ahead, has her sails airing in the spring sunlight and a smack converted for pleasure use, lies beyond. The saltings of the marsh stretch towards the low horizon of Peldon with new-leafed elms in the haze of a fine day.
Douglas Went

"Bill" Wyatt joined his father in the little business by the hard which subsisted principally on the patching and repairing of the many old smacks and small fishing boats then worked by West Mersea fishermen. He remembered the increasing numbers of new 10 and 12-ton smacks which were being built at Brightlingsea and Wivenhoe for West Mersea men during the 1880s and 1890s and his father saying: "Them new bots'll finish us, boy. They 'ont never want anthin' done to 'um." However, in that he was wrong as Bill Wyatt ministered to their maintenance for a lifetime. He also found new work in the small yachts with amateur crews which began to frequent West Mersea after the early 1890s in increasing numbers. Many began to lay up and moor there in mud berths and stores provided by his yard. Bill also built gun punts in the picturesque little black weatherboard boatshed which stood where the present Dabchicks Sailing Club House is built. He built his last punt in 1948 and I was privileged to be shown her under construction and have the finer points of punt design explained briefly by a master. She was launched from the nearby yard with eighty-five-year-old William at the paddles and a large red ensign flying from her stern. A little gathering of Wyatt's boatbuilders, Gowen's sailmakers and others witnessed the launch with informality and good humour typical of Mersea's waterside.

In old age Willliam continued to ride his bicycle from his home in Firs Chase, the few hundred yards downhill from the yard, usually walking it home. He never seemed to forget a face or a name and retained a keen memory into extreme age, his manner firm but kindly towards youngsters with little money seeking small boats they could afford.

William Wyatt became, perhaps unwittingly, the mentor of many commencing sailing, often retaining them as clients in following years. Both the boats I bought there were old, renovated craft; another of his yard activities. After 1945 with young boatbuilders joining him after war service, the little firm commenced building small yachts and motor skiffs for Mersea oystermen. There were numbers of existing yachts to renovate and maintain and increasing numbers of them arriving at West Mersea anchorage, where they had long outnumbered the remaining smacks. The first yacht built from my design was by Wyatts and was launched off the hard on a bitter spring day. Although we did not know it, she would be sailed to Greece, then to America and Canada, to be lost on the Grand Bank when homeward bound.

Wyatts specialised in rigging and refitting craft "on spec" for resale. Usually these were renovated by Mr Hewes, known as "Pinky" to his friends. The yard had a flair for painting craft they sold or built in light, contrasting colours; often cream topsides, red bottom, deep green sheerstrakes and thwarts and pale grey insides; an effective and workmanlike combination. Caulking was one of "Pinky's" accomplishments and many a smack and yacht has been "made tight" by his skilful iron. He is a rare hand at racing a bumkin on regatta day and thoroughly enjoys giving the fishermen a good race. The spring fitting out ritual of visiting West Mersea to buy black varnish and bass rope from Wyatt's yard was sheer enjoyment. "We want six fathoms of bass, Mr Wyatt," we asked, jingling the half-crowns in our palms invitingly at the office door. "Well, boys, if yew goo up to the third store there, yew can help yourselves, here's the key." We scampered into the dim-lit hut stacked with coil on coil of rope, all natural fibre then, hemp, manilla, sisal and coarse, hard to bend but mud-resisting bass; spun from coconut fibre and much used locally for moorings. Gleefully we measured off great long fathoms with arms stretched 8 feet wide. Cheekily we coiled the rope, with its excess of a fathom or so and confronted the "Admiral".

"How much, Mr Wyatt?"

"Well, well boys. Six fathom yew say? Well, put that on the scales, mate, 'cos that goo by weight." The twinkle in the eye I always remember, as well as our red faces.

Purchasing black varnish involved Fred Cutts, a partner in the firm who, years earlier, had worked at Rowhedge Shipyard, where we were then apprenticed. The request for black varnish was always met with, "Now we've gotta find the key." (Emphasis). This being brought from the "orfice" it was, "Now I suppose yew aint brought no tins?" These were sought from the yard dump. "Now we want a funnel." One was found and the rich smelling black varnish gurgled into the cans.

"That'll be three and six each." Knocking the last dregs from the spout. A muffled shout from the office. "What say, Mary?" "Oh, that's three and seven each. Thass gone up a penny, how things keep a'going up. How's old Fooksey, the yard blacksmith? Is Jack Smith still shipwrighting? I hear your a'building a huge great big tug . . ." The little boatyard, a maritime survival treasured in memory and now changed by a later generation into a thriving business, but still proud of its origins, directed by Fred Cutts' ever jovial son Harold, his wife and son.

While Wyatt's were building yachts of aromatic oak, pine, mahogany and Canadian rock elm, next door at Gowen's sail loft wise heads were bent over shapes and tapes on the polished floor, where masses of soft cotton canvas were being cut and patted into the flowing shapes of yacht sails. Can anything beat the feeling of quality of a new Egyptian cotton sail? After it, the hard, glossy slatting of its Terylene successors seems brash, but like many plastic things there can be no doubt of its calculated strength. Around the floor sailmakers and apprentices sat working at their benches. On it lay an embryo mainsail for an American yacht. In this English sail loft Mr French, the cutter, coaxed and patted into shape the leach of a sail which would first be hoisted in Maryland. Ken Gowen, owner of the loft and son of its founder, supervised and together they blended years of experience.

At the end of the nineteenth century A. A. Gowen, who had been at sea as a young sailmaker in large merchant ships, came ashore to become foreman at Hibbs, the Brightlingsea sailmakers. During 1903 he commenced business as Gowen and Company and just before 1914 removed his business to Tollesbury, attracted by the numbers of yachts then laying up there. During the 1914-18 war he opened a small loft at West Mersea and two of its men collected materials by rowing to Tollesbury and back in a smack's boat.

The changing trend of yachting to smaller craft and apparent post war stagnation at Tollesbury led to Gowen's main loft being moved to West Mersea in 1919, when the anchorage was beginning to attract many yachts and its future in sailing looked assured. However, a small loft was kept open at Tollesbury for a time. The firm prospered, making sails for craft from dinghies to ex-15 metres.

The staff of Gowen and Company sail loft at West Mersea, about 1920. Left to right—Charlie Woods, A. A. Gowen, Kenneth A. L. Gowen, Miss Gertie French (Mrs Stanley Farthing), Herbert Welham (foreman), Jack Gurton, Jack Wadley and Joe Jeckells.   *Gowen and Company*

Interior of part of Gowen and Company's sail loft during the 1960s. It has since been further extended.   *Gowen and Company*

The best racing yachts sails were then made from Egyptian cotton duck, hand sewn and most work was for the hundreds of cruising yachts and dinghies created for the sport's gradual expansion. Gowen's also continued to make sails for smacks. A. A. Gowen died in 1935, when his son Kenneth took charge of the business, which continued to expand until 1939 and remained busy throughout the war on government work; resuming pleasure sailmaking in 1945. Man-made fibres were soon to replace the creamy cotton canvas and in 1952 Gowen's were approached to make the first sails from the new material "Terylene", which in three years had displaced cotton as the bulk of their production.

In 1950 Paddy Hare joined the firm and assumed its direction when Ken Gowen retired in 1957. The loft was extended in 1966 and a testing mast was rigged on the waterside for sail evaluation. Sailmakers tend to remain at Gowen's and several old hands have spent half a century at the loft, including foreman Ernie Ponder. There are also younger men who not only make the sails but sail the boats which use them, part of the present sailmaking tradition and Mersea sails are sent to many countries for many types of yacht.

Gowen's made the sails for the first craft built for me, the day-sailer *Blue Peter*, constructed at West Mersea by Jack Emeny in his little boatshop at the back of the village, beautifully planked, single-handed by that patient craftsman.

During the past twenty-three years Mersea has been the home of a yacht design team who have had considerable success. In 1956 Cornishman Kim Holman settled at West Mersea. Always fascinated by yachts and boats and with a background of engineering, he had spent two years working with Woodbridge yacht designer J. Francis Jones before establishing his own practice. Cruisers and offshore racing yachts came from his drawing board, each with a distinctive classical style which with their sailing performance made Holman yachts outstanding. Whole classes of yachts such as *Stella*s and *Twister*s stemmed from this era and Holman was soon commissioned to design large offshore racers such as *Whirlwind* and *Fanfare*. In 1960 Donald Pye of Colchester joined the firm, which became Holman and Pye. They were soon involved in the design of yachts for the surge of building which commenced with the widespread use of plastic for yacht construction. Series building and commissions from builders and owners abroad have brought international recognition, with yachts up to 57 feet coming from their office in City Road.

Due to ill health Kim Holman retired from the firm in 1968 and since that time Donald Pye has been senior partner, with David Cooper, and the firm continues to design sailing yachts blending advanced style with a distinctive grace. They particularly specialise in craft suitable for offshore racing; a sport in which West Mersea yachtsmen have been prominent for over thirty years.

The noted marine artist Arthur Briscoe lived at West Mersea for some years. His works in oils and etching are well known but his prolific line illustration less so. At "Buzzon", Briscoe's house, noted cruising men and artists were frequent

34

callers, as were Mersea fishermen and wildfowlers, for Briscoe was one of the clan of "Gennelmen gunners". He was the founder of the Dabchicks Sailing Club, bustling about the creeks and river in a bumkin named *War Baby*. He could not foresee the growth of "The Dabchicks" to its present popularity but was content to see it flourish in a happy atmosphere with a subscription of half a crown a year. Briscoe also founded the Mersea Smack Insurance Society and was its first chairman, replacing the begging from local gentry which had been the earlier custom after loss or severe damage of a smack.

An annual regatta has probably been intermittently held at West Mersea for well over a century and there were lively ones in the early 1900s, with races for smacks and fishermen's boats and later for small yachts. In 1920 seventy boats raced in West Mersea Town Regatta and forty-five participated in the weekly races of the Dabchicks Sailing Club, which did not then possess a clubhouse yet had 240 members including fishermen, smack owners, oystermen, residents and visitors. That September, 150 members filled the Great Hall barn for the annual dinner and around improvised tables in the lamp-lit barn, decked with flags, ate, drank, smoked and sang in the informal fellowship of the east coast.

Regatta morning at West Mersea 1936. Smacks, yachts and dinghies muster for the day's annual races and fun afloat. West Mersea and Maldon smacks stretch down the Deeps in early morning sunshine, with the *Unity* inshore. All set a big staysail for the light air. Inset: the West Mersea Yacht Club "Sprite" class 14-footers reach towards the start.   *Douglas Went*

The enjoyable sail for many Mersea yacthsmen is from the anchorage, at a reasonable hour when the tides are around mid-day, across the Blackwater to Bradwell Creek. There, having navigated its short but tortuous course, they anchor and row ashore to *The Green Man* for beer and the conversation beloved of sailing people in the snug atmosphere of a pub which has catered for their needs for ninety years, and for the bargemen, fishermen and wildfowlers who preceded them.

Herbert Reiach, founder of the *Yachting Monthly* in 1906 and its editor until his death in 1921, made West Mersea his headquarters after 1918. This wise and gentle man, the most knowledgeable critic of yacht design and construction in his day and a trained naval architect until ill-health forced him to yachting journalism and other business interests in the printing world, became deeply fond of the east coast, so different from his native Clyde. He was happiest amongst the fishermen and fowlers, bargemen and boatbuilders and sailing friends of the Blackwater.

Fid Harnack, West Mersea's marine artist, sailing his sloop *Ben Gunn* in the Blackwater.

Others followed the artistic tradition set by Briscoe; Fid Harnack has sailed his small sloop and painted the east coast scene to perfection for fifty years. One of his oils hangs by me as I write; the grey dawn above a faintly wind-stirred creek, with oyster skiffs dredging and Mersea Island a blur in the background. It evokes the spirit of the creeks on an autumn morning. From his studio and house at West Mersea Fid has painted some of the most realistic pictures of the sea, particularly of small craft and the east coast. His seas wet the canvas, his sails bulge and draw, putting power into the picture; a man whose work is true and valuable sea art. Fid and his brother Edwin sailed together in the *Ben Gunn*, a clinker-planked, transom-sterned ship's boat converted to a gaff sloop during the 1920s by Mr Clarke, the Mersea shipwright. The addition of a rockered keel, uncompromising cabin top and well planned gaff sloop rig make her a joy to see beating out of Buzzon Creek, which is her usual mooring; her owner puffing a contented pipe, his eye noting every detail of the familiar scenes he captures so well on canvas.

Archie White, noted as a marine artist, was another Mersea yachtsman. His delightful line drawings of local scenes and craft, humorous personality and kindly manner combined with a deep understanding of local sailing traditions and of sailing itself made him and his able yawl *Concord* well known on the east coast and well beyond. He was master of using a fair wind and frequently sailed to Holland or Denmark instead of the Channel Islands; the oft avowed destination.

Up the lane at Feldy, his house looking westwards over the creeks and marshes to the fields of Virley and Wigborough lives Hervey Benham, sage of the Blackwater, whose knowledge and writings of the Essex coast have inspired many to enjoy the pleasures of sailing those waters and appreciate their history and traditions. Ownership of many craft led to his enjoying and absorbing the pleasureable freedom of sailing a working craft for fun. He bought the Mersea smack *Charlotte* from Charles Hewes in 1938 and as spare time from business allowed, sailed her until war commenced in 1939, fish trawling and dredging, racing in the regatta and cruising coastwise and across the North Sea to Holland and Belgium. His lifelong devotion to sailing and fishing allied to his skill as author has resulted in such fascinating books as *Last Stronghold of Sail, Down Topsail, Once Upon A Tide* and *The Stowboaters.* He has inspired many with his skill afloat and continues to sail and fish for pleasure from his favourite Blackwater, of which his friend and contemporary Michael Frost has written so expressively in his book *Boadicea C.K. 213.* Probably no one has wider knowledge of the natural features, the waters and fish, shores and wildfowl of the river and estuary than the owner of *Boadicea.*

These sailing men and scores of others enjoyed Mersea's golden age, the forty years when the village was sought and savoured by a few enthusiasts and before universal popularity of sailing began to dilute its magic. The Mersea they remember is still there at times, especially on summer weekdays when one turns out of a warm bunk in the Ray to see the sun of early morning behind the island trees. Aspens whispering in the chill, faint north-easterly breeze, bringing thin white mist off the creeks to enhance the contrast with the silhouetted village still sleeping under its red roofs and dark treetops, with the faintest trace of honeysuckle wafting down the lanes and voices carrying clear from the causeway, where a dropped oar loom rolls thunderously in the quiet.

In 1928 the West Mersea Yacht Club decided to encourage dinghy racing and sensibly sought a boat which would be useful for pottering in the creeks and Blackwater when not racing, and one which could also be sailed safely by children and not so agile adults. They chose a 10-footer which had been designed in 1919 by Herbert Reiach. About twenty were built and became successful. Most were built at Mersea by Mr Clarke, but three were constructed at Maldon by Walter Cook and Son, where Alf Last recalled they were rowed down to Mersea by a fisherman who arrived on the bus at high water and straight away stowed the gear in two boats, got out the oars of the third and with the other two in tow rowed off down the Blackwater on the long pull to West Mersea with the ebb.

The ten-footers provided wonderful sport for many years and a few are still sailing the creeks. Two are stored in my boatshed as I write, owned by my son and daughter who are fond of these chubby dinghies, which remain unaltered except for their Terylene lugsails.

About 1933 the West Mersea Yacht Club commissioned Robert N. Stone, the talented Brightlingsea small craft designer, to produce plans for the 14-foot "Sprite" one-design class, which provided keen racing for over thirty years. The boats were built at Brightlingsea by D. Stone and Sons and within a few years a fleet of 25-30 boats were racing regularly. Interest revived after 1945 when further boats were built for the Blackwater Sailing Club at Heybridge, at the head of the Blackwater. With 5 foot beam, moderate hull depth and 111 square feet of sail area the "Sprites" had some of the good qualities of the designer's splendid 18-foot Brightlingsea one-designs and remain a desirable type of day sailing boat, now sought by many.

The rush of enthusiasm for offshore racing in small yachts during the 1930s was as keen at West Mersea as anywhere. Increasing numbers of yachts were being moored there and though numbers of smacks were still working, their crews were increasingly seeking summer berths as yacht hands, some racing in the large class yachts such as *Lulworth, Shamrock V, Astra* and the two *Endeavours*. Harry Milgate of West Mersea was mate of the *Shamrock V* and Walter Mussett, who moved to Tollesbury, was skipper of the 12-metre *Vanity*, with a local crew.

The 1939-45 war brought the Royal Army Service Corps water division to West Mersea, their craft occupying the creeks and moorings. Giant amphibians rumbled up and down the hard and the yachts and smacks slumbered in mud berths and in corners of the yards, which were put to war work, along with Gowen's sail loft.

The yawl *Thalassa* was a stalwart competitor in British offshore racing for twenty years and is still sailing as a cruiser. Here she is as best remembered, big jib and mizzen staysail set, footing away for the mark with her owner, Alan Baker of West Mersea, at the tiller, boat on deck and a cheerful crew out to win.

Douglas Went

Yachts racing in the Blackwater, 1936. V. B. Harrison's wishbone-rigged schooner *Elver* was built at Lymington in 1923 and was a familiar sight in the Blackwater, with moorings at West Mersea until the 1940s.   *Douglas Went*

After 1945 the pent up longings of sailing people burst out with astonishing enthusiasm in an austerity ridden world. It has never subsided. The little cruisers and dinghies were soon sailing again and offshore racing regained a strong following from Mersea, where the larger yachts were mainly intended for that healthy branch of the sport. The fine yawl *Thalassa* was owned by Alan Baker, one of the early members of the Royal Ocean Racing Club and its Rear Commodore from 1958-60, besides being a leading spirit in the West Mersea Yacht Club for many years. Norman Richards' 45-foot sloop *Corinna* was queen of the anchorage and a regular supporter of the annual regatta, where her presence, with a few contemporaries, *Thalassa, Jocasta, Mehalah* (which weathered a notable gale when racing to Spain one summer), *Kismet, Windhover*, and the wishbone-rigged schooner *Elver*, lent some meaning to the pretentious title of "Big Class".

A then young contemporary, John Milgate of West Mersea, sailed during 1947 in Orson Wright's 50-foot Fife cutter *Kismet*, whose skipper was Merseaman Jack Chatters. His interpretation of racing rules was rather wide and led to many narrow escapes at the starts. That glorious season the *Kismet* won prizes at regattas all along the east and south coasts, besides racing in Cowes Week under a big topsail which John tended with a mastheadsman's care, the envy of us other youngsters. In 1949 it was decided that the smart *Kismet* would sail no more; her lead keel was removed to be sold and the graceful cutter became a houseboat along the Coast Road, where she still lies amongst the hulls of other racing and cruising yachts.

It was John who proved that gun punts can be sailed out of the water. He owned one rigged with a large lugsail. The tide left her at the top of the hard one morning when John was putting me off to my boat. Undeterred he set the lug mainsail and the foresail, gave her a shove and we were off, sailing down the weather mud to plunge into the creek and dart about, muddy but triumphant, amongst the anchorage, bringing terror to owners of shiny white topsides, at whom we grinned with meaning as the punt shot past.

Buzzon Creek and saltings, looking towards the Blackwater, about 1939. Smacks lie at moorings in the creek and although the photograph is entitled "The houseboats", the two craft in foreground are smartly kept seagoing yachts occupying mud berths preparatory to laying up. A hand from the small motor yacht is busy in her launch, astern. Beyond is a pointed stern yawl, one of several built by Cardnell Brothers at their yard on Maylandsea Creek, further up the Blackwater.

Bells Photo Company

The Houseboats, West Mersea.

Regatta days were a special joy, particularly if one was racing. The eager cycle ride from Fingringhoe in the crisp air of early morning to arrive, panting, at the waterside already filled with figures hurrying towards the causeway. Hiding the bike behind Wyatt's sheds in anticipation of the crowds of afternoon. The rush down the causeway and cajoling a ''Put off'' to the smack or yacht in which one had arranged to sail. The excitement of being a participant in this pageant. Mersea Town Regatta day is the greatest survival of informal waterborne fun in Essex, with ex-fishing smacks and bumkins coming to the line and rolling the clock back, followed by the latest fashions in hulls and sail plans of plastic-hulled offshore racers and cruisers, class by class, to the smaller handicap yachts, many of which have sailed from Mersea for thirty or forty years.

''The line'' at West Mersea Town Regatta watersports in the 1930s. Craft of many types form a floating grandstand for the afternoon's fun; an old and continuing tradition. *Douglas Went*

A youthful Harold Cutts edges along the greasy pole to take the flag and the prize at West Mersea Town Regatta watersports, 1947. The dense crowd of spectators and boats is typical of this popular regatta. The greasy pole event has a centuries-old tradition.   *By courtesy of Harold Cutts*

Dayboats and dinghies follow until the estuary is a mass of sails, white and tanned, and finishing guns boom from the committee launch anchored in the Deeps as the racers sweep home, the smacks cheering each other in the old tradition as they cross the line. Things change slowly in the organisation of these events and handicaps for some classes are still often decided by popular consent in the Public Bar rather than by formulae. Here is none of the embittered, frantic competition of the Solent classes. Keenness and rivalry, but if you don't win, why worry? There are the watersports to come—and then the fair. After lunch; a liquid one for many, spectator craft begin to crowd Mersea Fleet for the watersports. Traditionally, "The Line" as this temporary gathering of craft is called, centres around a sailing barge chartered for the day by the regatta committee and laboriously got into position broadside to the hard, the day before the event. When everything was stowed, her crew locked up and went home on the bus for the week-end. The watersports are famed locally and attract huge crowds of spectators afloat and ashore. Yachts and smacks, oyster bumkins and day sailers string themselves out in a long anchored line, crowded with people watching the two hour succession of events during the afternoon high water. Rowing and sculling races, swimming, blindfold rowing, pair and single oared races, the shovel race in which several smack's boats are propelled at amazing speed by three or four youths with shovels, followed by those climaxing favourites; the greasy pole, the "duck hunt" and the "Pull devil, pull baker".

The greasy pole is rigged out at right angles from the committee barge's side and in past times was well greased by William Wyatt and his nephew Ed, a tradition carried on by Harold Cutts. One by one the competitors venture on it, attempting to reach the flag on a stick at its outer end, with a few successes for the prize, which used to be a live pig. In the "duck hunt" the human "duck" in a wildfowl punt is pursued from the hard, across the water between the anchored craft and spectators by his human pursuers in boats, climaxing the performance by climbing to the topmast head of the barge and coming rapidly down the shrouds, hand over hand, along the mainsail headrope and down the sprit, perhaps to be caught on the deck or maybe managing to dive overboard and swim ashore to beat the time limit gun and win the prize for eluding capture.

Events end with the "Pull devil, pull baker", in which two rowing boats are made fast from their transoms with a length of stout rope and four men in each, often wearing comic dress at the start, pelt each other with bags of soot and of "flour" (chalk) as a rower in the bow of each attempts to tow the other boat in his direction. Excitement mounts amongst spectators and competitiors as black and white bags burst in clouds of dust, the dishevelled bakers and devils shouting "insults" at each other and finally, when ammunition is exhausted, boarding each other and pitching the rival crew overboard. So all end drifting in the tide and washing off the results of the battle. All these events are traditional and have been enacted at Essex regattas for many years.

After the tea time lull, a joyful prizegiving in the open air before the *Victory* pub and the spectacular evening "Colours" by the Sea Cadet boys band at the Yacht Club flagstaff. Then all thoughts are on the annual fair which was, by tradition, held each year on the tiny meadow behind the *Victory*. For days beforehand fair caravans have been arriving and lorries bearing all the gaily painted parts of the giant racer, the dodgems, swing boats, stalls and tents. Erecting and testing goes on until regatta day and by dusk all of West Mersea's population and seemingly that of the parishes around, joined by many from Colchester and elsewhere, flock into Mersea's narrow roads and lanes, converging on "the fair", attracted like moths by the bright lights and strident music beating out above the roar of generators, whose snaky tentacles drive and light the fascinating assortment of attractions which are appreciated by the generations, with grandfathers and grandchildren whirling round on the dodgems, wildly bumping exuberant young fishermen and yachtsmen and their girl friends, shouting, laughing, singing, shrieking; enjoying this one wild fling in the usually sedate village calendar. Old timers recall the days, into the 1930s, when the fair arrived towed by steam traction engines, whose earth-shaking beat drove the generators; youngsters have eyes only for the giant racer, twirling round at incredible speed with the young fare collectors riding nonchalantly on its rim, giving change at a centrifugal speed to test an astronaut.

With the fun of the fair still at its height it is time for the fireworks; the best display on the east coast, with a crowd fully rivalling the famous Friday night of Cowes Week. The crowds press thick along Coast Road, at the top of the hard, along towards Wyatt's in one direction and Clarke and Carter's in the other; up Firs Chase, to spill over on to the Yacht Club lawn and the little green opposite. Since mid-afternoon Brocks' workmen have been busy erecting the set pieces and preparing batteries for the rockets and Roman candles, Sharp at nine o'clock, with darkness almost complete, the two firework men appear with their lighted sticks and dodge, half seen amongst dinghies on the hard, to set off the thunderous maroon announcing commencement of the show. Rockets streak up, two and three together, bursting in clouds of brilliant stars which bring excited ''Oohs and Aahs'' as they soar and fall, followed by the rising, chanting count for the bursting rocket stars; ''One, two, THREE, FOUR . . .'' Coloured light, the smell of gunpowder, the fizz of giant catherine wheels and the sparkle of set pieces culminate with the portrait of the Queen and then—blackness, the murmuring of the crowds and the shuffling walk back home, or to the fair, where the young continue to enjoy its strident pleasures until midnight.

I have dwelt on West Mersea and its waterside because to many, including myself, it has represented that pleasant mixture of work and play which appeals most to the temperament of north-east Essex sailing people. I sincerely hope its atmosphere will not be ruined in the future.

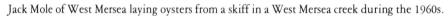

Jack Mole of West Mersea laying oysters from a skiff in a West Mersea creek during the 1960s.

Three Men Of Mersea

ONE man's experience cannot give a sufficiently broad glimpse into the way of life of the fishermen and yachtsmen of West Mersea and three island men have contributed their story. Jack Mole and Jim Mussett have a lifetime's experience afloat behind them, while John Frost is a young fisherman using modern methods, craft and equipment.

Jack Mole

Jack Mole was born at West Mersea in 1902, the son of a fisherman and one of four children. He left school aged thirteen to work afloat and could swim across the "Hove", a rill off Buzzon creek, then reckoned a necessary childhood accomplishment. He went as boy on board the 9-ton Mersea cutter smack *Daisy Belle*, under Thomas French, who worked her for Mr Capes, a retired resident. They both worked on a part wage system. The *Daisy Belle* spent much of the year trawling for shrimps in the approaches to the Colne and Blackwater Rivers, usually in the Eagle Deeps, breaking off to trawl dabs in April in the swatch between the flats off Sales Point at Bradwell and the Batchelor Spit and the Knowle Sands, often in company with a dozen or so Maldon smacks.

Jack's father was a member of the Tollesbury and Mersea Oyster Fishery Company and he was formally apprenticed for four years as an oyster dredgerman. The oysters were sold to several buyers at West Mersea including William Gasson, Mr Woolf, George Cutts (who also bought winkles) and Ted Mussett, for whom they were often landed on the beach at the foot of "Monkey House steps" near the church, so named for the glass-domed coastguard lookout which fishermen called the "Monkey House". He recalled their crew humping 30 to 40 bags ashore there from the smack at times.

The Oyster Company shares were of two types; "A" shares were for capital investors only. "B" shares were owned by dredgermen working the fishery and every man so employed had to be a shareholder, just as in the nearby River Colne fishery each had to be a "Freeman of the Company".

These small smacks carried three hands for dredging, each man working one dredge. They started at 6.30 a.m. and sailed out to the ground being worked that day and dredged until "elevenses", when they laid to an anchor or a dredge if it was fine, or hove-to for the three-quarters of an hour break. Then it was back to hauling and sorting until 2.00 p.m. when they invariably stopped work and the catch was transferred from each smack to those with a juryman of the fishery on board, to be carried in to the packing shed island at Mersea, where the day's catch was sorted by jurymen, only, standing at long benches culling oysters into the various grades for sale or to be re-laid as stock in the oyster pits on the nearby saltings.

There were then three watch smacks anchored in the Blackwater to protect the Company's grounds against theft or illegal dredging; the *Frolic*, which Jack describes as an ''ex-Revenue cutter'', lay off the Mersea shore at the ''meets'' or shore beacons which marked the lower limit of Company ground and lined up with others on the opposite shore at Bradwell, where the smack *Betsy* lay anchored about half a mile below the mouth of Bradwell Creek. The *Spy* was anchored in the mouth of Thirslet Creek to watch the upper parts of the fishery. All had one watchman on board, usually a juryman of the Company. The watch smacks were on station for long periods and became very foul from not being scrubbed. The *Frolic* was once brought into Mersea hard for scrubbing and painting when the weed on her bottom was so thick that a school of mullet played around her and the fishermen set a peter net around the hull, but, as ever, the wily mullet jumped it as it closed on them. There were also oyster policemen in the Blackwater during the 1920s, using the bulky cutter *Our Boys* which was built at Paglesham, on the River Roach, as a yacht but was converted to a police boat in which Constables Brown and Nurse patrolled the river under sail and power until the 1930s.

As a boy Jack went winkling, going away on Monday in a small smack with two or three hands to sail into the Ray Sand Channel, then in over the Dengie Flats to lie in the deep outfalls ''along the Main'' sea wall, where the smack was moored snug and took the mud at low water while the fishermen spread out gathering winkles which were plentiful in warm weather but became scarce on cold days. On Friday they hauled out, often barely finding room to swing the smack in the narrow outfalls. Then they sailed home with the week's ''catch'' filling sacks in the hold, to be put ashore for the buyer. In strong easterly winds they could not get the smacks out of the outfalls and off that lee shore, so often the crews had to walk the weary miles of sea wall to Bradwell for food and beer, and sometimes to row from there across the Blackwater to get home for the week-end. Some fishermen rowed from West Mersea down the Mersea Flats in search of winkles and a few ventured on the Main in superannuated yachts' dinghies and smacks' boats, setting a small lugsail for a reach or a fair wind. About 1912 some Mersea fishermen conceived the idea of using a bumkin for this work; a small clinker-planked, centreboard open boat rigged as a gaff sloop, varying from 15 to 18 feet long, beamy and deep but also capable of being rowed and capable of towing a single oyster dredge over a laying in the creeks.

West Mersea winkle brig *Kate* racing in one of the early races of the Dabchicks Sailing Club. She was built for William Trim.

The 18-foot *Kate*, built for William Trim, was one of the first and was also one of the original craft of the Dabchicks Sailing Club. Later the *Kate* was owned by Bill Wyatt the boatbuilder. *Ellen, Winnie* and *MaNabs* were some which followed and in 1920 Charles Kidby of Brightlingsea built the *Ivy* for Billy Vince, followed by the 16-foot *Jack* for another Mersea fisherman. The Mersea men preferred using bumkins for working on the Main as the two man crew could get home at night and avoid the expense of maintaining a smack to lie about three days of the week. The younger men naturally wished to get home if possible for courting and shore pursuits.

In 1919 Jack sought a summer berth in a yacht, as did most of his contemporaries seeking a good income from a summer's yachting to supplement the winter's small returns from oystering and winkling. It also held promise of adventure but he was young and inexperienced in yachting ways, so it would be a cruising yacht. Early in the year he heard that Bert Frost, the Tollesbury skipper of the Earl of Craven's 80-foot yawl *Sylvia* was looking for a hand and he cycled over to Tollesbury to get the job at the immediately post-war inflated wages of £3 per week, with an additional ten shillings weekly "conduct money". After fitting out, the *Sylvia* cruised down Channel and to France, making fast passages under her 3,735 square feet sail area. She returned, cross Channel, for Weymouth, encountering a gale in which the skipper would not take her into harbour and the *Sylvia* lay-to offshore until it moderated; an incident annoying to the owner. She returned to Tollesbury to lay up.

After a winter's oyster dredging and winkling, Jack again joined the *Sylvia* in spring, fitting out under another Tollesbury skipper for the 1920 season of cruising. After another winter's winkling he hoped to go again in 1921 but she

Tollesbury and Mersea oystermen at the oyster packing sheds at West Mersea, about 1904. The group includes A. Carter, Joe Pearce, Isiah Binks, Nehemiah Ward, A. Rice, John Redgewell, R. Page, William Collins, James Heard, Joseph Heard, Michael Heard, Peter Frost, J. Pettican and some of the Mole family of West Mersea.

did not fit out. However, he heard of a berth in the large cruising schooner *Halcyon*, fitting out at Brightlingsea, but was too late to get it. Instead, he took charge of the small Mersea smack *Fairy* which had been chartered to some visitors to the island for summer sailing. One day they wished to play golf at the East Mersea course and Jack sailed the *Fairy* around to East Mersea Stone, anchored and put them ashore with their clubs in the boat. The 42-ton cutter yacht *Thanet*, which then raced in the big handicap class under Captain Zac Burch of Rowhedge was anchored there. Jack sculled over to speak to her hands while he awaited the return of the golfers. He was excited to hear that the *Thanet* was a hand short but felt frustrated when the hands added that the skipper had just gone ashore to Brightlingsea to interview a man for the job.

Later Jack took charge of the 8-ton cutter *White Heather*, owned by Colonel Grimblewold, cruising on the east and south coasts with Jack as hand, living in solitary state in the little fo'c'sle. In 1922 he obtained a berth in the schooner *Halcyon* fitting out at Brightlingsea under Captain Joe Carter. This 120-footer was owned by Mr R. Ffenell, a South African and was capable of extended cruising. She was manned in the manner of contemporary larger yachts. There were, besides the skipper, Bob Howe of Brightlingsea as the first mate, a second mate, six hands, an engineer, three stewards and two cooks. She had a bulky paraffin auxiliary engine in its own engine room. The owner, his family, friends and guests did not, of course, have any part in the navigation and handling of the yacht, as was then customary, contenting themselves with an occasional spell at the wheel in fine weather, under the watchful eye of the skipper or mate. The *Halcyon* cruised down Channel and coastwise but an unexpected stomach ulcer ended Jack's yachting career when the *Halcyon* was laid up one winter and he had to go into hospital for an operation and rest, for which it seemed the owner paid as he never received an account.

This left a weakness and afterwards he settled to a life of oystering and winkling in the West Mersea tradition. In 1925 Jack placed an order for a new 15-foot bumkin with Charles Kidby. She was built complete for £27. 10s. 0d. Jack had not thought of a name but at the insistence of a young nephew he called her *Wheezy Anna*, after the then popular song. She proved a fine little sailer, though they still had to row to and from the grounds in a calm and Jack recalls frequent four or five hours hard pulling followed by five or six hours of back breaking winkling, then another four hours or so rowing home before the catch was landed and the winklers could go home to spruce up for the evening! A typical day's work might result in picking up 3-4 wash measures of winkles and sometimes 5-6 bushels.* Winkling seems removed from "fishing" to many, but it was a wearing trade.

Jack Mole's memory brings alive a picture of the Blackwater filled with working sail; smacks, bumkins and barges, scores of dredgermen, shrimpers and fish trawlers, some stowboaters and, as background, the size and briskness of the river's oyster trade. The Tollesbury smack *A.E.F.A.*, owned by Bowles, was carrying oysters from the Blackwater to Whitstable in Kent for the Seasalter and Ham Oyster Company to supplement their own carrier, the *Seasalter*. The Whitstable Company's cutter *Postboy* was also a carrier; all three making two trips each week in the season. Jessie French had the bumkin *Oyster* built for carrying oysters from the Maldon smacks dredging in the upper river, above Thirslet Creek, to his layings and pits at West Mersea. Later she was owned by his son Leslie and was sold for pleasure sailing during the 1950s. In 1960 I became her owner and have never enjoyed a boat more. Sam Francis' *Winnie* was also used for carrying oysters as he was the Mersea agent for the Whitstable Oyster Company. She was later sold to Mr Banks, another oysterman.

In the days before bumkins and motor oyster skiffs, the layings in the creeks were dredged in open skiffs by "tow hauling". Usually there were two men in a tow haul skiff, occasionally three. It was hard work hauling a heavy skiff along a bass warp anchored to the bed of the creek, towing a dredge astern, the men heaving at the warp until it was time to haul the dredge. If there was a strong wind, fair in one direction of hauling, a squaresail was set on a stump mast forward and they blew back, giving the haulers a rest. In heavy rain or very cold weather the squaresail was rigged as a "hullet" over the forward end of the skiff for shelter.

*A wash is 5 gallons 1 quart, $\frac{1}{2}$ pint: approximately $\frac{5}{8}$ of a "Winchester bushel".

Jack eventually owned a laying, using the *Wheezy Anna* and a tow haul skiff to work it. In the late 1930s he bought the motor skiff *Sally* from Lewis Worsp of Wivenhoe but retained the *Wheezy Anna* for some time. She was a regular competitor in the race for bumkins at West Mersea Town Regatta with Jack at the helm, out to beat his fellow fishermen. The *Sally* had a Brit petrol paraffin engine of a type preferred by West Mersea oystermen for their work which involves considerable time running at low speeds.

The Mersea and Maldon men were loath to fit engines in their smacks and Jack recalls the transom-sterned *Boy Kenneth* as the first auxiliary at Mersea during the 1920s.

The first full powered motor fishing craft Jack remembers in the Blackwater was the 40-foot launch *Dan* owned by the Tollesbury and Mersea Oyster Fishery Company. She had a turtle deck forward and bitts aft for towing smacks and skiffs. The noise of her hot bulb diesel engine could be heard for miles when it was started with a blow lamp. The coxswain, Laban Pierce of Tollesbury, kept her smart and until 1939 she frequently towed two or three skiffs with three men in each, dredging in the creeks, besides acting as a carrier for smacks dredging in the river.

Nine smacks beat up over the tide for the day's dredging in the Blackwater. Most set a two-reefed mainsail, staysail and a small jib; a rig suitable for dredging under sail in a fresh breeze.

Douglas Went

Jack Mole's working life continued untroubled except by fears of a harsh winter and by the war of 1939-45, which filled the creeks with moorings for craft of the Royal Army Service Corps and the foreshores with barbed wire, mines and regulations. But fish were still landed and oysters survived, tended as best they could be. His preoccupations were, as always, the work of oyster cultivation; clearing ground, laying culch, anticipating spatfall, dredging, hauling, sorting, relaying, carrying and selling in a world which quickly regained its taste for oysters amid post-war austerity.

The winter of 1961-62 changed Jack's way of life. The snow and frosts grew more severe until at last the rills, then the creeks and finally the shores of the rivers froze. Ice floes piled on each other at the saltings and tidelines, grinding up and down at each tide. At first there was some hope for the delicate oysters, soon it was hopeless and Jack and other oystermen knew their stock must be killed by the intense cold. As soon as it thawed sufficiently to allow, Jack took the *Sally* out to the laying and had a few hauls; all came up full of decayed and rotting oysters. The stench was as overpowering as the final realisation that all his hard work and investment had been destroyed by a few weeks of winter. He contemplated re-stocking but at sixty he would be close to retirement when he reaped any returns on four more years of hard work and risk. The laying was sold to Ted Woolf, a young oysterman having other grounds at Mersea and Jack went to work for him with the *Sally*, clearing the layings of dead oysters and re-stocking them for the future.

Jack Mole continued dredging and working for Ted Woolf until he retired in 1972 after a lifetime afloat. From his comfortable home in Victory Road he can potter in the garden and glimpse the river through the trees.

James Mussett

James Mussett, known to his friends as ''Jim'', was born at West Mersea in 1905, the son of Clark Mussett, a fisherman of one of Mersea's oldest established families. Jim was one of a family of three children and first went fishing in his father's cutter *Edith*, a small clinker-planked craft of about 7 tons which had been doubled to smooth her sides for oyster dredging. She had been bought from George Baker of Bradwell. In her they dredged oysters and gathered winkles and young Jim quickly became skilled in casting a dredge, walking the muds, pulling an oar, trimming a sheet and handling a tiller. When he was twenty-one years old he decided to try for a summer berth on board a yacht and in the early spring of 1926 he joined the cruising schooner *Halcyon* in which Jack Mole had earlier served. She was fitting out at Brightlingsea under Captain Joe Carter and Jim and some other Mersea men in the crew cycled over to East Mersea each morning and went across on the ferry from Mersea Stone to Brightlingsea to spend the day fitting out before returning each evening. The *Halcyon* completed for sea in Colne and sailed south to the Downs, to embark guests at Deal before sailing for Falmouth, where she was stored for a cruise to the Mediterranean. Jim's duties were the usual ones of a cruising yacht: handling sails, hauling ropes, tending gear, standing watches, scrubbing down and maintenance work. The crew lived in the fo'c'sle, flanked by its double tiered rows of pipe cots for each man, with polished pine locker tops under them as seats and the captain's little cabin opening off the side of the messroom in which the two mates and three stewards lived.

The *Halcyon* made her landfall on the west coast of Spain, then cruised along the coast to Vigo, where the owner decided to turn back because the weather was already unpleasantly hot and would become intolerable by the time they reached the Mediterranean. So the schooner turned for England, but called at many ports in Spain and Portugal; San Sebastian, Bilbao, Finisterre, Couronna, then on up the French Atlantic coast, where the Essexmen were interested to see the vast oyster centres of Britanny. The final passage home was to Brightlingsea in mid-October to dismantle and lay up for the winter, which Jim spent in oyster dredging and winkling in and around the Blackwater.

Early in 1927 he was approached by Harry Milgate, a Mersea man who was then second mate of the *Lulworth*, to sail as a hand in this first class racing cutter. The first mate, George Francis of Brightlingsea, had asked Harry to find five hands from West Mersea to complete the crew for the season and Jim was glad of the opportunity. The 125-foot *Lulworth* had been built in 1920 as the *Terpsichore*, designed by Herbert White and built at White Brothers' Itchen yard as a racing cruiser, rather than as a pure racing yacht. Her owner was R. H. Lee.

She was an unusually shaped cutter having considerable freeboard, 2 foot high bulwarks and prominent channels for the shrouds. The shape of the bow and counter was uncompromising but her underwater body was well formed and she often "got a flag". Like all large gaff-rigged racers of the 1920s her rig was frequently altered and heightened in the search for windward efficiency.

During 1926 she had been sailed by Captain Charles Bevis of Bursledon, on the river Hamble, Hampshire, but due to his illness she was fitting out under Captain Archie Hogarth of Port Bannatyne, Bute; a Scot who had commanded large racing yachts since the 1890s and valued Essex hands in his crews. The *Lulworth* had a mixed crew of 26, from the Clyde, the Colne, West Mersea, Tollesbury, the Solent and the west country. Harry Milgate got his five men; Peter Owen, Alf Farrow, Leslie Mussett, Tom Cudmore and Jim Mussett. They joined her at Northam, Southampton, and fitted out in a mud berth for the racing season.

Her first passage was to the Clyde under trysail gear; used by all large racers when passagemaking, the precious racing mainsail remaining stowed to avoid pulling it out of shape and besides, the racing mainsail was too large for serious sea work.

Jim Mussett of West Mersea first served as hand in a large racing yacht on board the 125-foot cutter *Lulworth*, whose sail plan of 11,000 square feet was set on a "Marconi" mast in the quest for windward efficiency. In 1927 her crew of 26 included five hands from Mersea.

They sailed down Channel, round Land's End and up the Irish Sea to race against the big schooner *Westward*, the cutter *White Heather* and the *Shamrock* (23-metre), sailed by Captain Sycamore from Brightlingsea. On the second day of the Clyde Fortnight, the northern equivalent of Cowes Week, the four racers were manoeuvering at the start when Captain Mountifield fell overboard from the wheel of the *White Heather* but was quickly rescued and taken ashore injured.

The *Lulworth* sailed for Belfast Lough and two races at Bangor regatta. Then a return passage "round the land" to race at Falmouth, then at Plymouth and up-Channel to prepare for Cowes Week.

Captain Hogarth did not look astern when racing and Jim recalls old Captain Charles Bevis sailing with them in the Solent regattas as racing pilot for local waters and Captain Hogarth at the wheel asking him what was going on astern, keeping his concentration for racing tactics and covering his opponents.

The major regattas of Southsea and Ryde followed. In the Royal Albert Yacht Club regatta, from Southsea on Thursday 11th August, the racing fleet started in a strong south-westerly wind and all were reefed for the heavy squalls. The *Lulworth, Shamrock* (23-metre), *White Heather* (23-metre), *Britannia* and the mighty schooner *Westward* started for the Albert Gold Cup.

The *Lulworth* was last but one over the line, followed by the *Britannia*, and these two carried full sized jib-headed topsails instead of the "thimble headers" set by the others, all being gaff-rigged. The fleet beat to the west in Spithead, the *Westward* leading and the others battling it out. Off Wootton Creek, on the Isle of Wight shore, *Lulworth*'s mast broke about 6 feet above the deck with a loud, cracking rumble as 9,300 square feet of sail, mast, boom, gaff and rigging fell, fortunately to leeward, leaving her plunging in broken water with the wreckage alongside. It took a long time to clear this and get most of it on deck. Then she was towed to anchorage off Ryde. As no life was lost the other yachts carried on and the *Britannia* won by 3 minutes 5 seconds from the *Westward*.

The disabled *Lulworth* was towed to Southampton and laid up at Northam as it was too late in the season to re-rig her for the remaining racing fixtures, so the crew paid off. By then Jim had had enough of the *Lulworth* for the same reason other men had been glad to leave; her gear was too heavy for a crew of 26. Earlier gaff-rigged cutters had been larger, with gear of equal or greater weight but they usually had 30-35 hands to provide adequate hauling power, as these yachts had none or very few winches for sheets and halyards and all hauling was done with tackles.

After another winter oystering and winkling Jim found a berth for 1928 in the 67-foot steel schooner *Sus* with skipper Stan Lewis of Tollesbury, fitting out at White's yard at Itchen, Southampton. Jim joined as hand and Arthur Bibby of Tollesbury was cook and steward. The three of them tried to sort out her gear, which was in store marked in Russian! The *Sus* had been built in Russia in 1905, and had a reputation for being a fast cruiser for her size. Why she came to England was a mystery. Her new owner, Mr Toogood of Plympton, near Plymouth, was a sick and cautious owner who insisted on installation of an auxiliary engine, so the *Sus* was consequently delayed and did not get away until July, anchoring in the Cattewater at Plymouth to await orders. Each morning Jim rowed in to the Barbican Steps, from which the Pilgrim fathers sailed from the port, to pick up the owner for a day's sail; often Mr Toogood sent his chauffeur instead with the message that he felt too unwell to sail that day. Usually they siled to the Eddystone light and back, but after a month or so the owner was not well enough even for that and they sailed the *Sus* back to the Hamble river and laid her up in Luke's Yard. While completing this, Captain Bevis of the new 70-foot Bermudian yawl *Gladoris* came on board saying he was short of a hand, so Jim joined her for the remainder of a long season. There were only three on board; the skipper, Jim as hand and a steward from Southampton.

That winter, while oystering and winkling, Jim heard from George Pullen of Mersea, who was a hand in the 75-foot yawl *Palmosa*, that her Tollesbury skipper, Billy Wilkinson, wanted a hand, so he applied and joined this cruising yacht which had in earlier days raced in a handicap class and is still afloat as a houseboat at Cowes. Jim and George were hands and George White was cook/steward. They fitted out at Tollesbury and sailed to the south coast where the owner, Mr Newbiggin, a noted London silversmith, joined her for weekends, then for a month's cruise to Deauville, the Channel Islands and then back to Torquay to enjoy the fun of the end of season racing and regattas. They finished the season at the Helford River where the Essex men found much interest in the local oyster fishery, so similar to their home activities. The *Palmosa* returned to Tollesbury to lay up and Jim remained a member of her crew for four seasons of enjoyable cruising.

Late in 1932 Merseaman Bert French, who was mate of the "J" Class racer *Shamrock V*, was asked by Captain Ted Heard of Tollesbury to find him several Mersea hands for the big racing cutter *Astra*, his new command. Bert suggested that Jim apply and he wrote to Captain Heard, who requested his references. He had none but referred the skipper to the captain of the *Palmosa* and as a result was shipped as a hand. The *Astra* had a crew of 18, nine of whom then came from Tollesbury. They joined her at Camper and Nicholson's Gosport yard to fit out in the spring of 1933.

At that time of economic depression racing crews received £2. 14s. per week, as wages had fallen since the early 1920s and were further reduced by 10 per cent during those years when anyone was fortunate to find employment, though north-east Essex with its then modest population was better off than most areas. However, Ted Heard contrived to get his men something extra for "special duties". Of course the mastheadsman and bowspritendsman received an additional 5 shillings each week for their often arduous and sometimes dangerous work, but the others were assigned an extra rating to justify payment. Jim became "lampey", trimming the navigation and riding lights, which meant keeping them cleaned and filled, with wicks trimmed for clear burning. Of course, wages were supplemented with prize money and each hand received £1 for a win, 15 shillings for a second prize and 5 shillings for a start. They also had 2s. 6d. each racing day for "Grub Money". During the season they came to know the crews of the other big class yachts well; *Britannia, Shamrock V*, and the new *Velsheda*.

Jim raced in the *Astra* for the seasons of 1933, 1934, 1935 and 1936. Other Mersea men in her crew at various seasons were Dick Haward during 1935-6 and "Chubby" Russell in 1937. At the commencement of each season the mate, Jack Gempton of Brixham, Devon, made out a list of duties for each man; a logical procedure followed on most large racing yachts for many years to ensure smart handling. Jim's duties in the *Astra* included making fast and letting go the main halyard and the spinnaker halyard. All halyards in large racers of that time led through a deck block at the foot of the mast and aft along the deck to belay on a cleat, allowing many men to haul with all their strength along the deck instead of pulling down in a cluster as they would otherwise have to do as there were no rattled-down shrouds to climb and "string down", as the crews did on the halyards of older, gaff-rigged racers. When the hands hauling had hoisted the sail Jim put the turns around the cleat in a twinkling and all hands melted away to the next job.

Jim recalls the tremendous power in those huge sails. This sometimes led to tragedy. In 1935 the American "J" Class racing sloop *Yankee* visited England to race with the large class, around the coast in the traditional series of regattas. She missed the opening regatta at Harwich and joined the racing fleet off Southend, at the mouth of the River Thames. A new and large spinnaker had just been delivered to the *Astra* from Ratsey and Lapthorn and Mr Lapthorn came with the sail to see they got the best out of it. So keen were he and the owner to try the new spinnaker that *Astra* started in this race when she might otherwise have laid at anchor in the strong wind, as did *Shamrock V*.

The order came to set the big spinnaker and up it went. Jim was making fast the halyard when the spinnaker sheet went out of control in the strong wind as hands on the foredeck were passing it round the forestay with the spinnaker boom run right forward. It lashed under the lee of the sail and some grabbed it but had to let go, except for George Lewis, a steward from Brightlingsea who held on and was thrown overboard amid shouts from forward. He flashed past the length of the roaring lee bow wave and quarter wave and a hand aft neatly dropped a lifebelt, always kept on the counter for the purpose, alongside his arms before the great racer was past and brought-to. The dinghy was launched in seconds and pulled furiously towards the lifebelt. But George Lewis, a non-swimmer, made no attempt to grasp the buoy and may well have been unconscious. When the dinghy got there he had disappeared. *Endeavour* lost her mast in the same squall and *Astra* scoured the area without trace of the missing man and returned to the Southend anchorage with a flag in the rigging; traditional sign for a drowned man. The steward's death cast a gloom over the commencement of one of the best yacht racing seasons ever experienced in the big class. The *Astra* called at Gosport for some alterations before racing at Falmouth. While there, news arrived that the body of George Lewis had been picked up by a sailing barge bound for the Thames and Medway barge matches and the inconsiderate authorities required her skipper to attend the inquest on the day of the opening match.

The mainsails of the ''J'' class were much smaller than those of the older gaff-rigged racers but still spread about 5,800 square feet of cotton canvas weighing just under a ton. It needed all hands to hoist and to sheet these in a breeze. When Jim first joined the *Astra* she had a conventional round-sectioned boom, which was soon changed to a deep rectangular boom, 6 inches wide and 30 inches deep, fitted with two tubular struts with bracing wires led over them, enabling the boom to be bent to the same curvature as the foot of the mainsail

Astra, in foreground, is led by the *Velsheda* and has *Endeavour* to windward at Harwich regatta, 1934. Captain Heard stands on Astra's quarter as she fetches towards the next mark off Felixstowe. The 115-foot long *Astra* was shortest of the big class racers, but was one of the most graceful.

Douglas Went

Jim Mussett of West Mersea as one of the crew of the *Endeavour*, 1937.

by setting up a rigging screw in the wire. The struts and wire had to be folded back to the boom before lowering the mainsail, which temporarily left the boom unsupported for side loads and liable to break if any weight came on the sheet. To speed lowering, Captain Heard ordered Jim to take the fall of the main halyard well forward of the mast and flake it across the foredeck when, as the yacht shot head to wind, Jim released the halyard from the cleat, allowing it to fall in a couple of seconds by its weight, while the writhing halyard fall shot upwards, with all hands keeping well forward.

Astra's 9 inch high bulwarks held some water on deck yet made little difference to the crew's safety as they were accustomed to racing and passage-making without the guardrails and pulpits now considered essential for seagoing yachts. Bound for the west country regattas, *Astra* met gales and sheltered overnight in the charming anchorage of Studland, under the lee of the west shore of Poole Bay, while the south-westerly roared through her rigging. Resuming passage next day she passed through the race off St Albans Head under trysail and foresail, the watch clustered aft by the wheel. Suddenly someone shouted and pointed at a large piece of timber whirling slowly past to leeward. Then they realised it was the forward fifty feet of bulwark, torn off by the vicious short seas. Next winter the bulwarks were reduced to 4 inches. British big class racing was in disarray for the 1937 season and the *Astra* was not to be fitted out. However, Captain Heard was loaned by Mr Paul to Mr Fred Sigrist, a close friend of Mr Sopwith, who had chartered the *Endeavour* from Herman Andreae to sail against the *Endeavour II* in the tuning-up races in American waters before the challenger raced for the America's Cup in September. Jim wrote to Captain Heard in February, hoping for a berth. Captain Heard replied offering Jim a berth as hand in the *Endeavour* at £3. 4s. per week, plus £1 per week extra, as soon as she left England until they returned, for her special work in tuning-up the challenger. All food was to be provided, so the hands cleared £4 weekly, then an exceptionally good wage. Jim was particularly pleased as the reply commenced with, "I have had you on my list for some time."

They joined the *Endeavour* at Gosport and were drawn from many places then sending hands into racing yachts. Jim recalls his shipmates as Captain, Edward Heard of Tollesbury: First Mate, Jack Gempton of Brixham, Devon: Second Mate, Lewis Wilkinson of Tollesbury: First Cook, Cyril Coates of Tollesbury: Second Cook, Joe Uglow of Looe, Cornwall: Steward, Ted Heard (Junior) of Tollesbury: Mastheadsman, Duncan Currie of Tinabruagh, Scotland: Second Mastheadsman, Bob Parker of Southampton: Hands, Bill Lewis of Tollesbury, Nevill Gurton of Tollesbury, Jim Stubbins of Tollesbury, Horace Chatterton of Tollesbury, Jim Mussett of West Mersea, Leonard Pengelly of Looe, Cornwall, Walter Pengelly of Looe, Cornwall, Jack Sargent of Looe, Cornwall, Dan Mutton of Port Isaac, Cornwall, Jim Cann of Port Isaac, Cornwall, Harry German of Brixham, Devon (who acted as stemheadsman), Harry (Jumbo) Randall of Hythe, Hampshire.

The *Endeavour* was fitted out for the ocean crossing with a shorter mainmast and a mizzen, temporarily converting her to a ketch setting a boomless trysail on the main and a stout staysail and jib forward. Her racing sails were at Ratsey and Lapthorn's Gosport loft and several of her crew, including Jim, were soon busy packing these huge pieces of canvas into hessian covers for shipment. As Mr Sopwith's big new motor yacht *Philante* was not completed, he chartered a powerful Belgian-owned trawler, the *Jon*, to tow the *Endeavour II* across the Atlantic and carry the racers spars and gear. The challenger was capable of sailing over under the reduced rig but the principal need was to get her to America as quickly as possible, without damage, to commence tuning up against the *Endeavour*, which was to be towed by the motor yacht *Viva*, also owned by Mr Sigrist.

When the *Endeavour* was almost ready, Captain Grint of the *Viva* requested two more hands from her crew to assist his men with watchkeeping during the long tow ahead. Jim Mussett and Jim Cann were told to report on board the *Viva* for this duty when the *Endeavour* joined up with her in Cowes Roads. A tug towed *Endeavour* there and she anchored awaiting the *Viva* from Southampton, but the motor yacht had stripped the teeth of her steering quadrant and was delayed for several days. Then Captain Heard, impatient at the delay, sailed the *Endeavour* up to Southampton where the crew had an evening ashore. When the *Viva* was ready the two Jims shifted their belongings from the crowded fo'c'sle of the racer to more spacious quarters in the motor yacht. The towrope was made fast to the bitts on the after deck and the long tow began, down the west Solent, past the Needles and westward, down Channel, through a fine day and a fine night, then through a thick fog in which the blue-hulled *Endeavour* could not be seen from the stern of the *Viva*. The two yachts left the short seas of the English Channel for the long rollers of the Atlantic, the crews of each keeping anxious watch on the towline and steering to ease the racer as much as possible, for sailing yachts are not happy being towed. Three or four days later they were approaching the Azores in mid-Atlantic, where they were to call at Ponta Delgada for fuel and supplies. During the 12 to 4 watch Jim was asleep when his mate roused him and other hands below with the news that the towrope had slipped from the bollards. It took all day to recover the 130 fathoms of chain rope and wire which was hanging down vertically in the water, as all they had to assist muscle power was a small electric warping capstan on the after deck, from which messenger ropes had to be seized to the rope and short hauls made. At last it was on deck, *Endeavour* again in tow, and the two yachts made port, where the *Viva* refuelled.

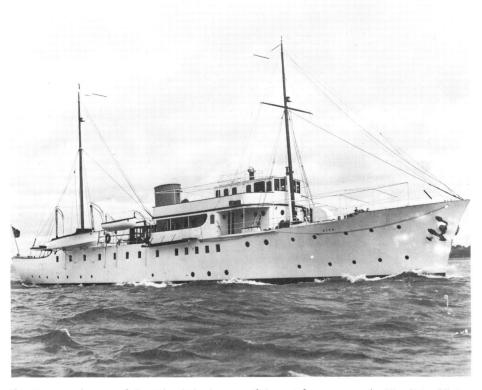

Jim Mussett twice crossed the Atlantic in the crew of the 178-foot motor yacht *Viva II* (ex-*Vita*) as one of two hands loaned from the "J" class racer *Endeavour*, which she towed and escorted during the America's Cup challenge of 1937.

They sailed next day into a northerly wind which increased during the second night at sea and the pounding seas caused *Endeavour* to slip the towrope and set sail. The *Viva* had to steer head to wind to recover the rope again, then lay-to the remainder of the short summer night, talking with the *Endeavour* on the radio telephone. The racer was making 6 knots under sail to the west, north west. The *Viva* was well north of her and turned back at daybreak to pick her up, with lookouts posted and the radio direction finder working, but the racer could not be sighted and after a wide search all day the *Viva* steamed for America, reporting by wireless that the racer was proceeding alone. A week later the *Viva* was in Newport, the Rhode Island harbour which is the centre of America's Cup activity throughout the races. Meanwhile an American Coastguard cutter, a powerful seagoing ship, had sighted the *Endeavour* and towed her until the *Viva* arrived to tow her to Bristol, the yacht port further up Naragansett Bay, where the racers were to prepare at the Herreshoff yachtyards and where the *Endeavour II* was already lying.

Jim Mussett and Jim Cann rejoined the *Endeavour* which commenced fitting out for racing in a frenzy of activity, before dropping down to Newport to lie at her buoy with all anchors and cables unshipped and stowed below in the bilges.

Captain Heard soon had the *Endeavour* and his crew ready for her work in competitively tuning-up the challenger and all hands were keen to show what the *Endeavour* could do against *Endeavour II*, practising starts and holding daily races against each other in the waters and conditions of the Cup course. Afterwards, while the *Endeavour II* was hauled out preparing, the *Endeavour* joined the New York Yacht Club cruise from Newport, eastward along the coast, around Cape Cod and returning, visiting some of the finest sailing waters of New England. The cruise included passage races against the American "J"'s, *Rainbow, Yankee* and the defending *Ranger* which, on one unforgettable day, was beaten by the *Endeavour*.

The *Endeavour II* was perhaps the most attractive yacht to race for the America's Cup. She was the longest of the British "J" class; 132 feet overall length, and 87 feet waterline. She set 7,500 square feet in mainsail, staysail and jib. Her largest spinnaker was 18,000 square feet in area and, roaring downwind she set this and her 5,000 square feet mainsail to total 23,000 square feet, handled by her professional crew of 26. She was well designed, built, manned and handled, but could not match the American *Ranger*. Both yachts were steered by their owners; *Endeavour II* by Thomas Sopwith and *Ranger* by Mike Vanderbilt. Both were clever racing helmsmen and had their respective professional skippers Williams and Monsell standing by, besides an "afterguard" of friends, ready with advice and assistance when required.

Endeavour II lost the first three races of the series to the *Ranger*. For the fourth race Jim Mussett and three others hands from the *Endeavour* were told to report on board the *Endeavour II* as extra hands, bringing the total number on board up to the thirty allowed by the rules; 26 professionals and the remainder amateurs. Both yachts sailed out to the starting line in a 15 mile per hour breeze and *Endeavour II* was over the line 8 seconds early at gunfire, gybing to recross 1½ minutes late. Both yachts short tacked every 1½ to 2 minutes, with *Ranger* increasing her lead to the weather mark, 10 miles away from the start, the first leg of the triangular, 30 mile course. The constant sheeting of the enormous headsails and the dozens of minor jobs to be carried out at top speed while tacking were very exhausting for the crews and though these races were of short duration, it was long enough at the pace and strain imposed. At the buoy the *Endeavour II* was 4½ minutes astern but as they reached away to the second mark she drew up on the *Ranger* and during the final leg she was slowly gaining, but the American maintained her lead and won by 3½ minutes, averaging 9½ knots for the 3 hours 7½ minutes of the race. It had been well sailed and in the English yacht racing tradition the *Endeavour II* crew lined her weather rail and led by Captain Williams waving his cap, "cheered the winner", the Americans replying. This was the last time large yachts raced for the America's Cup, all subsequent challengers and defenders being of the much smaller 12-metre class; "Nice little boats" the professionals termed them.

At Bristol the *Endeavour*s were restored to their passagemaking ketch rigs for the return tow home. As the new *Philante* had arrived the trawler *Jon* was sent home.

The same crew arrangements were followed for the return passage and Jim Mussett and Bill Lewis berthed on board the *Viva*, whose captain had warning of gales to the south and wished to leave quickly to avoid them. They sailed on Sunday, 12th September 1937, with *Endeavour* again on the end of her towline. 24 hours later the wind increased, freshening quickly to a severe gale which sent the racer plunging and straining astern, her deck hidden in clouds of spray as she pitched. Captain Grint was inclined to slip the racer to ease her but they held on into the night and the seas worsened as the *Viva* steamed full ahead keeping both yachts' head to sea. At dawn the seas were mountains high but the towrope trailed astern—without the *Endeavour* which was assumed to have slipped it in the darkness and made sail about 200 miles east of Nantucket Island. The *Viva* recovered about one third of the rope and requested all ships to keep a lookout for the *Endeavour* by radio. The French liner *Ile de France* answered. She was bound for Southampton and *Viva*'s owner, Mr Sigrist, was on board. She reported no sign of the racer. When the gale eased the *Viva* turned round and wirelessed continually for the *Endeavour*, without reply. The *Endeavour*'s set had fallen and could receive but not send. She steamed a zig-zag search course for that day, then gave up and returned to Newport to report. A

The graceful "J" class racer *Endeavour II* in which Jim Mussett raced during the America's Cup series of 1937. She was beaten by the American *Ranger*.

week later she again sailed and steamed back directly to Britain. As one of the
Viva's able seamen had damaged a hand, Jim Mussett stood his watches at the
wheel, rolling eastward across the Atlantic.

When the *Viva* entered Portsmouth harbour a launch came off from
Gosport with Mrs Paul, wife of *Astra*'s owner, on board with news that the
Endeavour had been sighted homeward bound under sail by the oil tanker
Cheyenne at the approaches to the English Channel. The *Viva* returned down
the Solent to look for her wayward charge, which was by now reported as sailing
up Channel, and the motor yacht brought up off the Needles at the westward
end of the Isle of Wight. The blue-hulled truant appeared the next day and the
towrope was passed for the haul up to Portsmouth Harbour to a tremendous
welcome of cheers and ships' sirens as they moored off Gosport; a fuss which
surprised her crew. After two weeks of work laying up the *Endeavour* Jim and
the rest of the crew were paid off and he returned to marry in November and
spend another winter of dredging in the smacks and winkling in his bumkin, the
Jack, which Jim bought in 1935.

At the commencement of the 1938 season, yachting prospects looked bleak for the racing men. The big class would not fit out (and never would again, though no one could foresee that), so Mr Paul decided to order a new 12-metre as that class were being keenly raced around the coastal regattas and were usurping the allure of the "J" class yachts for owners who could race them with much less expense as they only carried a skipper and three hands, in keeping with their small size of 70 feet overall and 1,900 square feet sail area in a sloop rig.

The new Paul 'twelve was launched from Camper and Nicholsons as *Little Astra* but Mr and Mrs Paul decided to have the *Astra* fitted out to sail round the coast with her and act as their floating home for the summer and as tender to the 12-metre. *Astra*'s mast was shortened by being cut off at the upper crosstrees and the mainsail was consequently cut down to the equivalent of two reefs; a handy cruising rig for the crew of 14-16 hands which was shipped, most of whom were the same men who had sailed with Jim in the *Endeavour* the previous year. Captain Ted Heard was skipper of the *Astra* and also of the 12-metre when she raced, but at all other times she was in charge of Lewis Wilkinson of Tollesbury with a crew of three hands including Joe Uglow of Looe as cook and steward, also on deck when at sea or when racing, and Edward Heard (junior) who left the *Little Astra* when his father came on board to race, thus maintaining the correct number of professionals on board in accordance with the class rules, returning to her after each race.

However, the *Astra*'s crew did have some racing as they were a ready source of experienced "extra hands" for the other racing yachts in the big handicap classes and if necessary, the 12-metres. As extra hands they received £1 a day, which went towards replacing their previous income from prize money. The *Little Astra* and her tender were at all the major regattas on the east and south coasts and when 12-metre racing finished the *Astra* cruised to Devon and Cornwall for two weeks before returning to Gosport to lay up for the winter. While the *Astra* was at Plymouth a cruiser was launched at Devonport Dockyard and as Mrs Paul wished to see this, the launch was sent away up river in charge of Jim and Jack Sargent. After the event they found that the propeller was fouled and Jim leaned over the side struggling to free it. After several attempts he cleared a mass of coconut matting from it but in doing so his chest had come in violent contact with the launch's transom several times. When the yacht arrived at Torquay he visited a doctor, who said he had strained chest muscles and told him to report to his own doctor as soon as he arrived home. Two weeks later Jim's doctor diagnosed heart trouble and ordered him to take two months rest.

The Pauls did not have *Astra* fitted out for the 1939 season and Jim and the rest of her crew had to find other berths. However, Ted Heard wrote that Mr Glen Tyrell needed four hands for the cruiser-racer *Diadem*, which was fitting out with Jim Stubbings of Tollesbury as skipper. He was not an orthodox yachtsman, having served 12 years in the British army before doing two or three winters fishing from Tollesbury and being picked for the crew of the Cup challenger *Endeavour II*. He had also sailed in the *Astra* and the *Endeavour*. Mr Tyrell liked Jim Stubbings as an active type but Michael Heard, an older Tollesbury yachtsman, was also engaged. Jim Mussett was selected for mate and Ken Cudmore, another Mersea man, was cook and steward. Jim received a weekly wage of £3. 5s. 0d., then quite good money. He did the navigating.

The 67-foot *Diadem* had been thoroughly refitted and re-rigged as a Bermudian cutter for the large handicap class which looked like replacing the big class racing yachts for some time. The class included some fine yachts such as *The Blue Peter, Erivale, Joyce, The Lady Anne, Noriene, Cariba* and others. After visiting the Crouch the *Diadem* raced at Harwich regatta against her great rival *The Blue Peter*, whom she allowed one minute on handicap. After a hard race these fine cutters came in as a dead heat at the finish; something no one could remember ever happening before. They did not enter the Harwich to Southend race but raced twice at Southend before going on to race at Ramsgate, at Cowes, then at the west country events at Torquay and Torbay. By the time they arrived at Dartmouth the owner was convinced that war was imminent and they did not race but sailed at once up Channel to lay up. The *Diadem* became a houseboat at Mersea in 1947.

Like all able bodied men Jim was called for medical examination for war service and here the effects of his accident with the launch off Devonport became apparent as the doctors diagnosed heart trouble and he was rejected. Jim joined Gowen and Co. whose sail loft was turning over to war work, where his ability at splicing and ropework made him a valuable hand on the various government contracts for the many specialised items they produced.

Jim Mussett was mate of the 67-foot racing cruiser *Diadem* when this photograph was taken in 1939. The owner, Mr Glen Tyrell, is at the wheel, racing in the big handicap class.

65

After the war the loft soon returned to sailmaking and Jim and others were put to stitching seams of hand sewn sails, when he was not doing the loft's rope work and rigging jobs. Gowen's received a contract for sails for a large yacht and as Jim stitched his way across the long seams his thoughts turned increasingly to the open spaces and windy vastness of the days he had spent "on the mud", winkling and oystering. He left the loft and as the oyster trade was reviving, spent most of his time "ebbing"; picking up year-old oysters for sale to the merchants for relaying. He cycled to the Flats at East Mersea each morning in company with Jack Mole and many other Mersea men, spending the low water time walking the flats and filling his "tendle" basket. The winter of 1946-7 was severe and killed off many young oysters but Jim and others soon found alternative work picking up Portuguese oysters on Thirslet Spit, in Colliers Creek, walking the muds with "splatchers" on their feet and gathering the walnut sized "Ports" which were sold to Ted Woolf, the Mersea oysterman. Jim and Jack Mole worked together and were sometimes joined by Jim's father. By then Jim had bought an Aldeburgh beach boat with a motor, with which he often towed the *Jack* to be loaded with oysters and sometimes with shram, as local fishermen term the shell used for the basis of oyster layings and hards. This was loaded in sacks and they gathered about four tons each week for Charles Prigg's chicken grit business. By about 1960 there was "Nothing much doing on the mud" as Jim puts it and as Jack Owen, Gowen's veteran rigger, was retiring, Jim rejoined the sail loft to take his place at rope and wire work, using all his sailor skills at tucking neat splices and working rope.

Jim Mussett carried on until the age of sixty-five, then reduced to part-time work in the mornings and when the loft had a slack spell he retired for good, to spend his time on the garden and enjoying village life amongst relatives and old friends from days afloat.

John Frost

The little Mersea sailing bumkins attracted youngsters fond of the subtle blending of sailing and fishing they represented and many were sold for pleasure use. During the early 1960s one named *T.D.* was owned by young John Frost, a son of Michael Frost, owner of the sailing smack *Boadicea*. John passed through the Colchester Boys' High School and from an early age the sea lure held his imagination. During a brief entry into the Royal Navy at Shotley training school he returned to West Mersea and at weekends to sail the bumkin for amusement and learn more of the ways of the Blackwater. After leaving the Navy John went as mate for two years in barges of the London and Rochester Trading Company and spent a further two years with Prior's barges, gaining sea experience on the coast.

Afterwards he fished part-time, drifting for herrings in the heyday of that revived Blackwater fishery during the 1960s, selling catches through Richard Haward. During the summer days from 1968 to 1972 John also worked as the West Mersea Yacht Club launchman, taking off and landing yachtsmen and acting as the Club's general handyman afloat. He was soon fishing with the *Curlew*, a converted naval motor cutter, drifting for herring with reasonable success. In winter he went spratting with Douglas Stoker, using the surface trawls which replaced the old stowboat nets in the early 1950s.

During 1973 John ordered a new 26-foot, plastic-hulled motor boat from a firm at Witham and she was fitted out by John Milgate, a Mersea boatbuilder, in business at Peldon. She was launched as the *Gill*, C.K. 143, and John was joined by Mersea man Don Mole as crew for the new venture. Don had been in the sailing barge *Lord Roberts* and was skipper of the motor barge *James P*. Besides herring drifting, the *Gill* was beach seining for mullet and bass, selling to Dick Haward, the Mersea fish merchant to whose shrewd business management John reckons Mersea fishermen owe much. Then, in autumn and winter, it was back to the herring drifting in the Blackwater and its approaches. The days of the traditional "Herring voyage" by hundreds of steam and later motor drifters up to 70 feet long from east coast of Scotland and East Anglian ports had ended twenty years earlier. Bulk catching by large numbers of European and Russian trawlers using huge surface trawls had decimated the stocks and the herring are now protected. Fishery scientists predict the permissible annual catch and a herring management committee of fishermen and marketing men allocate catching quotas. Since Peter French of West Mersea revived the traditional Blackwater herring fishery in the early 1950s, Mersea fishermen have increasingly participated, until they now usually land three-quarters of the herring caught in the Thames estuary. All herring in the North Sea are protected from fishing by British boats and it has taken considerable effort by West Mersea's Bill Read and Ken Green from the Colne to stop closure of the Blackwater fishery also. All of this underlines the changed attitudes of the present-day Essex fishermen.

At Christmas 1975 John ordered a new and larger boat, having a plastic hull moulded at Tonbridge, Kent and fitted out at Mersea by Clarke and Carter to be launched as the *Gill Too*, C.K. 227. At 30 foot length John regards her as the optimum size for his work and he has successfully used her between the Wash and the Solent, which he considers as the reasonable limits for the trade. John's new boat fished out of Lowestoft, Suffolk, during an autumn season of successful herring drifting off Happisburgh, in company with two other Mersea boats. In summer they went gill netting for mullet and bass and John had a fancy to try fishing in the Wash, off the coasts of Norfolk and Lincolnshire, amongst the fierce tides and desolate shoals of that treacherous area.

67

During 1976 the *Gill Too* was motored south to the Solent with two other Mersea boats seeking mullet and it was an unexpected pleasure for me to see the familiar letters "C.K." on their bows from the windows of the hovercraft, on the way to the office.

Despite modern aids the hazards of fishing in all weathers are ever present. One night, shooting monofil nets, the meshes caught Don's fingers and he was carried overboard. John jumped from the wheel, stopped the engine and after Don was clear of the prop managed to haul him on board. They returned to Mersea to work at oyster dredging, filling in time between fishing seasons. In summer the *Gill Too* fishes with monofil nets set on the sands off the Essex coast with specially made anchors, tended each tide by the boat. She has modern equipment including a hydraulic net hauler, radar, V.H.F. radio and a fish finder. A Decca Navigator system, in which John has great faith, will be added soon.

The herring fishery remains the present mainstay of the Mersea fleet of twenty or more boats; a trade usually needing a 12-18 hour day, five days a week, in line with the restrictions for conserving stocks. The landings average each boat's quota of 50 stone per day; all fresh fish fetching a good price from the merchants. A 30-footer is the smallest boat desirable for the work but the crews have the satisfaction of getting in quickly when working off the Essex coast. Herring drifting in the Swin brings problems in adjusting the depth of the nets and with ships fouling and dragging the long curtains of net strung in the tideway, despite use of lights and warning radio contact.

The energy and outlook of John Frost and his contemporaries, their search for new fishing methods and outlets and unassuming seamanship make them worthy successors to the old timers of the sailing days.

John Frost of West Mersea on board his fishing boat *Gill Too*. Typical of the modern craft now working the inshore fisheries from the Essex coast.   *Ernest Graystone*

The West Mersea fishing boat *Gill Too* alongside at Lowestoft with a capacity catch of herring. Owner/skipper John Frost is at the extreme right with his mate Don Mole and a youthful helper, proudly wearing his seagoing rig.   *Ernest Graystone*

CHAPTER FOUR

Where Plough Met Sail

B RADWELL, on the south shore of the Blackwater entrance, was unattainable in my first boat, an old 9-foot dinghy in which I voyaged down the Colne to dig cockles on the Cocum Hills, seaward of East Mersea Stone. The separating four miles of wide and often rough estuary lent allure to its prospect. Through the old binoculars I carried on those expeditions I could scan the horizon for craft, perhaps the tan sails of barges, maybe one of Cranfield's Ipswichmen with a white ball in her topsail or the distinctive grey hull of a big Everarder, possibly the *Will* or the *Greenhithe*, bound through the Spitway. Further south, triangular sharks' fins of leaning sails showed fast bermudian rigged yachts from Burnham, hurrying through the Ray Sand Channel on the ebb, bound for the Blackwater, hardening sheets through the Knoll Channel and standing miraculously to windward past the long spit running off from Sales Point, forming the northern edge of the vast St Peter's and Dengie Flats, stretching south towards the Ray Sand and the invisible mouth of the River Crouch. In those days fighter-bombers practised attacks on targets set offshore on these muds, the almost inaudible drone of the approach suddenly erupting into the delayed chatter of machine gun fire and the echoing boom of bombs and rockets.

In contrast, the Bradwell shore had an enduring natural dignity. The green sea walls of Sales Point were backed by distant elms and by big south-westerly clouds. At this lonely spot overlooking the entrance to the Blackwater and Colne, and southward to the approach to the River Crouch, the Romans built a fort and its commander, styled "Count of the Saxon Shore", commanded its garrison of about 600 men called "Fortenses" or "Braves"! He had jurisdiction into Norfolk, to the north, and was watchful for marauding Saxons landing on the Essex and Suffolk coasts. As the power of Rome dwindled in her outposts, the stronghold was evacuated and gradually fell into ruin. Britain was divided into petty kingdoms and this part of the east coast was ruled by Sigbert, King of the East Saxons. The teachings of Christ were advancing in the population and Sigbert sent to Oswy, King of Northumbria, which was a stronghold of Christianity, for assistance. Oswy sent Bishop Cedd and a band of followers who built a small chapel, using stone and tiles from the ruined fort.

The chapel's foundations were astride the crumbled walls of the fortress and gave the chapel its name of "St Peter's on the Wall", when it was consecrated in A.D.654. It was a simple church measuring only 49 feet 6 inches × 21 feet 6 inches with an apse and a porch at the west side surmounted by a tower. From this windswept chapel bands of preachers roved the coutryside spreading the gospel and King Sigbert became a convert. Bishop Cedd died in 655 and long afterwards the chapel remained a centre of Christianity but eventually decayed and was desecrated. During Tudor and Stuart times it was used as a beacon to guide shipping and by the nineteenth century had become a barn. In 1920 an unknown benefactor caused it to be repaired and reconsecrated. It was infrequently used until interest in it was renewed in July, 1954, on the thirteen-hundredth anniversary of the chapel's founding, when a bishop and many interested locals and visiting yachtsmen walked from Bradwell village along the road to the sea wall, and a service of thanksgiving was again held in St Peter's, which remains a restored example of a Saxon church, fascinating by its age and associations.

Close by, in a small cottage and garden on the seaward side of the sea wall lived Walter Linnett, a professional wildfowler, earning a living with his guns and punts into the early 1950s. We always looked for his little home when sailing into the Blackwater and thought of his lonely life dominated by the tides, which, at low water, ebb a considerable distance from the cottage. Walter Linnett was a quiet, fair haired man, skilled at his calling and the last of a once considerable company in these waters. He had a wonderful knowledge of fowl, and the developed instincts of a hunter. He was resourceful and resolute, as such men are, and once saved two amateur gunners whose great punt gun blew their punt to pieces out in the loneliness of "the Main"; the wide, windswept tidal expanse stretching south and south-east from the sea walls of the Dengie Hundred, south of Bradwell, towards the Ray Sand Channel and the distant Whittaker.

By 1947 Walter Linnett was the sole surviving professional wildfowler on the Blackwater, though about thirty fishermen from Maldon, Mersea and Tollesbury also shot in winter when bags were likely to be worthwhile. He continued to earn his living by his fowling guns and punts, eel spearing and lining for fish; a gaggle of open, Blackwater-type punts lying beyond the fence of the little garden, with its bullace and damson trees. There were once professional punt gunners from Poole to the Cromarty Firth on the east and south coasts, but Walter Linnett was probably the last to earn his living in this way.

Walter was the son and grandson of wildfowlers who had also lived there and possibly his ancestors were amongst those who shot wildfowl with crossbows or snared them in various ways, before shot guns were introduced during the sixteenth century. His father participated in the notable shoot of 32 punts which surrounded about 5,000 Brent geese off the Bradwell shore. Every punt except one discharged her gun and 704 dead geese were recovered. The loaded punts were rowed to Bradwell Creek towing strings of birds. The wildfowlers gathered at the *Green Man* to spend some of their money while over 250 more geese were picked up alongshore by shore gunners and boys. The proceeds were shared out but it had been noticed that when the order to shoot was given one punter did not discharge his gun, hoping to save powder and shot, and at the share out he received nothing and was thrown out of the gathering. The elder Linnett, with James Chaney and John Basham of Maldon, were amongst the 18 punters who fired off Bradwell one night and bagged 360 geese.

These are some of the high watermarks of the Victorian wildfowlers in these waters which then teemed with fowl in winter.

Walter Linnett, professional wildfowler of Bradwell, punts out from the shore by his home in 1939. The grey-barrelled punt gun lies ready, stretched between the stem head and the thwart supporting its stock. Walter lived in the wooden cottage built on the seaward side of the sea wall (left) close by the chapel of St Peter's (right), the oldest Christian church in the area.

Douglas Went

Upstream from Sales Point, Bradwell Creek leads off the Blackwater's western shore, now dominated by a giant nuclear power station. Bradwell village snuggles round its church, well inland, but there are houses by the Creek and its hard. The Creek has a twist in its channel but if strangers keep the leadline (nowadays more often the echo sounder) going, the best water should be readily found as there is not much time to look at a chart if one is beating in or out. Bradwell became increasingly known to small yachts and their crews with the increase in amateur sailing in the 1880s and has remained frequented by them in increasing numbers.

I first sailed my own boat into Bradwell Creek thirty years ago, when access to the waterside was free and unhindered. The barge quay was in disrepair and a few small yachts laid in the Creek which was crowded on Saturday nights and Bank Holidays with visiting craft. Daily in summer, Rube Pullen's blue motor launch *Pedro 1* nosed into the Creek with a load of Mersea visitors having an afternoon trip to the delights of this sleepy village and the *Green Man*, beloved of generations of visiting yachtsmen and then little changed from descriptions written fifty years previously.

The village shop at the top of the road sold almost everything, and the whole place had an atmosphere of peace which even the building of the giant wartime airfield sprawling over the fields could not destroy. The runways which launched Mosquitoes and many other aircraft on their missions were beginning to crack and decay, like the scattered Nissen huts and control tower. The gusty marsh winds echoed through the once crowded buildings and cornfields again sprouted over the fields. As late as 1961 there were not more than a score of moorings in Bradwell Creek and we sailed our old West Mersea fisherman's boat *Oyster* up the Creek to pass its upper shallows and circumnavigate Pewit Island; the marshy bulk which protects Bradwell from west and north-west winds, emerging into the Blackwater in the windy and lonesome St Lawrence Bay.

Although Bradwell never attracted large yachts or any wealthy yachtsmen in the grand period of the sport, it played a prominent part in organising early sailing races and regattas on the Essex coast at the end of the eighteenth century, when the Blackwater's broad estuary saw some spirited sailing by local smacks. Regattas of any kind were a novelty and as few yachts existed, competitors were principally fishing craft and revenue cutters, while the ''pleasure yachts'' were usually onlookers and committee boats.

In 1783 Bradwell's parson Bate-Dudley organised a sailing race for Essex fishing smacks, held in the Blackwater and won by a Burnham cutter. The regatta craze caught on and a few months later Captain Hopkins of Wivenhoe organised a similar event for smacks belonging to Wivenhoe, Rowhedge, Brightlingsea and Mersea, which raced for a silver cup and a suit of colours, which were respectively won by Captain Cooke's *Mayflower* of Rowhedge and George Wheatly's *Two Sisters* of Wivenhoe. The race had become established by the following July when six smacks competed for the "Annual silver cup and suit of colours" won by the Brightlingsea cutter *Cleverly*, Captain Tobor, with Captain Worrel's *Mayflower* of Mersea second. The event seems to have lapsed next year but was certainly held in 1786 when the *Essex Chronicle* published the following spirited account so typical of these early Essex races:

> "By nine o'clock on Monday morning the sea between Mersea and Bradwell was crowded with pleasure yachts, sloops, etc. decorated with various colours. At ten the Bradwell yacht (aboard which were several of the principal gentlemen of the county) got under weigh and fired a signal for commanders of the cutters entered for the prize to go on board the yacht, draw lots for the weather gauge, and receive their distinguishing colours.
>
> As soon as their several pendants were hoisted and the cutters got into their destined stations (they started from anchor) a second gun was fired as the signal for starting, when eleven fine, well trimmed vessels got under weigh, and with clouds of sail stood out to sea under a salute of guns from the surrounding yachts etc. The whole forming a very striking naval spectacle.
>
> The contest lay principally between the *Two Brothers* of Rowhedge, Captain Shakeshaft, and the *Batchelor* of Mersea, Captain Overall, which was very sharply disputed, till the last time doubling the Eagle buoy, when a heavy squall coming on, the *Batchelor* found it prudent to strike some of her sail, which at this moment unfortunately going overboard threw her so much to leeward that she was unable to recover her station.
>
> About five o'clock the *Two Brothers* passed the starting flag on the middle buoy, and, receiving a general salute, went on board the yacht where being drank to by the donor, received the cup . . . The *Pink* of Burnham, Captain Richmond, coming in second, received the second prize, viz. a full suit of St. George's colours; the *Friendship* of Paglesham, Captain Wiseman, was the third vessel; but the others came in so close that it was impossible to class them."

The cup and colours for the 1787 sailing match were donated by gentlemen members of the Colchester King's Head Club and ten smacks sailed the usual estuary course for them, the Burnham *Friendship* winning, with the *Batchelor* of Mersea second. No regattas appear to have been held in 1788 but next year the White Hart Club of Colchester put up the prizes and invited contestants from Rowhedge, Wivenhoe, Brightlingsea, Mersea, Tollesbury, Bradwell, Burnham and Paglesham to meet at the Mersea *White Hart*, which is presumably where the club members foregathered for conviviality, well away from Colchester and disapproving wives or families, or possibly they were "pleasure sailors" who kept their craft at West Mersea. The meeting discussed holding a race that September but there is no record of its having taken place.

Thus local fishermen had, by inclination and working necessity, a sound knowledge of racing under sail and similar local regattas were also organised along the Devon coast and in the Solent, with Cowes holding its first in 1776 and Southampton shortly afterwards. In Suffolk, Woodbridge held a regatta in 1784 and there were sailing matches at Ipswich in 1791 and 1792, which were probably for commercial craft. In all these events yachts were present as a minority of the onlookers and few existed before 1800, when there were probably not more than seventy in the country, mostly used for day sailing or cruising.

A few smacks were owned at Bradwell, including Jack Spitty's *David and Eliza* and a smack now named *Taffy* and still sailing as a yacht, then worked by "Fan" Hewes and his son, who had earlier sailed in the *Fiddle*. The *David and Eliza* also engaged in the Blackwater winter herring fishing which with the May-July mackerel drifting in earlier times, often provided work for a few smacks from Mersea, Tollesbury, Bradwell and Wivenhoe, which were the only places to work it as far as I know.

The spritsail barges *Mayflower* (left) and *Lord Warden* (right) at Bradwell Quay about 1912. The *Lord Warden* was built at Sandwich, Kent, in 1891 and for many years was owned by John Adams of Ramsgate. When this photograph was taken she was one of the fleet of Clement Parker, the Bradwell landowner whose craft carried cargoes of grain, hay and straw to London, returning with manure. They were also in general trade.   *Bells Photo Company*

Because of its location on the west shore of the Blackwater, near to the river's mouth and offering a lee from the south-westerly winds, Bradwell Creek was a natural choice for the stationing of a fast cutter to combat the smuggling which became rife on the east coast during the latter half of the eighteenth century. The revenue cruiser could lie safely off the Creek mouth and could slip out of the river at any time in any wind. She was kept busy.

During the eighteenth century the scale and value of smuggling increased until by its end gangs were running cargoes through the countryside and challenging the revenue men, and large cutters were often landing contraband cargoes in daylight on the coasts. Many of the smugglers were large; such as Stephen Marsh's 140-tonner manned by 34 hands. The revenue cutters too, grew in size and the *Repulse* of Colchester, built in 1778 as one of a series of six of that name owned by Captain Harvey of Wivenhoe, who hired them out to the authorities and provided the crew and often acted as commander, was a typical 210 tons and had a crew of 50 men and a boy. She mounted 16 carriage and 12 swivel guns and used the Colne as an anchorage but ranged far afield in pursuit of smugglers and prizes, as did most of her contemporaries. In 1768 a Custom house smack chased a sloop from Helvoelstuis on the Dutch coast for many hours and finally came up with her in the Blackwater, finding she had 48 tubs of gin, 40 of brandy and tea and muslins. She was taken round to Leigh where the cargo was unloaded and the sloop was burned. One must remember that contrary to the romantic tales usually woven around old time smuggling, much of it was carried on by seafarers to whom the risk of transportation, imprisonment or death was worth it compared to a lifetime of grinding poverty which was then the lot of most.

Until 1775 the Blackwater smugglers had an easy time as the yawl *Queen* was the river's sole anti-smuggling vessel and was kept at Maldon for the use of Thomas Sherman, the "Tide Surveyor". She was easily spotted whenever she slipped down on the ebb and Sherman complained bitterly of lack of support from his masters. In 1777 the collector of Customs at Harwich recorded that 30 or so small cutters were constantly smuggling between the Naze and the mouth of the Thames, eluding the deep draught revenue cutters amongst the sands and channels to land cargoes in the rivers and creeks, working from Holland and Belgium. Tea, gin and other spirits, silks and tobacco were the principal commodities.

With all this activity it is not surprising that the revenue cutter *Badger* was stationed at Bradwell in 1775; a typical clench-planked, powerful hull with a large sail area, long bowsprit and topmast and carrying a squaresail for running. She had ten guns on deck and was well manned. Such a cutter was usually a match for the largest smuggler and disabled or unwilling prizes of considerable size were commonly towed in under sail by such craft, which made light of a barge or smack which they had caught. In 1818 the revenue cruiser *Rattlesnake*,

Lieutenant Neame, R.N., was stationed in the Blackwater and her commander arrived in the lugger *Falcon*, which is believed to have remained on station as her tender.

Things became more difficult for the smugglers when the Coast Blockade, the forerunner of the Coastguard, was established in 1817; and the Coastguard came into being in 1831, after which large scale smuggling became unprofitable. The Coastguard was a branch of the Navy, manned by officers, petty officers and blue-jackets stationed all round the coast and usually based in watch vessels; old hulks of small warships, usually brigs, which were moored or beached in creeks and estuaries. There were two in the Blackwater; one at Bradwell and the other at Stansgate.

The revenue cutter *Badger* was stationed at Bradwell in 1775 to counter smuggling in the Blackwater and Colne. Her long bowsprit, clench-planked hull and powerful rig with squaresail and square topsail were typical features of these fast cutters.

The smugglers resorted to subtlety and subterfuge and this was the pattern of the trade subsequently, until it virtually died out by the 1880s. A coastguard station was maintained at Bradwell into the early twentieth century but there was little major smuggling into the creek as confined access to its waterside rendered it easily watched.

Jack Spitty who at one time lived at Bradwell, went in for occasional smuggling along with many of his contemporaries from the Colne and Blackwater. Usually runs were small scale and consisted of spirits and tobacco cunningly concealed in the smack's structure or cargo of fish. Even Clement Parker's Bradwell barges were not above a little profitable subterfuge; bringing home a bottle or two hidden behind the hold ceiling or perhaps in a drum of paint in the fo'c'sle store. But such misdemeanours were very minor after the bold runs of the late eighteenth century, which "the trade" has never seen again.

Sea transport was much easier than land until the early nineteenth century and there were about 100 quays in Essex during the reign of Queen Elizabeth. In 1630 most farmers of the Dengie Hundred, to the south of the Blackwater, sent their corn to London by water and vessels from Bradwell, Maldon and Burnham enjoyed the privilege of landing goods free in London after 1665 because these craft had continued to supply the city during the great plague.

Bradwell and its surrounding countryside was principally dependent on agriculture for its living but local farmers were also barge owners and the village was a home port of bargemen and barges which carried cargoes of grain, hay, straw and root crops to London, returning with horse manure and general goods, besides engaging in general trade. Thomas Kirby and his five sons were all barge owners and skippers. Their best barge was the *Water Lily*, built in 1902 at Rochester, Kent, a handsome 58-tonner which was later owned by James Spitty. She left an unforgettable impression on the author when he came up with her off Bradwell one day in 1948. She was fresh off the ways from being rebuilt, with Bill Kirby at the wheel, though she had long since passed to Wakeley's blue and white bob.

William Hatch was a local owner and T. Goymer of West Wick Farm, another, whose craft worked to the village quay and included the *Bradwell*, the *Dover Castle*, the *Mary Ann* and the aged *Denton*. He was a better farmer than a shipowner and after a few years the barges were sold, leaving the quay dominated by the heart and hand flag of the Parkers of Bradwell. James Parker's barges were sailing from the creek in the mid-nineteenth century and by its end Clement Parker was operating a fleet of well found and sometimes notably fast barges, besides farming vast acreages. His barges were smartly kept and even hoisted their owner's "Bob" on flag halyards; and it had to be lowered when alongside the quay. These included the *Violet Sybil, Nellie Parker, Verona, Duchess, Fanny, Daisy, Triton, Champion* and *Princess*. The *Mayflower* was reputedly another of Parker's barges and may have been built at Milton, Kent, in 1882. He acquired Kirby's *Water Lily*, which was his pride, but the fast *Veronica*, built on the Thames by Shrubsole was pride of his fleet and amongst the fastest spritsail barges with her well formed hull.

The face of the sailorman. Bill Kirby of Bradwell was skipper of the *Water Lily* and one of a noted family of barge owners and skippers from the village. *Arthur Bennett*

Clement Parker first entered his barges in the races on the Thames and Medway, where in 1905 the *Violet Sybil* won the coaster class and his new *Verona* was second to the famous Thames *Giralda* in the topsail class and was first in the Medway race. Bradwell men and their small community were exuberant; they felt like "giant killers". Next year was the Parker fleet's triumph; the *Violet Sybil* won the Thames and Medway races and the newly launched *Veronica* the topsail class in both races with the *Verona* second, putting the *Giralda* third. The 56-ton *Veronica*, built at East Greenwich, was the fastest of Parker's fleet and amongst the fastest of all sailing barges, whether racing or working. She was once reputed to have loaded a stack in the creek and sailed at noon, to begin discharging at Woolwich, in the Thames, 26 hours later. One of her skippers was H. Bell who recalled the keenness of Parker's crews to get their craft going well. "I have known skippers tie a piece of spun yarn around the standing part of the forestay fall as a mark for the best position of the block, and this would be moved half an inch at a time until the best rake of the mast was found—that was our usual practice in the *Veronica*. When one remembers that it was a three fold purchase, the infinitesimal difference that one half inch could make to the rake shows to what lengths we would go to get the best out of these lovely craft."

Parker's barges were allowed one week a year to refit. Each barge in turn loaded a freight for Bradwell and went on the blocks at Bradwell waterside where the mast was lowered, sails unbent, and these were taken up the "hill" to be spread on a small meadow where they were renovated and often recut by the owner's sailmaker, "Yankee" Bill Phillips, before being dressed with the usual mixture of oil and ochre to the rich, supple tan colour this preservative gave the flax canvas.

Parker's fleet engaged in many trades, often far from the Blackwater, in the heyday of the sailing barge, between about 1900-1927; from stone cargoes from Portland up Channel to London and elsewhere, to coke and coal to French Channel ports during the 1914-18 war. Many were in the stack trade, loading at Bradwell or at the various outfalls along the long sea wall between the mouth of the Blackwater and the Crouch.

Bradwell was a centre of the stack trade until 1914 and loading a sailing barge with hay or straw which filled the hold and formed a stack on deck followed a procedure well understood by Blackwater bargemen. It is a remarkable tribute to the barges and their crews that a stack of hay ten feet above deck and protruding outboard about a foot from the rails on each side could be sailed to windward around the coast and up the Thames to London, though such carriage was also done by craft in other countries including Germany, India, and on the west coast of America.

Stacks were built from trusses made in the farm hand lever hay presses; straw was tied with straw; the hay with three string bindings. The trusses were carted to the barge and carried on board, but the crew built their own stack. When the first trusses were laid in the hold, sufficient space was left for a man to put his back against one and feet against another to press them to a tight stow. The space was then filled tightly with trusses. When the cargo reached the coamings the outer trusses were laid on deck with one end over the rail and the other on deck, so the sides of the stack canted inboard and gained stability. Six stack irons were placed in rail sockets; one pair forward, a pair amidships abaft the shrouds and another pair aft. Three eight feet long irons shipped into square sockets in the rail. The trusses of the deck stack were pressed against these and the shrouds to pack the stack tight against shifting. Three main hatch covers were left off, and all the covers of the fore hatch. Throat lashings were rove from the stack irons, through a scupper in the rail; one pair forward, two pairs aft. A pair of wire breechings were made fast to the mast and were taken around the stack, aft to an eye in the rail on the opposite side.

When a hay stack was built the top was given a covering of two layers of straw trusses to give firmer foothold, and the unshipped hatch covers were placed on top; two forward; one each side of the mast and two abaft the mast. Three 24 foot square stack cloths covered over all, lashed down by the bights of the throat lashings. The stack was held in place by the stability of its construction and its weight. The lashings were merely to hold the protective cloths down to prevent rain and spray penetrating the stack top. Another cloth was lashed over the after side of the stack to protect it from sparks from the cabin stovepipe.

The two-man crew were expected to build the stack in a day, coping with the heavy work of lifting and placing the trusses and the intermittent arrival of more waggon loads, with country boys flinging trusses on to the barge. Much of the barge's sailing gear was buried under the stack, including the foresail horse. So a temporary rope or wire-rope horse was rigged over the stack for the sheet of the small "stack foresail", used when loaded. Extra cleats were permanently seized to the shrouds of barges in the stack trade, ten feet or so above those used from the deck. A spider band was clamped to the mast to provide belaying pins for the topsail halyard and sheet. The main brail was taken from the winch on deck, near the mast, and was led to the dolly winch on the bitts. Lower brails were unnecessary as the bottom of the mainsail was reefed to clear the stack, using the second set of reef points fitted to a stack barge mainsail, or a reefing line led through eyelets in the sail. As the stack projected outboard through the shrouds, ratlings were not fitted and the mate, going aloft to stow the topsail in an unladen stacky, had to scramble up the lower shrouds in the manner of a racing yacht crew.

Although the stack barges appeared unhandy sailing craft, they sailed in any reasonable weather. The skipper at the wheel could not see directly ahead and relied on directions from the mate, on the stack. In open water he might steer by observing the wake and angle of a buoy passed (a trick re-discovered by minesweeping crews during two world wars). In some tiller steered stackies the skipper rigged lines from the tiller, through blocks to the top of the stack and could sit on top and see where he was going. A loaded stack barge had so much windage at anchor that she usually kept sheering to it, checking on the scope and then sailing off on the other "tack". So familiar was this constant movement that if it ceased her skipper knew she was dragging.

The cargoes were consigned to wharves and quays serving the horse fodder trade over a long sweep of the Thames, from well below to well above the Pool of London. The Westminster bank of the Thames immediately above the Palace of Westminster was crowded with stack barges lying bows in, sheer to sheer, discharging cargoes of hay and straw to wharves until 1914; the clean smelling cargoes overlying the foul grime of the river and its then constant traffic of tugs and lighters, and bringing a whiff of the sea and the farms to Members of Parliament and the Lords. If bound above the Pool of London to discharge, the centre trusses of the stack were cleared away to allow the mast and rigging to be lowered so the barge could pass under the many fixed bridges. These were removed from the mast case (tabernacle), working aft. The after end of the stack on the centreline was not completely removed as once the sprit was down on it, the stay-fall holding the mast was surged and the momentum buried it a foot or so in the top of the cargo. When the barge was alongside the wharf, the mast and rigging had to be hove up again before the crew commenced helping to unload, which was often complicated. A dock just above Lambeth Bridge accommodated just two barges, bows inwards, so each truss had to be carried ashore up a plank off the fore-stack. The bargemen placed one hay truss weighing 56 pounds on their head or took two straw trusses, each weighing 36 pounds, under each arm. The payment for all this labour was 5 shillings a ton for hay or 3 shillings and 6 pence for a load of straw of 36 trusses. One half of this sum was shared between skipper and mate.

London's horse traffic began to decline about 1912 and the introduction of motor buses to replace horse drawn vehicles led to a marked falling off of stack work soon after.

The Parker fleet grew to 26 barges, complementing the vast acreage of their farms and connections with the land. But when Clement Parker died in 1932, the barges were laid up and sold, and the hand and heart flag was lowered for the last time.

The barges have gone but Bradwell Quay remains, with its tall, braced piles which prevented the barges from lodging on its edge during a high water spring. Only dinghies and small yachts use the Creek now and crowd the yacht harbour excavated from the saltings by the waterside, where the breezy tinkle of unstopped halyards on aluminium masts drowns the call of the curlew.

The spritsail barge *Nellie Parker* thrashes to windward in the Blackwater. She was one of Clement Parker's fleet from Bradwell, built at Ipswich, Suffolk, in 1899 and trading into the 1950s.

CHAPTER FIVE

Mehalah's Country

THE Strood Channel leads past West Mersea's waterside to the causeway
which carries the road from Colchester to the Island; site of a Roman ford
and later of a water mill which stood on foundations remaining on the east side
of the causeway at the Peldon end. The mill was built in 1734 and seems to have
been demolished only thirty-five years later but the mill pool remains alongside
the road and the mill quay was last used for commerce in the 1940s when
Wakeley's sailing barges called there to discharge cargoes of Kentish ragstone for
repair of the sea walls, then usually unloaded by gangs of German prisoners of
war. Forty years earlier stack barges loaded there, bound for London with hay
and straw from surrounding farms. The crews walked up the road to Peldon's
Rose for beer, as yachtsmen sometimes still do having landed in a dinghy at the
Strood causeway, which divides the Strood channel from the waters of Pyefleet
Creek; a tributary of the River Colne which continues Mersea Island's separation
from the mainland to the eastward.

A long tapering spit of low land called The Ray divides the Strood Channel
from the upper end of Thornfleet Creek, which is locally called "up the Ray".
Coarse grass, bushes and stunted trees cluster to make the Ray resemble an
island, which it becomes when spring tides flow over the marshes at its upper
end. The shingly beach landing on its north side has made it a favourite picnic
place for Mersea people for generations, though during the 1960s it became
subject of dispute of ownership and right of public access and it is now owned by
the National Trust. The Ray was the fictional home of Mehalah, heroine of
Baring Gould's novel of the title which, if one disregards the lurid Victorian
melodrama of the story, contains accurate observation of this countryside
between Mersea and Salcott. He describes the marshes; ". . . yet it is not without
beauty. In summer the thrift mantles the marshes with shot satin, passing
through all graduations of tint from maiden's blush to lily white. Thereafter a
purple glow steals over the waste, as the sea lavender bursts into flower, and
simultaneously every creek and pool is royally fringed with sea aster. A little later
the glass-wort, that shot up green and transparent as emerald glass in the early
spring, turns to every tinge of carmine.

When all vegetation ceases to live, and goes to sleep, the marshes are alive
and wakeful with countless wild fowl. At all times they are haunted with sea

mews and roysten crows; in winter they team with wild duck and grey geese. The stately heron loves to wade in the pools, occasionally the whooper swan sounds his loud trumpet, and flashes a white reflection in the still blue waters of the fleets. The plaintive pipe of the curlew is familiar to those who frequent these marshes and the barking of the brent geese as they return from their northern breeding places is heard in November.''

Baring Gould ascribes the place name to ancient inhabitants who built a fortified camp or ''rath'' of wooden logs on the spit, though this seems to have been conjecture. One of his novels featured in a strange wartime experience of Walter (''Navvy'') Mussett, a West Mersea fisherman and yacht sailor who has spent most of his life sailing out of Tollesbury. Joining-up early in the 1914-18 war, he was serving in the British army fighting the Germans in Belgium when their trenches were overrun by cavalry. Navvy and other survivors were taken prisoner, to be transported into Germany and then to Poland to work in the coal mines. Arriving at a labour camp there, the prisoners had to give their particulars to a German officer. At Navvy's turn the officer said ''Mussett! Do you come from West Mersea?'' Walter said he did. ''Then you know the Nass and you know Bill Wyatt?'' ''Yes, I do,'' said Navvy. ''And so do I,'' said the officer, adding: ''Have you ever read Mehalah?'' Navvy said he had not and the officer offered to loan it to him. Afterwards Navvy discovered he had kept a small yacht at Bradwell before the war.

Spacious marshlands stretch westward from the Thornfleet sea wall and have a magic of their own. In 1971 my son David and I were cruising and anchored for the night in West Mersea's Thornfleet. In the evening we rowed across the creek, filled salting-high with the still of high water and clambered up the sea wall, just below the indentation of Sampson's Creek. From its crest a vista of surprising beauty unfolded. Feldy Marsh, hundreds of acres in extent, held areas of ripe corn rippled in burnished waves by the faint south-east breeze. Beyond, Fresians browsed on marsh fields and wildfowl chittered on the fleets. The evening light was changing from a smoky blue in the east, through turquoise, to a brazen west, with the orange sun a ball dipping into a fine weather haze of intensity graduating from fine upper layers to near milky white over the distant, shaded fields of Virley, where elms drooped, reviving in the cooler air of evening. The sun dipped to a red Humpty Dumpty, the evening breeze shivered through the spiky marsh grass, then it was gone and the chill sent us rowing back to the warm cabin. I doubt if I will ever forget the evening light on Feldy Marsh.

The top of Ray Creek reaches into marshland at Peldon, an agricultural parish whose maritime connections were the usual local ones of sailing barge trade during the nineteenth and early twentieth century. Men from Peldon and Salcott also fished over the centuries and were cited in an Inquiry held in April 1377 regarding a method of fishing on the Essex coast and rivers. Most works on fisheries have it that trawling was "invented" by the Brixham or Barking fishermen during the eighteenth century. However, fishermen from Brightlingsea, St Osyth, Fingringhoe, Alresford, Tollesbury, East and West Mersea, Salcott, Peldon and Heybridge were before an inquiry of Colchester justices accused of causing damage to fisheries in the Colne, Blackwater and Wallet by using primitive trawls called "wonderthons". These had been in use for sixteen years and were said to be causing severe damage by overfishing. Certainly the wonderthon was a great advance on lines and drift nets, and fishermen were trawling "plaise and buttes" in great numbers, being accused of burying 20,000 fish which remained unsold.

Richard Clark of Brightlingsea was trawling the Wallet with a wonderthon having an eight foot beam and a net four fathoms long with a mesh "so close that no fish can escape, however small". Another wonderthon was described as having a ten foot beam and three fathom net with two inch meshes and a leaded groundrope with stone rollers. These new trawls promised spectacular returns and it was recorded that a "great quantity of labourers have withdrawn from the business of agriculture, such as the carters, ploughmen and shepherds, plying these nets because of the gain and excessive wages they receive, to the no small damage of the whole people". The inquiry condemned the wonderthon for inshore fishing but recommended its use for deep sea work.

Wakeley's sailing barge *P.A.M.* discharging a cargo of Kentish ragstone for the sea walls at the Strood, 1946. The unloading gang are Ukrainian prisoners of war. *Arthur Bennett*

Peldon was a quiet place, yet its inhabitants were once influenced by fiery John Ball who would now be considered a militant Socialist. His beliefs contributed to the Peasants' Revolt in 1381, with his verse "When Adam delved and Eve span, who was then the gentleman?" The resulting riots and disturbances spread throughout south and east Essex.Fisherman and fowlers of the Thames estuary produced the spark that fired a workers' revolution. Fobbing-by-Tilbury men, aided by others from the Thames villages of Corringham and Stanford le Hope, resisted arrest with open violence and on 2nd June there was an affray at Brentwood where some men were killed. The Admiral of the Essex coast, Edmund de la Mare of Peldon Hall and the sheriff, John Sewall of Coggeshall, had their houses ransacked; la Mare's papers being carried on a pitchfork at the head of the triumphant fishermen and farm workers. Other manor houses were sacked in that period of change from the feudal manorial system.

This was the sole violent excitement to disturb Peldon's peace over the centuries and it has remained pleasantly agricultural, though Peldon men have become sailmakers and shipwrights at West Mersea and a West Mersea man, John Milgate, has established a thriving little boatyard at Peldon, at the marsh pool leading off the head of Ray Creek, known as "the parlour". Here he repairs and refits craft up to 50 feet sailing smacks and yachts, and winter finds a collection of both laid up there. Once a year the smacks race to Peldon from a start in the River Blackwater; up the Quarters, through the Thornfleet and up the Ray to finish at Peldon and be welcomed by John and his family in their house on the sea wall.

This is countryside where plough meets sail and from the country road which straggles from Peldon through the villages to Tollesbury and on to Maldon one obtains tantalising high water glimpses of brimming creeks and waterways with perhaps a distant view of a tan-sailed smack or barge, or the white sails of yachts in Mersea creeks. Long fingers of salt water probe inland and in the days of sailing commerce the worlds of farmers, bargemen and fishermen met at now decayed barge quays, jutting in isolation from sea walls, where carts and tumbrils brought hay and straw cargoes and took back muck, lime or five-fingered starfish, to fertilise the fields.

The parishes of Great and Little Wigborough have no maritime associations and seem to have passed the quiet centuries in the grinding toil of pre-mechanised agriculture, rudely shattered for a few weeks when the large German Zeppelin L.33. crashed there on the night of 23rd September 1916, after a raid on London. The returning raider awoke the inhabitants of Little Wigborough with the roar of its engines flying low over them, out towards the River Blackwater. Circling, it returned and landed in a field near two cottages in this tiny hamlet. Either the Zeppelin was damaged or was deliberately set on fire by her crew for the 700-feet long aircraft was soon a mass of searing flame, to the terror of the inhabitants. The cottages narrowly escaped because the wind was away from them. The German crew walked the lanes towards Peldon and gave themselves up to an astonished village policeman. They were later taken to West Mersea and were locked in a barn before being taken to Colchester by an escort of soldiers. The night's events were terrifyingly exciting but next morning Little Wigborough had never seen anything like it, before or since; all roads and lanes leading there were thronged with sightseers anxious to view the huge skeleton of the burned out airship, which was guarded by men of the Lancashire Fusiliers until it was broken up, though a few relics remained in local homes for many years afterwards.

Sailing smacks crowd the berths at John Milgate's boatyard at Peldon after the first Peldon Smack Race in 1975. *Essex County Newspapers*

I found echoes of another war when walking through this countryside in 1947. A man was repainting a footpath signpost green, with neat white lettering. He sang as he worked. His black ex-Army beret was stained with spots of green paint. His bike, with the then inevitable camouflaged gas cape lashed to its carrier, lay in the hedge. We chatted. He had fought in the desert (there was only one desert then) and later through Italy; an Eighth Army man. Now he was very glad to be painting signposts in rural Essex with a modest wage but a contented mind in that time of scarcity; of rationing; of coupons.

Further west, along the road, the twin villages of Salcott and Virley face each other at the head of Salcott Creek which winds inland from the top of Mersea Quarters, past the Sunken Island and skirting the south of Wigborough marshes. Salcott is probably a corruption of Salt cote, signifying that salt was made here long ago. Its twin village reputedly gets its name from Robert de Verli, a Norman lord whose property it became. Later it was known as Salcott Verley while the other village became Salcott Wigborough and flourished during the fifteenth and sixteenth centuries as a small market centre for this then isolated district. Two centuries later Salcott and Virley were used by Essex smugglers and runs of goods were sometimes concealed in the church.

It was at tiny Virley church that the proud but fictional Mehalah was married to the villanous Elijah Rebow of "Red Hall" with a ring of iron.

Baring Gould, one time rector of East Mersea, wrote of nineteenth century smuggling:

Mehalah's country. From the saltings on the Mersea side of the Strood Channel, divided from Ray Creek by the tapering tip of Ray Island. The smack *Mersea Lass* dredges against the hazy backdrop of Peldon on a spring morning. *Douglas Went*

"The traffic was carried on with an audacity and openness unparalleled elsewhere. Although there was a coastguard station at the mouth of the estuary on Mersea 'Hard', yet goods were run even in open day, under the very eyes of the revenue men. Each public house on the island and on the mainland near a creek, obtained its entire supply of wine and spirits from contraband vessels. Whether the coastguard were bought to shut their eyes or were baffled by the adroitness of the smugglers, cannot be said, but the taverns found no difficulty in obtaining their supplies as often and as abundantly as they desired. The villages of Virley and Salcott were the chief landing places and there horses and donkeys were kept in large numbers for the conveyance of the spirits, wine, tobacco and silk to Tiptree Heath, the scene of Boadicea's great battle with the legions of Suetonius, which was the emporium of the trade. There a constant fair or auction of contraband articles went on, and thence they were distributed to Maldon, Colchester, Chelmsford and even London. Tiptree Heath was a permanent camping ground of gipsies, and there squatters ran up rude hovels; these were all engaged in the distribution of the goods brought from the sea."

Salcott was a rural barge port, with craft discharging and loading at Church Wharf at the head of the creek which, lower down, is one of my favourite anchorages. Trade was principally agricultural; hay and straw outward and London muck inward, with occasional other cargoes of coal, grain and road or sea wall stone. There were then two coal yards at Salcott and a post windmill ground grain grown on the surrounding broad acres. Usually there were four men to discharge a barge, often carrying the cargo ashore in wicker baskets. Hay was tied into trusses and bundles and this work went on between loading or unloading cargoes. Once, the unloading at Salcott was stopped by the finding of a bag of gold sovereigns amongst the muck and swill in a barge's hold. These were shared out amongst the delighted workmen.

The Salcott Creek "huffler" who assisted barges up and down was adept at putting them ashore "accidentally" at just the right spot to help the deflected tide scour away a growing spit.

Jack Spitty, son of the noted smack skipper of the same name who we have met elsewhere in this book, skippered the barges *Lord Warden* and *Victa* as a young man in the coasting trade. Just after the First World War he worked up the tortuous upper reaches of Salcott Creek to berth the 50-ton *Lord Warden*, then owned by Clement Parker of Bradwell, near the church. This was a prime example of the versatility of the spritsail barge; loading a haystack in the heart of a village for delivery to the bustle of the capital. The berth was later dammed against flooding.

Of course not all the barges arriving at local wharves were manned from the Blackwater. One Mistley skipper, who was also a lay preacher, carried his tricycle in the hold and on Sundays away from his home port would put on his best suit and bowler and pedal off the weary miles to Mistley to fulfil his duties.

The integrated economy of the district was reflected in the barges owned by Robert Seabrook who farmed extensively at Tolleshunt D'Arcy, a village withdrawn from the water, between Salcott and Tollesbury.

The *D'Arcy*, *Defender* and *Pride of Essex* were all designed and built by John Howard at Maldon and skippered by Thomas West, Harry West and a Mr Keeble. The *Defender* was a fast barge with a reputation for overhauling almost all other barges. All three often worked to a small wharf at Skinners Wick, at Tolleshunt D'Arcy.

The village was the home of Dr J. H. Salter, one of the Blackwater's notable "gentlemen gunners" who was wildfowling and shore shooting for three-quarters of a century, until his death in 1933.

Many boys from Tolleshunt D'Arcy were sent to sea at an early age in the nineteenth century when local farms could not employ all of the large families of the village population and many youngsters straight from rook scaring or stone picking were packed off as apprentices, a title then synonymous with cheap labour afloat, on board Tollesbury smacks, some to become prime seamen in the harsh work of the fisheries.

CHAPTER SIX

Dredgermen, Shrimpers and Stowboaters

TOLLESBURY, facing West Mersea across the expanse of marshes and creeks between them, was perhaps the most vigorous of the Blackwater's seafaring villages. Its seamen have dredged, trawled and stowboated under sail and power, owned and manned barges, built smacks, yachts and small boats, manned yachts of all sizes, including some of the most famous racers, and have carried these traditions into the mid-twentieth century. Unlike West Mersea, nestling amongst its trees and sheltered from the north-east winds, Tollesbury is less compact in its siting and as much of it was built between 1890 and 1914, is generally as architecturally uninspiring as its contemporaries Brightlingsea, Wivenhoe and Rowhedge, on the Colne, whose mariners often rivalled Tollesbury men afloat in fishing and yachting.

From seaward the approach to Tollesbury is most unpromising. Its creek leads westward off the Quarters, inside the Nass Spit and forks into the North and the South Channels at the eastern tip of the Great Cob Island which divides them. Abreast of Shinglehead Point the South Channel turns north-west, skirting a long sea wall enclosing the marshes of Tollesbury Wick. Then a westward offshoot leads to Tollesbury, while the South Channel continues, to join the North Channel and lead into Old Hall Creek and into the marshes. The twisting little creek which runs up to Woodrolfe Hard looks impossible from the entrance, but anything up to 10 feet draught can get up at high water springs and all around are the cosiest mud berths, sheltered from every wind.

These creeks have at various times over many centuries been used to produce oysters and there were many "layings" leased from local landowners or owned by individual fishermen. The Heard family have long been fishermen and mariners out of the Tollesbury district and in 1377 John De Heerde of Salcott was recorded as dredging brood oysters and laying them in fleets to fatten. At the close of the eighteenth century and the commencement of the nineteenth, William and Thomas Sanford of Wivenhoe owned and worked three layings there and between the years 1810 and 1828 "haled", to use Sanford's expression, 9,022 wash of marketable oysters from them, the price varying from 1s. 2d. to 1s. 9d. a wash. This total was approximately twice the quantity of brood oysters laid and the value of Sanford's stock on the layings was maintained at around £400.

Many local smacks dredged oysters on free ground in the River Blackwater and adjacent waters, alongside others from the River Colne, from Burnham and some from Whitstable in Kent; an oyster centre to which large quantities of brood oysters were sold by the Essex fishermen.

There seems to have been more than just business connecting the oyster dredgers of Tollesbury and those at Whitstable, in Kent, who bought or dredged Blackwater oysters. The cutter-rigged dredging smacks of Whitstable were locally called "yawls" and this contradictory term is also found in several references to Tollesbury cutter smacks during the nineteenth century. In 1823 Martha Lewis, a widow of Bradwell, sold to John Lewis the "yawl" *Defiance* which had been built at Maldon in 1802. The contract of sale gives the following description:

"The vessel has one deck and one mast, her length from forepart of the main stem to the afterpart of the sternpost aloft is twenty four feet ten inches, her breadth at the broadest part above the main wales is ten feet three inches, her height of hold five feet, and measures ten tons 9/94. She is a square sterned carvel built yawl, and has neither galley nor figurehead" (contemporary ship terminology).

She was sold with fishing gear, for £42. 10 shillings; then an average price for a craft of that size and type. Later Tollesbury smacks were usually larger, up to 50 feet long and though still rigged as cutters, had deck room and sailing length increased by the "lute" stern, an early form of counter, and later by the full counter stern in the many carvel planked clippers turned out in large numbers by yards at Brightlingsea, Wivenhoe and Rowhedge, on the Colne, which built most of the Essex smacks and bawleys for many other villages including the fishermen of Tollesbury and West Mersea.

Smacks were built at Tollesbury from time to time and my great-grandfather's husky 17-tonner *Prince of Orange* was launched there in 1788, long before his ownership, in which she fished, salvaged and smuggled from Rowhedge, on the Colne. During the nineteenth century many boys from Tollesbury and some from neighbouring agricultural villages were apprenticed to oyster dredgermen, often for a term of seven years, the "master", owning the smack, agreeing to supply the apprentice with stipulated clothing and to pay him £5 at the end of his apprenticeship; a system of cheap labour which also usually produced prime seamen.

By the 1890s the agreements required a payment of a small wage to the boy, often six (old) pence weekly during a four year term. The boys, on their part, had to conduct themselves in an obedient manner, obey the lawful commands of the skipper and be honest and sober.

The Tollesbury smack *Daisy*, C.K.6, in winter with quarter boards shipped. The rig is typical but her steeply raked counter is not. She was later owned at Wivenhoe. She is towing two yachts' boats, possibly from an end of summer regatta.

Summer was the harvest time for brood oysters, dredged to be re-laid on other beds in the Blackwater or Colne, and many dredged from the Blackwater were sent to Whitstable in Kent. A report from the Maldon Customs House in 1846 included a statement by A. Chatterson, a Tollesbury oyster merchant, that between 350-400 smacks from the Blackwater and the Colne town and villages, carrying on average four men and a boy, were engaged in dredging brood oysters in the summer months. It must be remembered this was before the tremendous expansion of yachting as a summer employment, which took place a few years later, particularly from the Colne. In 1862 Tollesbury was described as a "thriving fishing village" with a population of 1,193, most of the men and boys manning about 50 smacks of 7-30 tons, mainly engaged in oyster dredging. Several inhabitants described themselves as oyster merchants, including William Antony, Frederick and William Banyard, James and John Bowles, Adam Chatterson and Zacchariah Lewis, who was also a shipwright. Robert Lee was blacksmith for marine or agricultural items and William Last worked a duck decoy.

The Tollesbury and Mersea (Blackwater) Oyster Fishery Company (Limited) was established in 1876-7 when 260 men from Tollesbury worked at dredging oysters in 70 smacks of various sizes, generally not exceeding 18 tons. At West and East Mersea there were 120 dredgers owning 47 smacks. Of these, 380 dredgermen became shareholders in the new Company, which it was hoped would protect stocks and stabilise returns; oyster dredegermen then earning an average of 10 shillings weekly. Daily management of the Company was by a "Jury" or committee of twelve members who were drawn from Tollesbury, West Mersea and East Mersea men. The jury decided the rota on which members' smacks worked at dredging in the river, thus fairly distributing any gain from the fishery, which was invariably less than the wages to be earned as crew in yachts and particularly so compared with the prospects of prize money in a racer. Hence the Tollesbury men's, and some West Mersea men's, desire to participate in the considerable and long standing involvement of the Colne seamen in the sport.

Some idea of the quantities of brood oysters dredged from the Blackwater a century ago was that in 1882 five-and-a-half million were dredged in three months, to be sent to Whitstable for relaying at that Kentish oyster centre, which was then principally supplied from the Blackwater. As with oysters everywhere there was danger of theft and Watch smacks were anchored in the Blackwater; one off the South Shore of Bradwell, one at the mouth of Thirslet Creek and a third off the North Shore, aligned with "meets" on West Mersea shore.

A ground near the Bench Head buoy at the mouth of the Blackwater and Colne was a vast repository of culch and shell, which was valuable for spatting oysters on this common ground. About 1893 smacks from Burnham on the Crouch began dredging culch there and this caused tremendous resentment amongst Tollesbury and West Mersea oystermen, who threatened the Burnham men that they would run them down if dredging did not stop. The Burnham smacks *Emmeline, Alma, Wonder* and *Rose* continued to dredge and were almost filled one day when three Tollesbury smacks, with two or three men on deck, sailed towards them. One boarded the *Emmeline* and a dozen yelling fishermen sprang up from the hold brandishing sticks and shovels, overawing the Burnham fishermen, who made little resistance. The other smacks boarded the *Alma* and the *Wonder* but the *Rose* was a different task. Her young crew, named Rice and Ambrose, sailed up to see what was happening. One of the Tollesbury smacks left a prize crew on board her captive and sailed towards the *Rose* but got more than they expected when Ambrose came on deck, coolly loading a gun, which he levelled at the Tollesbury smack's crowded deck, threatening to shoot anyone who tried to board him. The growling Tollesbury-men kept their distance while the *Rose* stood by helplessly as the holds of the captured smacks were emptied overboard and, it was said, quantities of cocoa, tea and tobacco were extorted from their crews, before the craft were released with threats that if they reported anything they too would be thrown overboard another day. The Tollesbury fleet departed and the Burnham men sailed home in a fever of indignation. Reprisals were proposed but instead the Burnham men went to law and the case against the ''Tollesbury Pirates'' was heard at Witham in April 1894 when twelve Tollesbury fishermen were charged with piracy and assault, and of stealing the smacks' cargoes. The court was crowded with oystermen; 200 from Tollesbury, about 100 from Mersea and many from Burnham. The defendants claimed they acted to preserve a valuable basis of the oyster fishery which was free to all for dredging spat and brood but they refused to allow removal of the culch which was its foundation. Five were committed for trial and all were acquitted by the judge, who had some scathing remarks for the magistrates who had allowed the affair to get beyond an elementary stage of common sense justice.

By the early 1900s about 70 smacks of various sizes were owned at Tollesbury and in those days before chemical fertilisers, winter and early spring found many Tollesbury and a few West Mersea smacks joining others from the Colne in dredging five-fingers, or starfish, to be sold to fish merchants on the Colne or Blackwater, or direct to farmers, for field fertiliser. For this work the smack carried a crew of four men, each working four dredges with the net slacked back from the hoeing edge to avoid rubbish. Favourite grounds were on the Kentish shore and in the Wallet. Tollesbury smacks in this work had the hold divided into four by shifting boards radiating from a centre post in way of the main hatch. These prevented the cargo of five-fingers from shifting when the smack was under sail. This dredging was hard, backbreaking work. The smacks sailed on a Monday for the Kentish shore and dredged until Friday or until they filled the hold, when they sailed back to Tollesbury or its district to discharge perhaps 5-6 tons, or more if they were lucky. The smacks often discharged at Woodrolfe where the cargo was weighed on wooden scales before being tipped into the waiting cart or tumbril, the number of baskets being recorded. The loaded carts were drawn by two horses up through the village to the farms. Five-fingers were sold for 6½d. a bushel during the mid-nineteenth century, when a local farm might purchase about 2,000 bushels in a year, for fertiliser. The labour of five-fingering often did not end with sailing home, if the cargo had to be sailed up a narrow and obscure creek so the smack could berth conveniently for the farmer, often on a night tide, and one of the crew had usually to walk miles to rouse the farmer with news of arrival, so the carts could be sent down first thing in the morning. It was an unusual and a hard trade.

Mr Jack Owen, that veteran West Mersea seaman, recalled dredging five-fingers in Jack Spitty's *David and Eliza*, landing at £1 per ton. Spitty chanced on a thick patch of them off Frinton, just below the telegraph cable to the old Gunfleet lighthouse. Word went round and a few days later a score of

Rowhedge, Wivenhoe and Tollesbury smacks appeared to reap this harvest. However, the cunning Spitty anchored a skin buoy right over the cable and dredged around it with dredges hanging just below the surface. Down came the others, many with sixteen dredges apiece and, with warps straining, fouled the cable and each other, losing many dredges and their tempers. With a satisfied grin Jack Spitty retrieved his buoy and sailed off into Harwich, returning next morning when he filled his hold without another smack in sight.

Smacks fitting out on Woodrolfe Hard, 1938. These deep-hulled 18-tonners were similar to the Colne smacks and worked in the same trades. Others lie in the creek's mud berths. Drake Brother's slipway carriage and rails occupy the foreground.

In winter many Tollesbury smacks favoured sailing with the topmast housed and its heel lashed to the rigging, ready to send up when required. Others sometimes laid the topmast ashore for the winter and sailed with a short topmast aloft, known as the "chock pole". On this they often set a topsail with a spar on its luff. In winter the Tollesbury smacks could generally be recognised at some distance by their topmast shrouds which were coiled up and lashed, swaying like giant earrings from each crosstree. One Tollesbury smack caused a ribald sensation by arriving at Wivenhoe railway quay to discharge sprats with "Beecham Pills" painted in white letters across her mainsail.

Twenty or so Tollesbury smacks, with two hands in each, spent the summer shrimping from Harwich before 1914, but the remainder were laid up in the creeks and rills while their owners and crews were away yachting. The development of east coast seaside resorts during the Victorian period brought a demand for seafoods, especially shrimps. Leigh fishermen were shrimping before 1840 and when the railway reached Harwich twenty years later, that port took to the trade on a large scale. After about 1870 Leigh bawleys started working out of Harwich during the summer and were joined by others from Harwich and other smacks from the Colne and Tollesbury, with some from Kent. One day during the 1880s a record fleet of 180 shrimpers sailed from Harwich for the grounds, which varied but included the Goldmer Gat off Walton, the Sledway, the Sunk and the Swin.

The Colne and Blackwater smacks used the beam trawl for shrimping, which needed a crew of two. Shrimp nets were of fine mesh, which not only destroyed many immature fish but on good ground filled the deck with a writhing grey mass of shrimps with the crew knee deep in them, rapidly riddling them through a sieve and culling a stream of offal overside, attracting a cloud of gulls around each smack. Quality of the catch was checked by a "tell-tale", a small net on a dredge-like frame towed ahead of the trawl. The culled shrimps were tipped into a large domestic copper filled with clean salt water, with salt added to taste and kept boiling in the hold. When cooked the Essex coastal shrimp turns pink, while Thames shrimps go brown. The catch was despatched to market in wicker baskets, called "pads", and was and is sold by capacity measure.

The cutter-rigged smacks could always sail faster than the beamier, transom-sterned bawleys from Harwich or Leigh, working alongside them, but the bawleymen had the best of it while trawling as the beamy hulls did not heel so easily and were more comfortable to work aboard, compared to the narrower decks of the smacks. In the 1890s shrimps fetched 3d.-4d. a gallon and shrimping was ill rewarded. Shrimping ended in September but the Tollesbury shrimpers always sailed home for the annual village fair. Tollesburymen sometimes worked smacks for other owners. Harry Williamson and Lew Heard fished the little 10-tonner *Valkyrie* out of Harwich for Myall in the shrimping trade, but sailed her home for Goseberry Fair.

At the end of the nineteenth century a few Tollesbury smacks joined others from West Mersea and Bradwell drifting for winter herring in the Blackwater estuary. It is probable that large rowing boats were built for this work as a race for "Herring Skiffs" pulling four oars was included in Tollesbury regatta in 1904. This "White herring" fishery was worked with drift nets suspended in the water like a curtain, often from strops with buoys at the surface to obtain the correct depth for efficient fishing. They shot at night, soon after high water and drifted the tide down, hauling near low water, then shot again with the first of the flood, landing the catch in the morning. This fishery was not worked for many years until revived by Mr Peter French, one of West Mersea's most enterprising fishermen, during the 1950s. It afterwards developed to a major fishery for Blackwater boats.

In earlier times larger Tollesbury smacks might bring an occasional cargo to the village and Joe Hume's *Waterlily* was one of the last Essex smacks to sail to the Channel Island of Jersey for new potatoes; a delicacy once regularly sought in spring by mariners from Tollesbury, the Colne and elsewhere.

Smacks were a fine nursery for seamen but the return for fishing under sail was always poor. As late as 1907 the skipper of a smack might average earnings of 16 shillings a week throughout the winter months, compared to a yacht hand's wages of 23 shillings weekly in summer. With the refitting of many smack hulls for pleasure sailing, a use which would have sorely puzzled their original owners and crews, it is well to remember what a Tollesburyman who went fishing and yachting before 1914 wrote of his last winter fishing under sail: ''. . . thank God that was the last time I went in a smack. I think I had my share of it.''

Tollesbury smacks laid up in summer while their crews were away yachting, circa 1900.
from a painting by Tom Simpson, in the author's possession.

By the 1890s, a few Tollesbury mariners sought berths in steamboats for the winter, usually in the home or short sea trades, so they could conveniently return in spring to ship as hands in yachts; a practice also followed on the Colne and the Solent. The size of the marshes and contiguous farms led, in those days of horse-drawn transport and tortuous roads and cart tracks, to establishment of discharging berths in many now isolated and abandoned places. At Old Hall, to the north-east of Tollesbury, on the edge of the creek by the broad expanse of Old Hall Marsh, a thriving community of about 50 people lived in cottages around the *Hoy Inn*. Here barges loaded cargoes of hay, straw, root crops and grain and discharged London muck, coal, chalk, timber and stone. Chalk was burned in a kiln to become lime and there was a coal yard. Bricks were made in a kiln and supplied Tollesbury builders and others. Flints for roadmaking and Kentish ragstone for maintenance of the faces of the sea walls were also landed, along with some other cargoes.

Some Tollesburymen went barging, including the families Payne, Lee, Say and Fisher during the early nineteenth century and Frosts, Bowles, and Wests in later years. Barges loading stacks of hay or straw or unloading cargoes of London muck were a common sight at Woodrolfe Hard, which also occasionally saw Fisher's fine coasting spritty proudly named *Tollesbury*, built at Sandwich, Kent, in 1901 and later owned by Paull's of Ipswich; a fine looking barge, one of my favourites, which in 1940 brought back over 200 troops from the beaches of Dunkirk.

Tollesbury owners had several boomsail barges, rigged as ketches with boom and gaff mainsails and mizzens. Joe Culf had the *Mary Kate* and James Bowles ordered a fine boomie of that name from Robert Aldous at Brightlingsea in 1865. Later she was bought by William Frost, another barge owner in the village, who manned her principally with his sons. They later took charge of his other boomies *Empress of India, Darnet* and *Lord Hamilton*. These craft were often in the coal trade and voyaged to many North Sea and English Channel ports with cargoes of various kinds, the strangest being a complete wooden chapel shipped from Colchester Hythe to Bursledon on the Hamble River.

William Frost's barges were frequent coal carriers, and the day before one was expected to berth for discharge at Woodrolfe a crier went round the village with a handbell exhorting the housewives to place their orders. The men discharging her would receive 2d. a ton for the work. If the coal was taken at the barge it cost around 18 shillings a ton in the mid-nineteenth century, or £1 a ton if delivered to the road outside the household.

Besides the barges, much coal was brought in by brigs from the north-east coal ports on the Tyne and Wear; deep draught, tubby little vessels which required careful handling to berth safely at Old Hall or Woodrolfe. The inward bound barges and brigs lay in Mersea Quarters awaiting the pilot and sufficient water to get up to Old Hall or Woodrolfe. John, Samuel and William Lewis were pilots and hufflers (those who assisted craft up and down river to these places) at the end of the nineteenth century. Some of the larger Blackwater smacks also occasionally carried a coal cargo. The *Providence* of Maldon, owned by a fisherman named London, was reputed to be intending to land contraband hidden under a cargo of coal for Old Hall, in 1840. Like many other Colne and Blackwater seafarers, Tollesburymen were involved in smuggling until well into the nineteenth century and in 1772 a cargo of silks, gloves and ruffles was seized at Woodrolfe Creek. Amongst the 25 vessels captured during the first six months of 1778 by the Harwich revenue cutters *Argus* and *Bee* was a "small smuggling cutter of Tollesbury, 24 tons". It is interesting that she was described as "small" as she would have been about 50 feet long, indicating the large size of many contemporary smugglers. Like the other captures, she was probably condemned and burned at Harwich, the usual fate of local free traders.

In 1779 a run of 210 tubs of Geneva was captured at Old Hall, near Tollesbury. Coastguards were stationed at Tollesbury in 1843, and later also at Goldhanger, to guard the lonely creeks and marshes between Mersea Quarters and Heybridge, which were ideal smuggling country. Tollesbury's coastguard then comprised a chief boatman, five boatmen and a private of the mounted guard. There was smuggling at Old Hall during the 1860s and during the 1880s eight or nine barges or brigs were arriving at Mersea Quarters with inward cargoes each month and most were boarded there by the customs. A barge belonging to Stevens of Purleigh Hall was once chartered by them as a watch boat against smuggling at Tollesbury. The officers boarded her at Gravesend and remained below while she was sailed by her crew to Tollesbury, where she lay in the creek. The smuggling smack came in and when her boat put off to run goods ashore, the Customs men swooped, catching the smugglers. The barge owner received £10 and Garrod, the skipper, £5 for their assistance, but for some time bargemen would not work up to Skinners Wick, where she was bound. A new coastguard station was built at Tollesbury in the 1890s and remained manned until the early 1920s.

The ketch barge *Empress of India* was one of four similar boomsail barges owned by William Frost of Tollesbury. These were often in the coal trade, besides voyaging about the North Sea and English Channel with various cargoes.
By courtesy of
The Nottage Institute

Amongst the many gentlemen wildfowlers attracted to the Essex coast was the Count de la Chapelle; a French born lawyer who came to live at Tollesbury in 1907 to indulge his passion for salt water gunning at week-ends. He lived at Heron Lodge, near Woodrolfe Farm, overlooking the Wick Marshes, and owned the gunning yacht *Scoter*, built at Maldon by John Howard and the smaller *Teal*, besides a double-handed sailing punt, and smaller ones. Chapelle was a great observer of fowl and, with a Tollesbury man as hand, sailed and shot the Blackwater and the Main until his death in 1931. He often complained that the Tollesbury district was not good for wildfowling, being too overshot by fishermen-fowlers and he would not shoot on areas on which the Maldon and other gunners sought part of their living, but each autumn he shot over the Main with Walter Linnett, the Bradwell gunner. He was regarded locally as a fine shot, though he, like many continentals, felt no bird too small to escape his gun and once shot larks on the marshes.

Will Leavett of Tollesbury was his wildfowling companion for many years; a master hand in the Count's two big punts named *Grebe* and *Heron*. Once, during the 1914-18 war, these two were punting in the lower Blackwater on a misty morning when a motor launch racketed up towards them with gun manned and all hands ready to fire into the "submarine's conning tower", which their hazy silhouette suggested. They sprang up, shouting, in time to avoid being blown to pieces.

Tollesbury smacks appear to have commenced stowboating for sprats during the early 1890s and their entry into the fishery caused some resentment amongst Colne men. Their participation coincided with the decline of the big old Colne first class smacks; 20 and 30-tonners which were being superseded by the more economical 15- and 18-tonners; 48- or 50-foot smacks which could work a stowboat net with four hands instead of the six needed in the bigger smacks.

Autumn spring tides saw the smacks floated from summer mud berths to lie on the hard, which resounded all day long with the ring of caulking irons and the chaff of seamen bending canvas, rigging gear and tarring hulls. Along the shore road men bore on their shoulders the big stow nets and their cumbersome wooden baulks. The delicate mesh of the long, brown funnel-shaped nets had been carefully bated before these were dressed in bubbling cauldrons. Then the nets were put on board and triced up to mastheads to air. The square spars of the upper and lower baulks, each some 24 feet long, were shipped, together with a powerful stowboat anchor and many fathoms of stout cable.

The cumbersome stowboat nets; close meshed and funnel-shaped, were suspended beneath the smack at anchor when fishing, like a standing trawl about 240 feet long and capable of catching 10 or 12 tons of sprats. The anchor had to hold both net and vessel against strong tides, wind and sea, the net riding to it, mouth to tide, under the smack's bottom and away astern by a leg of cable made fast to the lower baulk which was ballasted with iron to steady the net's mouth. The upper baulk was held horizontally above it by the "templines"; ropes which made fast to the ends, passed up to belay on either side of the smack's forward rail.

When the net was streamed and fishing its mouth might be 24 feet square. It was closed by a chain, the winchain, which started from the lower baulk and passed through a ring on the upper one, over a sheave at the end of the baulk davit, fitted in winter on the opposite side of the stem to the gammon iron for the bowsprit, and around the barrel of the handspike windlass. To recover the net this chain was hauled in, bringing the two baulks together and to the surface where these were hauled up the side by a tackle, leaving the hopefully well filled net to be griped in alongside with ropes and the catch to be boarded from its cod end in quantities which were taken below deck through small hatches, into the fish hold.

It was an old gear, dating back to the Middle Ages and because of the comparatively shallow channels and heavy ship traffic of the Essex coast, was used by the fishermen in preference to the drift nets used elsewhere. The "stall boats" as these were originally called, were banned in 1488 by an Act of Parliament which was perpetuated in 1491. However, it must have been repealed as many stall boats were working again in 1547, when boats from Colchester, Fingringhoe and St Osyth, on the Colne, and East Mersea and Maldon and Harwich, were landing sprats near the Tower of London.

A stowboating smack needed four hands, often three men and a boy, and sometimes shipped six if she was a large smack with a big net. Crews worked on the share system and a smack with four men shared the proceeds of the catch in six shares, one for each, one ''for the boat'' and one ''for the net''.

The ''Stowboaters'' as they were called, usually fished in the Wallet, the Swin and in the approaches to the Thames, the skippers seeking the tell-tale signs of clouds of feeding gulls and discoloured water, marking the path of the big sprat shoals along the coastal channels. Occasionally stowboating smacks would make good catches under the Bradwell shore within the River Blackwater itself, though this was most unusual. The Tollesbury *William and Emily*, more usually known as the *Odd Times*, once made a freak catch of pilchards when stowboating. Undeterred, skipper Walter Mussett and his crew got them aboard, sailed the 12 ton catch to Wivenhoe and sold the lot to the canning factory.

Most catches were landed at Brightlingsea and were sold to one of the town's sprat merchants and curers, for processing or to be pickled in barrels for export to Europe and Russia. Some were smoked and relished as a delicacy. During the winter of 1911 smacks landed over 570 tons of sprats there, besides the many catches landed at Rowhedge, Wivenhoe and Tollesbury. Stowboating was a maritime gamble; a large catch after scarcity could bring a big return but more usually heavy landings were met by a glutted market and hard-won catches sold for a few pence a bushel as manure. Sometimes days or even weeks went by without a worthwhile landing and during that time the fishermen earned nothing, and there were no unemployment benefits in those days. It was a fickle living, which the Tollesburymen shared with their contemporaries from the Colne villages. All depended on the movements of the shoals. But Tollesbury's vigorous and far-seeking fishermen seemed to thrive on the hard work and in some ways the village developed as an isolated community in the Blackwater. Because of their participation in yachting and winter stowboating, they came to have more in common with Brightlingsea, Wivenhoe and Rowhedge than their neighbours at West Mersea or Maldon.

In 1922 Tollesbury smacks were amongst the first locally to install auxiliary engines, usually 15 h.p. Kelvins, and within two years most had them, with the Brightlingsea, Wivenhoe and Rowhedge smacks soon following. These enabled them to extend their range when stowboating and to keep going in calm and fogs. Another use was to ease strain on the cable in a strong wind or seaway by steaming slowly ahead. The smack could also be easily sheered across the tide to intercept a passing sprat shoal and could shift her berth more quickly, besides easing anchor work. For some years they remained fully rigged but as the auxiliaries proved reliable and more powerful engines came in, sail was gradually discarded. At first the long topmasts and topsails were laid ashore, then the bowsprits and jibs, leaving the mainsail and staysail. A few smacks adopted the

Tollesbury smacks discharging sprats in Brightlingsea Creek during the 1930s. The *Guide* (left) was originally owned at Shoreham, Sussex. The *Gladys* (right) was owned by Albert Lewis. A fisherman tips a bushel basket of sprats into a barrel in one of the beamy skiffs for transfer ashore to the curing yards.   *Douglas Went*

bermudian rig during the mid-1930s as convenient auxiliary and emergency canvas, obtained from cut-down yachts' mainsails; the Brightlingsea *Wonder* and Tollesbury *A.E.F.A.* amongst them.

Until 1939 Tollesbury was still sending about 25 smacks and 150 men fishing each winter and its mariners served in many ways during the 1939-45 war. Some continued to fish, incurring a few casualties. The *Alpha* was mined in the Whittaker but returned to be rebuilt. The *Thistle* struck a mine in the Wallet and another damaged the *Rosena* close by, while the *Express* was lost off the Kentish shore, followed soon after by her successor, the *Little Express*, with loss of the owner and his son.

After 1945 the energies of the Tollesbury men, like those of their Colne contemporaries, were to be gradually deflected into new ways of finding a living but the old order of summers yachting and winters fishing lingered there for a few years for some.

The big stow nets were still braided by hand in the village during the 1940s but stowboating ended about 1948 with the introduction of mid-water trawling by pairs of smacks towing a Larsen net and working with echo sounders and radio navigation aids. It brought a short resurgence of spratting and during the early 1950s Tollesbury fishermen formed Tolfish Limited; one of the few, perhaps the only co-operative founded amongst the fiercely independent Essexmen. The Company leased a quay for landing sprats at Brightlingsea, where an office was established, linked to the smacks by radio. The Tollesburymen also joined many other Essex fishermen from Leigh to Harwich who dredged white weed to be dried and dyed as fern-like domestic decoration. So profitable did this "fishery" become during the early 1950s that the Kent and Essex Sea Fisheries Board rebuked them for neglecting more orthodox fishing, but the boom was short lived. By 1959 only four Tollesbury smacks were spratting, using the Larsen trawl in pairs. Two others had gone to the Wash to try their luck there for the winter and four more were laid up in the creek. Tolfish was wound up soon after.

Since the 1940s the Essex coastal fisheries have passed through a period of great change, perhaps reaching a peak during the early 1960s, a decade which saw the entry of a new generation of young fishermen, particularly at West Mersea, and the re-birth of drifting for inshore herring. Now there is an emergence of more economical one- and two-men boats as costs increase and catches change with depletion of stocks and altered demand.

Although some fishing craft continue to berth at Tollesbury, it has become a modern yachtsman's waterside. Fishing craft are sometimes built at Frost and Drake's boatyard, but the majority of the village's population now look inland for their living. However, many take their pleasure afloat, following in the traditions of the Tollesbury yachtsmen, whose story is told in the next chapter.

Walter Mussett, stowboating.   *Hervey Benham*

CHAPTER SEVEN

The Tollesbury Yachtsmen—1

TOLLESBURY, alone of the Blackwater towns and villages, achieved a continuing tradition of professional yachting and produced captains of racing yachts to rival the Colne seamen in that specialised and exacting sport which became their pride, art and financial salvation. Tollesbury men do not appear to have participated in crewing yachts until the 1870s and then they served in yachts for some years before any became yacht skippers, usually of cruising craft. In 1884 Henry Appleton was recorded as master of the small yacht *Wind Hound*. The village lacked a long tradition of yachting and yacht building and was without the convenience of rail communication with London to encourage owners to lay up yachts there; all advantages long enjoyed by Wivenhoe, Rowhedge and Brightlingsea, on the Colne. Tollesbury village was withdrawn from the water, reached only by a comparatively shallow creek, which dried out at low water and there was no direct access to a deep water anchorage such as that at the mouth of the Colne, off Brightlingsea. No matter, Tollesburymen thrived on overcoming such obstacles. Some were shipped as hands in the racing classes by the 1890s when they usually sought a berth in spring by walking the twelve miles to Rowhedge or Wivenhoe, enquiring at the yards where the racing yachts were preparing to fit out or seeing their skippers who, while making up crews which were predominantly Colne men, had to begin taking others, for expansion of the sport and increasing size of the yachts was stretching the capacity of Rowhedge, Wivenhoe and Brightlingsea mariners to man them. Others had been finding berths in cruising yachts, usually small ones with from one to five hands. During the several weeks needed for fitting out they walked to the Colne on a Monday, starting from Tollesbury at about 5 a.m. and arriving on board about 8 o'clock to start work for the day, walking home again on Friday night. Like all communities who come late to established opportunity, the Tollesburymen had to try that much harder than their Colne contemporaries, had perhaps to set themselves a high standard of endeavour, and certainly realised their goal in becoming able skippers, mates and hands in yachts of many types.

With the Colne surging ahead in yachting and navigation classes being held each winter at Wivenhoe and Brightlingsea, Tollesbury awoke to opportunities the sport offered to its seamen and their village. Navigation was the first essential and Captains Isaac Rice and William Frost gave classes during the winter. By arrangement with the village schoolmaster, Captain Rice taught some of the older boys navigation and when the sun served at noon, they took a sight with sextants; a bath of water forming an artificial horizon. The school realised the needs of its young community of potential seafarers and provided knitting and darning classes and, for older boys, cookery lessons.

One of the earliest Tollesbury yacht captains was Alfred Carter, born in 1837. His most noted command was the 53-ton yawl *Hyacinth*, built by Payne at Southampton in 1886, which occasionally raced in the handicap class. Besides a house of their own the ambition of most Tollesbury yacht skippers was to own a pony and trap. By 1900 the Tollesbury yacht skippers' club was formed, largely by the energies of Captains Frost, Redhouse and Carter, and amongst other activities it promoted the village regatta, the first of which was held in 1900.

By 1901 the yard and slipways of Messrs. Drake showed a good selection of moderate sized cruising yachts laid up in winter, with larger ones moored in the saltings, and W. A. Snape and Co. and Williams and Phillips were busy refitting them in spring. That year five Tollesburymen were picked for the crew of the *Shamrock II* and others were sailing in racers skippered from the Colne and elsewhere. The increasing numbers of yachts being brought to Tollesbury by their skippers to lay up increased demand for refitting facilities. A James Drake was a journeyman-shipwright at Old Hall in 1851 and later moved to Tollesbury waterside. By 1899 Messrs Drake were applying to extend a slipway at Woodrolfe and to dredge the creek adjacent to this yard, which besides repairing yachts and hauling them up on the slipway to be struck over for the winter shored up under winter covers, also built boats for yachts and other craft and constructed small yachts up to about 24 feet. The yard was probably busiest between 1900 and 1914, when yachting flourished at Tollesbury and craft as large at 15-metre racing yachts, about 76 feet long and 10 feet draught, were hauled out, stored and refitted in the home village of their skippers.

A A. Gowen, a sailmaker, started in business in 1903 and removed to a sail loft at Tollesbury about 1912. His business was removed to West Mersea in 1919 where it was carried on by his son, the late Ken Gowen, and continues to flourish with an international reputation. By 1902 between 20-30 yachts were laid up there, an increase from the 20-25 brought there for the few previous winters. The Colne watched the increasing involvement of Tollesbury in yachting with jealous regard for its century-old eminence in building and manning for the sport.

About 1902 the Tollesbury Yacht Mud Berthing Company was formed, probably spurred on by the spirit of enterprise in the place. A light railway from Kelvedon was proposed, the first train of this Great Eastern Railway branch reaching Tollesbury in 1904, giving rail access to Liverpool Street station in London and hopefully attracting yacht owners to keep their yachts at Tollesbury, besides offering carriage for fish cargoes which previously had only reached the rail via Brightlingsea, Wivenhoe or Harwich. What Tollesbury needed was a deep water anchorage, so a pier was built out into the Blackwater, to the south of the village, approached over marshes, and the railway was extended to serve it. The pier opened in May 1907 and offered 10 feet draught alongside its end at low water. A few days later seven sailing and one steam yacht were anchored off and Tollesbury felt it was at last starting to rival the Colne. By 1910 it was proposed to deepen Woodrolfe Creek but this project was stopped by the 1914-18 war. Meanwhile, Tollesburymen continued to advance themselves in yachting, some rising to become skippers and many serving as hands on board yachts of all types. Thus Tollesbury had much in common with contemporary Rowhedge, Wivenhoe and Brightlingsea rather than West Mersea or Maldon, its Blackwater neighbours, and was developing in yachting and fishing until 1914.

Five Tollesbury men served as hands in the crew of 35 manning the 129-foot 6-inch America's Cup challenger *Shamrock II* under Captains Edward Sycamore and Robert Wringe of Brightlingsea. This racer spread 13,490 square feet in her cutter rig, an area almost doubled when her spinnaker was set.

Steven Barbrook was a rising skipper of this period. He was a native of Steeple, on the south shore of the Blackwater, above Tollesbury, and worked in smacks as a boy before seeking a summer berth in a yacht. Eventually he graduated to racers and in 1895 walked to Rowhedge to be shipped by Captain Thomas Jay of that village in the 30 man crew of the 283-ton racing cutter *Ailsa*, preparing on the Clyde for her racing debut in the big class. Tom Jay took her out to the Mediterranean to race against the Prince of Wales' *Britannia* during the Riviera winter season, returning to England in spring to fit out for the season's racing in home waters. In 1898 Steven Barbrook was again in Captain Jay's crew of the huge 300-ton racing schooner *Rainbow*, where he was fo'c'sle caterer in addition to his racing duties. He learned further of the racing ways in other yachts and later became a skipper noted for boldness and resource in racing.

When big class yacht racing temporarily collapsed after the 1898 season, the 52-foot Linear Rating cutters became the largest British yachts racing as a thoroughbred class, from 1896-1906, when the type was altered to 15 metres rating by a change of rule. The class was dominated by skippers from the Colne and racing was extremely close, often only 15 seconds separating each boat at the finish and the yachts were very lightly built for their seventy feet overall length. Going to windward in a breeze it was possible for a hand to sit in the fo'c'sle, on one of the side lockers with feet on the opposite locker, and feel his knees working! In 1903 J. W. Leuchars joined the 52-foot class with *Moyana*, designed by young Alfred Mylne, and Steven Barbrook of Tollesbury was appointed skipper. *Moyana* was his first important racing command and he thoroughly justified the owner's confidence in a comparatively unknown skipper by ending the season with a long string of prize flags. He raced her during 1904, when *Moyana* finished the season second to the new Fife cutter *Maymon*, sailed by Charles Bevis of Bursledon; but Captain Barbrook continued to race *Moyana* with considerable success in an extremely competitive class for four seasons before she was laid up during 1907.

At that time racing hands received 26 shillings weekly basic pay. Men with special duties received additional money; bowspritendsmen 2s. 6d. per day and mastheadsmen 5 shillings. Prize money was then £1 per man first prize, 16 shillings for second and, win or lose, there was ''starting money'' of 10 shillings per race. An allowance of 2s. 6d. per day was paid when racing as it was not desirable to cook or prepare meals on board.

In 1905 Captain Fred Stokes of Tollesbury had the distinction of sailing an English 52-footer designed and built by the famous American yachtbuilder, Nathaniel Herreshoff, who was commissioned by Mrs Turner-Farley to build the *Sonya* because she considered British designers had exhausted their ideas in that class. Captain Stokes was present at her sailing trials off Newport, Rhode Island, with designer Herreshoff, then came home aboard the ship in which the *Sonya* was shipped to London, where her Tollesbury crew joined her and sailed her round to Tollesbury to fit out for racing. However, she lacked balance in design and was frequently altered before being laid up in 1908 and sold in 1909. The owner was one of the two ladies ever to have actively owned a racing yacht of the larger classes, the other being Mrs Workman with the 21-metre *Nyria* in 1920. In 1906 *Sonya* and her principal rivals *Britomart* and *Moyana* sailed 45 races in less than 12 weeks, but she was least successful due to the frequent breaking of her gaff jaws.

The 52-footer *Sonya* rustles through the Solent under her spinnaker in 1905 with Captain Fred Stokes of Tollesbury at the tiller. She was designed by the American yachtbuilding genius Nathaniel Herreshoff for Mrs Turner-Farley to race in a keenly sailed class.

During the depressed state of big class yacht racing between 1897 and 1908, which reflected economic conditions as much as yachting fashion, there was great enthusiasm for rejuvenating old racing yachts, and racing in the handicap classes. The old forty-raters *Creole* and *Carina* had many battles in the small handicap class. The *Creole* was built by Forrestt at Wivenhoe in 1890 to the design of George Watson of Glasgow for the then hotly contested "forty" rating class and was sailed by Captain Tom Skeats of Brightlingsea. She passed to the command of Captain John Redgewell of Tollesbury when Tom Skeats left her to sail the big *Bona* in 1899. She was then long outbuilt in class racing but her owner, Colonel Villiers Bagot, was very proud of his yacht and entered her in most events around the coast, where she was very successful. After Captain Redgewell's death in December 1904 she was sailed by another Tollesburyman, Captain Charles Leavett, whose great rival was the *Carina*, sailed by Captain William Goff of Brightlingsea, and by 1905 the ex-forty rater *Vendetta* had joined in with another Tollesbury skipper at her helm.

In 1908 Captain Barbrook sailed the 23-metre cutter *Brynhild* for Sir James Pender. She had come out the previous year and was the unluckiest yacht ever built. At her launch on a Friday the cradle killed a shipwright, and old sailors shook their heads at this omen of disaster. During her first sail in the Thames matches one of her mastheadsmen fell from aloft and was killed, and a few weeks later a hand was lost overboard and drowned in the Solent and there were other mishaps to make sailors growl she was ill-fated. Racing eastward of the Isle of Wight, *Brynhild* lost her topmast and when the raffle of gear had been cleared away the owner's wife suggested to Charles Nicholson, her designer, that they should give up and return to Gosport to have a new topmast made. Knowing the keen watch kept on racers built by the firm, when in sight of lookouts in the yard, he replied: "I expect it's half made by now, madam."

The 23-metre cutters were fast but very wet boats, setting 10,000 square feet of canvas without the equally large spinnaker, and each had a crew of 22 hands. They cost about £12,000 fitted out; a tremendous sum in those days and a season's racing cost the owner about £5,000. Captain Barbrook took *Brynhild* over from her previous skipper, well knowing this background of tragedy, and set about improving her performance against the slightly smaller *Nyria*, sailed by Captain Steven Ray of Gosport with a crew from the Solent and East Coast, and the 23-metre *White Heather* built by Fife in 1907 and splendidly sailed by Captain Charles Bevis of Bursledon, with a Solent crew. All of them had a formidable competitor in the newly-launched 23-metre *Shamrock*, built by Fife for Sir Thomas Lipton and sailed by Captain Edward Sycamore of Brightlingsea, with a crew from Colne. Until well into the season *Shamrock* and *White Heather* were most successful, but in a terrific spurt during Cowes week and the subsequent west country regattas, Steven Barbrook brought *Brynhild*'s first prizes up to eight, against *Shamrock's* twelve and *White Heather's* five. She also won seven second prizes. Sir James Pender was delighted; always an enthusiastic owner, he wore a special striped guernsey for racing, woven in *Brynhild*'s racing colours of red and black.

The crew's work aboard a large racer, such as the *Brynhild*, followed a pattern evolved over generations of yachting in Britain. All hands turned out at 6 a.m. and shammied down the brightwork and scrubbed decks, making the most of any dew to avoid scouring the varnish. The headsails and spinnakers were made up in stops or, if the weather was threatening, they put a reef in the mainsail. Breakfast was at 7.30 a.m. and after it the mainsail was set, followed by the headsails and topsail, ready for the start which was usually about 9 o'clock, or a little later. With guests aboard and the yacht under weigh, all hands were at racing stations; the skipper at the wheel, mate and two hands in charge of the headsail sheets, two hands were at each side at the runner tackles and foresail sheets; the second mate and two hands at the jib-topsail sheets, mainsheet and topmast backstay tackles. The mastheadsmen were aloft and the remainder of the crew were alert on deck to haul where required on sheets or halyards. Usually the cook and stewards had charge of the sails prepared below in the fo'c'sle, ready to send them up as required, through the forehatch.

The day's racing might be round a fifty mile course, sometimes longer, and after it, with the owner and guests probably gone ashore to the club or to his steam yacht, the racer anchored, all hands lowered and stowed the sails carefully for the next day's racing. With everything checked and neatly stowed, minor repairs and maintenance carried out and decks washed down, all hands had tea and tried to dry their almost invariably soaked clothes round the fo'c'sle stove or on the bowsprit shrouds if the sun was still shining. A smoke and a yarn and its was time to turn into the rows of pipe cots lining the fo'c'sle, ready for the next day's racing.

The *Brynhild* was not fitted out in 1909 and Captain Barbrook went as skipper for King Alfonso of Spain in the new 15-metre yacht *Hispania* which had been built at Pasages to designs of William Fife. He raced her at San Sebastian in July, when she won her maiden race, and sailed her in England for Cowes week, but had a Spanish crew who were poor racing hands. For several days at the beginning of the week he did not dare bring the *Hispania* to the line in the heat of class racing against William Burton's new *Ostara* with Captain Albert Turner and Colne crew, or the new *Vanity* which Mylne had designed for Mr Payne.

The 15-metres were the best sporting class in British racing from 1907 until 1914. These 76-footers cost £3,500 to build and the crew's expenses were generally as follows: captain £150 per year; mate, 22 weeks at 32 shillings—£35 4s.; cook and steward 22 weeks as 32 shillings—£35 4s.; five hands at 26 shillings—£143; "Grub money" at 2 shillings and sixpence per head for fifty starts—£50. Prize money was paid to the crew from the yacht's winnings, as

The 40-rater *Creole* was built at Wivenhoe in 1890 and after 1899 was skippered by Captain John Redgewell of Tollesbury. After his death in 1904 she was sailed by Captain Charles Leavett, another Tollesbury man. She raced in the handicap class with considerable success until 1914.

follows; £2 to the captain for each first prize and £1 for each other prize; £1 to each of the crew for each first prize and 10 shillings for each other prize; 5 shillings to each man when no prize was won—known as "starting money". Other expenses included; an average of 30 shillings to a racing pilot for each race where he was necessary; entrance fees and other expenses—£100; clothes for captain and crew—£69; hauling up the yacht and scrubbing for racing—£60; insurance—£35; laying up the yacht for winter and sundry items—£100. The yacht might hope to win about £250 prize money during an average season which, when depreciation is taken into account, cost the owner about £1,500; a large sum in the days when "a sovereign was a sovereign". Although she did not race in England until Cowes week, *Hispania* proved to be a fast boat and her owner was well pleased.

In 1910 Captain Barbrook and his crew fitted out the *Brynhild* at Gosport and she had alterations carried out to her mast step, to increase the height of her sail plan. She competed in the passage race from Southend, at the mouth of the Thames, to Harwich, for the regatta, a race opening that season and for which no prizes were given. At the Orwell Corinthian Yacht Club regatta off Harwich on 23rd May, *Shamrock, White Heather* and *Brynhild* started, and near the weather mark, the North Cutler Buoy, *Brynhild*'s mast failed below deck, drove down through her bottom and sank her in fourteen minutes. She was leading at the time by about 2 minutes. The dinghy was quickly launched and *Shamrock* and *White Heather* launched theirs, but with a crew of 22 and 6 guests, all were quite full and fortunately it was comparatively calm. A destroyer came steaming up and launched her whaler, which took many on board. The *Brynhild* filled slowly at first, then lay over on her side until her mast was lying on the surface. Sir James Pender insisted on being rowed over to cut her racing flag from the masthead and a few minutes later the fine cutter sank. The owner, his guests and crew were landed at Harwich. Sir Thomas Lipton sent the launch from his steam yacht *Erin* and took the *Brynhild*'s crew on board for a hot lunch and gave them some clothing to supplement their racing gear in which they were picked up, all their other things having gone down with the yacht. The mate ascertained where each each man came from and Lipton kindly paid each man's train fare home, as what money they had was also lost. Captain Barbrook did not have a yacht for the rest of the 1910 season.

1911 was notable for the great international regatta which was to be held in the Solent and for the introduction of the 19-metre class; fine 100-ton cutters, 95 feet long and setting 6,200 square feet of canvas, handled by a skipper, mate, and 12 hands. They could race in any weather short of a strong gale and could have been the nucleus of a healthy class of large racer. Four were built; Captain Barbrook was appointed to sail Almeric Paget's and Mr Hennesey's *Corona*, designed and built by Fife, who also launched the *Mariquita* for A. K. Stothert, sailed by Captain Edward Sycamore with a Colne crew. The *Octavia* was designed by Alfred Mylne and built by McAllister at Dumbarton for William Burton who, as usual, sailed her himself, with Albert Turner as skipper. The fourth boat, *Norada*, was designed and built by Nicholson for Frederick Milburn, but had a crew from the owner's cruising yacht, only one of whom had previously sailed in a racing yacht, so she had little chance. These boats were one of the finest classes of British racing yachts, sailing to Kiel, where they had keen racing, then back across the North Sea to Aberdeen, through the Caledonian Canal and round the Mull of Kintyre for the Clyde fortnight, before sailing down the Irish Sea and up channel to the Solent regattas, finishing the season along the west coast regattas.

Octavia topped the class, winning 15 first prizes in 48 races, *Mariquita* being second with 12 and *Corona* third with 10. *Norada* proved an excellent design and won 9 firsts.

Captain Barbrook and his crew raced the *Corona* again during 1912, when her mast was lengthened to 116 feet, making her tender, and as it was a rough season she only won one first and five second prizes, in 16 starts. By then most Tollesbury seamen were settled into the rhythm of summers yachting and winters fishing and as on the Colne, income from yachting, particularly yacht racing, brought some prosperity to the place, financing the building of houses and a few smacks and generally supplementing the meagre earnings at the fisheries. A racing yacht hand then usually earned 26 shillings each week, of which 5 shillings was given to the fo'c'sle "caterer" for food. As a comparison, the brothers Drake, partners in the Tollesbury yacht yard, earned £1. 10s. weekly between 1900 and 1910.

In spring, when fitting out, by custom, each yacht hand received an allowance of yachting clothes of the best quality, paid for by the owner. A typical outfit comprised two guernseys, with the yacht's name and initials of the owner's club worked on them in white, on the chest, two pairs of pilot cloth trousers, a seaman's cap, a pair of canvas deck shoes and one of black leather, and a suit of oilskins. As a similar outfit was provided each spring when fitting out these clothes were a valuable supplement to income.

As in the Colne, Tollesbury's annual regatta was held when the yachts had arrived to lay up and their crews and the village's other fishermen were fitting out the smacks for the winter's fishing. Before the pier was built the regatta was held at a part of the sea wall known expressively as "The leavings" but afterwards its venue was off the pier, in the Blackwater. Early in the twentieth century it was organised by the Tollesbury Yacht Skippers' Club and included sailing and rowing races. The 1904 regatta was typical and the *Essex County Standard* recorded; "Yacht handicap race, not exceeding twenty-five tons; first class smack race (open) 18 tons or over; Yachts' Cutters (open to Tollesbury) crew not to exceed two; Coastguards' sailing race in service boats—a stiff and very interesting contest, the crews having to row three times round the ordinary course; single handed dinghy race for ladies (open to Tollesbury); race for four oared Yachts' gigs; Yachts dinghies single-handed race; pair oared dinghy race (ladies); pair-oared Yachts cutters; single-handed dinghies; Single handed race for fishermen; Single handed dinghies (Fisher lads under 19); Fishermen's four oared race; four oared herring skiff race; Pair oared race for Fishermen; shovel race in smacks' boats; Punt race (open)." As at Mersea regatta there was a "duck hunt", "walking the greasy pole" (rigged out from the committee boat) and the "pull devil, pull baker" event.

115

The volunteers of Tollesbury, August 1914. This photograph, taken outside the *King's Head* at Tollesbury, shows the first men from that village to volunteer for the army and navy. Seated on the car is Sir Laming Worthington Evans, M.P. for Colchester and with him, in a straw boater, is the Rev. William Carter. Almost all these men were fishermen and yacht hands, as the yacht's guernseys testify. How many lived through the holocaust to come is unknown, but one wonders what their thoughts were as the camera shutter clicked on an England which would never be the same again.

There was considerable rivalry in the smack races and the *Bertha* owned by Steven Redgewell was probably the fastest Tollesbury smack. The notably fast smack *Sunbeam*, owned and sailed by Captain William Cranfield of Rowhedge who skippered such large racing yachts as the *Valkyries* and *Yarana*, once came round to compete at Tollesbury and won the cup. She sailed home after crossing the line and leaving Captain Stephen Cranfield, the owner's brother, to collect the cup and bring it back to a smoking concert to be held at Rowhedge.

116

However, they waited in vain, for Stephen did not arrive for three days and then with a terrific hangover! When the *Sunbeam* next appeared at Tollesbury regatta smack race she was not allowed to compete on the grounds that she had a white mainsail. The *Bertha* tried several times to rival the *Sunbeam* and the crack racing smack *Neva* also from Rowhedge in the Colne regattas but was beaten, despite having her bottom enamelled one year. She was nevertheless a very fast smack and well sailed.

A brass band was then a necessary accompaniment to any village regatta and the Layer band entertained by the water during the day and in The Square during the evening, when the fair was in full swing with steam horses and roundabouts, swing boats, a steam organ and stalls.

When Sir Thomas Lipton challenged for the America's Cup for the fourth time in 1914, Nicholson of Gosport designed and built the radical but small *Shamrock IV*; the command of Wivenhoe's Captain Albert Turner. Edward Heard of Tollesbury, who had been a hand in *Shamrock III* in 1903, was first mate and there were other Tollesbury men in her crew, who were also from the Colne and the Solent. She was the last gaff-rigged challenger, having a very tall sail plan and many surprisingly modern features. The triple-planked hull was aluminium framed and the deck was plywood. The bulbous hulled *Shamrock IV* came out with a sloop rig but after a few trials with the huge single headsail and tussles with the sheeting of its 2,300 square feet in a breeze, the rig was changed to the conventional two headsails of the cutter.

America-bound *Shamrock IV* suffered from the First World War. In tow of the steam yacht *Erin* when hostilities broke out, the yachts were diverted to the southern American coast, then made their way to City Island, New York, where the *Shamrock* was laid up awaiting more tranquil times while her crew, mostly naval reservists, found themselves manning a cruiser instead of a yacht.

Tollesbury's seafarers served afloat and ashore during the 1914-18 war from which some did not return. However, though none could foresee it, Tollesbury men were to enhance their place in yachting during the glorious Indian summer of yacht racing between 1920 and 1939, when another war put an end to the professional racing yachtsman.

CHAPTER EIGHT

The Tollesbury Yachtsmen—2

L IKE THE Colne, the Solent and the Clyde, Tollesbury's yachting prospects looked poor after the 1914-18 war. Most of the yachts which had laid up there until 1914 had been sold to owners in prospering neutral Scandinavia during the war, but a few remained. Drake Brothers' yard offered two or three slipways and several cruisers and racing cruisers were hauled up there and the yard built a number of the 18-foot Thames Estuary one-design class centreboarders designed by F. Morgan Giles for the Alexandra Yacht Club at Westcliff, near Southend.

In 1919, racing hands' weekly wages had risen from the pre-war 26 shillings to £3. 17s. 6d. and the cost of labour and materials for repair and maintenance of yachts had rocketed, so it is not surprising that many thought the big racers would never revive, but they were soon proved wrong. That winter King George V decided to have the royal racing cutter *Britannia* fitted out for the 1920 season; his lead stimulated other owners and a big handicap class turned out to race around the coastal regattas as in pre-war summers. The cutter *Moonbeam* was ordered from Fife, with Captain Tom Skeats of Brightlingsea in command; the great cutter *Terpsichore* was built at Whites of Itchen and the 23-metre *Nyria* was converted to bermudian rig; the first large yacht to be so rigged. She was sailed by Captain Bob Diaper of Itchen. Sir Charles Allom brought out the 23-metre *White Heather* sailed by Captain Mountfield of Gosport and these were joined by the 385-ton racing schooner *Westward* sailed by Captain Sycamore of Brightlingsea and some large cruising yachts. Since 1913, when Captain Jack Carter of Rowhedge had left her, the *Britannia* had been sailed by Major Hunloke, the King's representative, who insisted on steering her when racing. However, he had to find a professional captain to command her, as the yacht had to be brought up to racing trim and a crew had to be selected and trained to work as a team, and he was not capable of navigating and sailing her around the coast, from regatta to regatta. Tollesbury Captain Charles Leavett, who had skippered the forty-rater *Creole* for many years, was lent by his owner, Colonel Villiers Bagot, as *Britannia*'s new skipper, with his son S. Leavett acting as "captain"; a unique arrangement.

For the first few races of her post-war revival the Royal cutter failed to win a flag but improved as the season progressed. She was still in cruising rig, the equivalent of one reef, and did well to be third in the class, which encouraged the King to order her rig to be altered and modernised. With bowsprit and boom shortened and bulwarks renewed she became a true racer again for 1921. An incident occurred that year which led to another change of skipper for the *Britannia*. In one race the skipper gave the order, "In spinnaker!", which was instantly countermanded by Major Hunloke, who ordered it to be re-set. Captain Leavett, who was a very experienced racing skipper, properly regarding himself as the man to give orders, went below and shortly afterwards Major Hunloke was looking for another skipper. She did not fit out the following year and in 1923 Captain Albert Turner of Wivenhoe joined her as professional skipper until her withdrawal from the big class on the death of her owner in 1935. They had a fine season.

The 92-ton yawl *Sumurun* was skippered by Nat Gurten of Tollesbury. Here she leads the large handicap class on a summer's day under 5,580 square feet of canvas.

119

The 1920 yachting season was enlivened by the series of races for the America's Cup off Newport, Rhode Island, between the American defender *Resolute* and Sir Thomas Lipton's *Shamrock IV* commanded by Captain Albert Turner of Wivenhoe, who was often relieved at the wheel by Sir William Burton, the first amateur to steer a cup challenger and a most experienced racing helmsman. *Shamrock IV* had several Tollesbury men in a crew also drawn from the Colne and the Solent. Edward Heard of Tollesbury was first mate and as the yacht had been hastily laid up at Newport on arrival after the outbreak of war in 1914, he had a formidable task to see that everything was in first class condition for the races and the crew worked hard alongside the yacht yard riggers, shipwrights and painters. She came closer to winning the series than any previous challenger, but the *Resolute* retained the Cup. In 1921 the big class changed again; the *Westward* dropped out and the *Susanne* was sold and in 1922 the big yachts did not fit out, but in 1923 the class revived with *Britannia*, *Nyria*, *Terpsichore*, *Cariad* and *Valdora*.

In 1924 Sir Thomas Lipton had his 23-metre *Shamrock* fitted out to race with Captain Charles Leavett in command and Sir Charles Allom's *White Heather* joined her. The *Terpsichore* was sold and, renamed *Lulworth*, was sailed by Captain Charles Bevis. The *Britannia* came out again, rebuilt and in charge of Major Hunloke, the King's sailing master, and with Captain Albert Turner of Wivenhoe in charge of her crew. The big yachts were again racing all round the coast and the structure of yachting in Britain had regained much of its pre-war glory.

By 1926 Captain Edward Sycamore was back as skipper of the 23-metre cutter *Shamrock* which was thoroughly refitted and soon proved a competitor to be reckoned with in the big class. She was driven as hard on passage as when racing and Gus Spinks of Rowhedge recalled her, bound for Cowes from the Clyde fortnight, storming up-channel under trysail and small jib, with her deck swept and streaming as she roared past ten knot steamers.

No more gaff cutters were built for racing and in 1928 the Fife-built cutter *Cambria* and the Nicholson-built *Astra* arrived to prove finally the superiority of the bermudian rig in the big class.

The big handicap class also raced around the coast and during the late 1920s was dominated by two beautiful yawls built by Fife and sailed by Essex crews. Sir William Burton's *Rendezvous*, launched in 1913, was an elegant 87-footer sailed by Captain James Barnard of Rowhedge and his great rival was Hugh Paul's *Sumurun*, a fast 79-footer sailed by Captain Nat Gurten of Tollesbury. Both boats set 5,500 square feet of canvas and, immaculately kept and sailed, were examples of the very best type of yacht produced by any period of the sport.

The big cutters had revived but the 12-metres, seventy-foot sloops, were the class of the future which provided great racing and a chance for many racing skippers from the Colne, Tollesbury and the Solent, to show their skill. Typical of them was Edward Carrington Heard, born at Tollesbury in 1879. He fished in the village smacks and in 1899 was selected as a hand in the 52-foot class racer *Penitent*, skippered by Captain Dan Aldrige of Rowhedge. In 1903 he went to America as a hand in *Shamrock III* along with Tom Sampson and William Riley, the two other Tollesbury members of her 40-man crew. In 1914 he was first mate of *Shamrock IV* under Captain Albert Turner, also racing in her postponed attempt for the America's Cup in 1920. In 1925 the Norwegian-built 12-metre *Noresca*, launched for Sir William Burton and R. G. Perry the previous year to designs by Johan Anker, was sold to R. Ellis Brown and F. G. Mitchell, who engaged Edward Heard as her skipper. The *Noresca* was a big, powerful looking boat, bermudian rigged, 68 feet long, and setting 2,150 square feet in a sloop rig. Captain Heard proved himself to be a dashing tactician, with a reputation for taking great risks. *Noresca* had a remarkable season, winning two King's Cups; at the regattas of the Royal Northern Yacht Club, on the Clyde and the Royal Ulster Yacht Club, Belfast, finishing the season with 17 firsts, 3 seconds and 4 thirds in 38 races. She was hard pressed by John Payne's *Vanity* but won £500 prize money and made the name of her captain in the racing world.

From 1924 until 1939 the 12-metre class provided some of the finest sport in British yacht racing, and at the modest cost of £4,500 for a new boat, restricted to a professional crew of a captain and three hands to handle a sail area of 2,000 square feet, and a spinnaker of greater area. The class raced all round the coast in the traditional manner, besides racing at Ostend, Le Havre and Deauville.

Next season four new 12-metres were built and competition hardened. It became general for more and more gear and movables to be left ashore on race days, to lighten the yachts; even to taking off the skylights and leaving them in the dinghy, on the mooring. The 12-metre conception had been for fast but seaworthy yachts whose owners and guests could live aboard throughout the season. But good accommodation meant weight and some owners began to live aboard a steam or motor yacht which followed the racing fleet around the coast. They arrived on board in a launch an hour before the start, and left her shortly after the finish. There was also development and decadence in the rig; the *Iris* Scottish owner designed his own 12-metre and took her mast height to the limit with a mainsail 86 feet in the hoist. The 12-metre class flourished and four other Tollesbury skippers came into the class, and for a time Drake Brothers yard had several of these sleek boats hauled up, each winter, standing high above the saltings like a badge of village pride, with the ex-15-metre *Ma'oona* and some other larger cruisers such as *Palmosa*, amongst them.

121

The crew of the *Shamrock V*, America's Cup challenger 1930. Captain Edward Heard of Tollesbury centre back row.

In 1927 Edward Heard had to contend with Sir William Burton's new *Iyruna*, skippered by Captain James Barnard of Rowhedge, which beat the class. Thomas Sopwith's remarkable 12-metre *Mouette* came out in 1928 with a Solent crew and gave *Noresca* tough competition, winning the first three matches of the season, but in the race for the King's Cup at Harwich, Captain Heard beat her by 16 seconds, despite, or perhaps because of the large headsail set by *Mouette*. But *Noresca* was outclassed by the new boats and finished sixth in the class. During the four years that he sailed her Captain Heard won 116 prizes in 137 starts; a splendid record. In 1929 Captain Heard was offered command of the *Shamrock V*, the last of Sir Thomas Lipton's green hulled challengers and the first British yacht built to the ''J'' class of the American universal rating rule. She was designed and built by Camper and Nicholson's at Gosport and commenced her season at Harwich. Her crew of 19 from Tollesbury, the Colne, West Mersea and the Solent, were jubilant when she proved her weatherliness by sailing clean through *Cambria*'s lee, also well beating the *Candida*, skippered by Captain Jim Gilbey of Emsworth, Hampshire with a Hampshire crew. This despite what many of them thought was her comparatively small sail area of 7,600 square feet and the weight of her wooden mast and elaborate rigging. *Shamrock V* was rigged as a bermudian yawl for the passage out to America, making a 24 day crossing from Brixham to New London, Connecticut. Lipton's steam yacht *Erin* escorted her and towed the challenger whenever conditions permitted, which was not often, to the crew's relief, as the racer was much easier under her double reefed trysail and storm jib than corkscrewing along through long, steep Atlantic seas behind a towline. Sometimes the *Shamrock* lost touch with the *Erin* for days and was becalmed in mid-ocean, with the crew vainly trying to get her along with a big headsail and squaresail set; boxing about for a time before the western horizon darkened again with shrieking squalls and days of big seas and wind which forced them to crawl about the heaving deck at the change of the watch, or to tend the badly chafing running rigging. The foc's'le became almost uninhabitable in pounding seas and some hands shifted to the sail locker in the long, flat counter, whose slamming in the seas was as noisy as the booming of the long, outreaching bow, but drier. Often, at meals, the saloon skylight would darken with a green sea and cascades of water roared down over the watch below.

The America's Cup challenger *Shamrock V* on passage in mid-Atlantic, 1930. She carried this ketch rig for the ocean passages out and home. A photograph taken from a passing steamship.

At last they arrived in America and raced the more lightly rigged *Enterprise*, sailed by amateur Harold Vanderbilt. *Enterprise* defeated the *Shamrock* in each of the seven races but Vanderbilt wrote of Captain Heard and his crew: "In defeat lies the test of true sportsmanship and they have proved themselves— quite the finest it has ever been our good fortune to race against." A fine tribute. *Shamrock*'s crew received a friendly welcome in the United States. The American observer who sailed aboard during the races noticed Captain Heard was fond of bananas with his sandwich lunch, served when racing, and next morning arrived on board with a big bunch under his arm! A dinner was given for the crews of both yachts who sat opposite each other at table, under Captains Heard and Monsell, and enjoyed themselves in the friendliest spirit. *Shamrock V* returned to England and, Sir Thomas Lipton dying soon afterwards, she was sold to Thomas Sopwith.

In 1932 it was back to 12-metres; Captain Heard taking charge of the eight-year-old boat *Morwenna*, previously *Moyana II*. Although she started 37 times and was sailed with skill and verve, she won only 4 firsts, and was outclassed by *Flica*, *Zoraida* and *Veronica*. Captain Heard was offered command of the 23-metre *Astra* which had been designed and built by Camper and Nicholson in 1928 and was previously sailed by Captain Pound, of Gosport, with a Solent crew. In 1931 she was bought by Hugh Paul, one of the Ipswich milling family, and soon improved her fortunes with Captain Heard at the wheel.

By 1930 the composition of crews in the big racing yachts had changed; no longer did a skipper strive to keep most of his crew from his native village, or even from the same district, but accepted men from other places, provided they were smart hands. Brixham men had come into the big racing yachts as hands when King George V requested that a proportion of *Britannia*'s crew be drawn from that port, in those days of meagre employment and opportunity; and later a few from Looe were added. In the *Astra*, Captain Heard had a Brixham first mate, Jack Gempton, and hands from Itchen and Southampton in his crew, besides men from Tollesbury, the Colne and West Mersea. Good racing hands were beginning to be valued more than ever before and many owners were paying a £1 weekly retainer to their crew in winter.

The *Astra* was an especially happy yacht and Mr and Mrs Paul were keenly interested in her crew. She fitted out in her builder's yard each spring, when a pleasant little tradition was maintained; *Astra* lay on the buoy in Portsmouth harbour, the Pauls came down by rail from London and the launch met them at the harbour station. As they came alongside *Astra* Captain Heard met them at the gangway, cap in hand, to welcome them and, as the owner stepped aboard, the burgee was broken out at the masthead. *Astra* was painted white for many years but one season Mrs Paul, when motoring down from London, saw a green coloured rick cover on a stack and decided the yacht would look splendid repainted to that shade, and so she remained until 1939, and Captain Heard

124

remained her skipper. *Astra* seemed a lucky yacht; rarely suffering damage and never losing a mast like some of her larger opponents. But the season of 1935, when the curtain came down on the glorious climax of big class yacht racing, brought tragedy to the *Astra*.

In June 1935, *Astra, Endeavour, Velsheda* and the visiting American sloop *Yankee* assembled at Southend for the Thames racing which opened the season. *Astra* was recalled at the start and returned to start again, behind the others, in the south westerly wind which was freshening to half a gale. The lee mark was the Mouse light vessel and the *Yankee* gybed at the West Oaze buoy but the British yachts continued and ran by the lee only to be forced to gybe at the Mouse, where disaster struck all three. *Velsheda* broke her boom, *Endeavour* was gybed before the backstay had been properly set up and the mast went overboard, fortunately clear of everyone aboard, but, saddest of all on the run to the Mouse, *Astra*'s spinnaker went wild and its sheet took charge. George Lewis of Brightlingsea, *Astra*'s steward, tried to check it but was flung into the sea.

When Thomas Sopwith had the *Endeavour II* built by Camper and Nicholson in 1936, to challenge for the America's Cup during the following season he had only the old *Endeavour, Velsheda* and *Astra* to race against. The *Britannia* had been scuttled, in accordance with the King's wishes, after his death, and *Yankee* had returned to America. The challenger tuned up in a background of depression amongst the big class but the 1937 challenge was probably the best organised there had ever been. *Endeavour II* was to be sailed by her owner, with Captain Williams of Hamble in charge of her crew of 30, and to tune her up in America, Herman Andrae, who had bought *Endeavour I*, lent her to Sopwith as trial horse. Captain Heard was released by Hugh Paul to sail the *Endeavour I* against the challenger. The two racers were rigged down as yawls for the transatlantic passage but were to be towed across; *Endeavour II* astern of the Belgian trawler *Jon* and *Endeavour I* by the motor yacht *Viva II*. The challenger had an uneventful voyage but *Viva II* lost her tow two-thirds of the way across and Captain Heard set sail and arrived unaided.

Captain Heard, sailing the *Endeavour I*, beat both the American defender *Ranger* and the previous defender *Rainbow*, in trial races before the start of the Cup matches in which *Endeavour II* was well beaten by the *Ranger*. *Endeavour II* was towed home, safely, by her owner's new motor yacht *Philante*, but during the passage her skipper, Captain Williams, was taken ill, died, and was buried at sea. The homeward bound *Endeavour I* with Captain Heard and his crew from Essex, Southampton and the West Country, again came into the headlines.

In tow of *Viva II*, *Endeavour* left Newport, Rhode Island, on the afternoon of 12th September, but 24 hours later, when approximately 230 miles east of the Brenton Reef light vessel, the weather, which up to then had been fine, deteriorated and a strong south-south-easterly breeze brought up a heavy sea from that quarter. Because of the violent pitching, the speed of the tow was

The "J" class cutter *Endeavour* which Tollesbury's Captain Edward Heard and a crew from Tollesbury, West Mersea, Southampton, Brixham, Cornwall and the Clyde sailed as trial horse in America against the 1937 America's Cup challenger *Endeavour II*.   *Douglas Went*

reduced, first to 9 knots and then to 5, to lessen the strain on the yacht's hull and her crew. As evening advanced the weather continued to worsen, and preparations were made to stream the sea anchor in case it became necessary to slip the tow-rope. *Viva II* was kept informed of this by wireless telephone. However, by 10 p.m. the wind reached hurricane force and, owing to the heavy seas which were constantly sweeping the decks, it was impossible for any man to go forward to slip the tow-rope. All sails, with the exception of the small mizzen, which was later to be so important, had been stowed and everything movable on deck was securely lashed. Just before midnight it was found that the 9 inch hemp towrope had parted and the sea anchor was streamed. In the weather conditions it was impossible to get the 70 fathoms of towrope inboard so it was left hanging from the stem head, acting as an additional sea anchor. When everything on deck was secured all hands were ordered below and the yacht battened down. For the next 12 hours the yacht lay with the mizzen set and riding to her sea anchor. The motion was extremely violent and wireless communication with the *Viva II* broke down when seas broke the skylights of the after cabin and flooded the set.

The *Endeavour* suffered no damage while hove to and by the following morning the weather fined away sufficiently to enable the towrope to be recovered. Shortly before noon there was a fair wind and the sea anchor was recovered; the yacht squared away on an east south easterly course under staysail, trysail and mizzen, with a fresh wind. Meanwhile the *Viva II* was searching anxiously and wirelessed the American Coastguard for assistance in her search. Cutters and seaplanes carried out a wide sweep, without success, and anxiety rose for the *Endeavour* and her crew.

On 15th September the *Endeavour* sighted a seaplane flying low in the distance, but of course they were unaware of the dramatic fears for their safety which the press and radio had propagated. On 19th September a schooner was sighted but not spoken, and the yacht continued to roll slowly eastwards until the wind freshened next day and she began to make knots. On 21st September the *Endeavour*'s crew, listening to the wireless receiving set which was still working, heard a broadcast which said that the American Coastguard had called off their search and that the yacht was presumed to be lost. Desperately they tried to get the transmitter to work, but this message was never picked up.

The *Endeavour* sailed on in everything from light breezes to half a gale, when the rubber mast wedging had to be reinforced with wooden wedges driven up from below. On 27th September the wind came ahead and the yacht spoke to the British tanker *Cheyenne*, who reported them. For two days they beat against head winds and sighted the Bishop Rock light in the early hours of 30th September, 19 days out from Newport. The *Viva II* had crossed the Atlantic and, when she was almost at the Needles, the message that *Endeavour* was sailing home reached her and she turned back at full speed. The *Endeavour* had a triumphal return up-channel and her welcome in Portsmouth harbour on 1st October could not have been greater if she had been the returning *Victory*.

During the 1920s and 1930s sizeable yachts continued to be hauled out at Drake Brothers yard and others spent the winter in the mud berths of the creek. The largest was the 500-ton steamer *Alice*, in charge of Captain Drake Frost.

By 1935 social customs and yachting fashions were changing and inshore racing in class yachts, which had been brought to near perfection in the 12-metre class, and to excess in the rig of the bigger cutters, was proving too expensive and unattractive to the rising generation of sailing men. Their enthusiasm and means were attuned to the sport of passage racing in comparatively small yachts which had been established in America before 1914, and had spread to England during the 1920s, where enthusiasts established the Fastnet race and the Ocean Racing Club, later the Royal Ocean Racing Club. Although a few of these early offshore racers, such as *Halloween*, carried a full professional crew, the majority were almost totally manned by amateurs, usually with one professional hand, and professional helmsmen were banned.

Many Tollesbury men manned the 12-metre class boats which were racing in the West Country regattas a few days before the outbreak of war in September 1939. Within weeks many were serving afloat with the Royal Navy, others were fishing in the smacks, facing daily peril from mines and aircraft attack, and some found work as riggers on government contracts making anti-submarine nets and similar jobs, while the racing yachts slumbered in the yards where they had been hastily laid up, never again to race in their pre-war classes.

Several older Tollesbury yachtsmen found work as watchmen on board the many large merchant ships laid up in the Blackwater as a result of war damage or which were surplus to post-war requirements. Captain Edward Heard was amongst them, ending a lifetime still doing a useful job afloat. He died in September 1947, respected as amongst the greatest yacht racing helmsmen.

Tollesbury men recommenced yachting after the war's end in 1945 and for a time it seemed that the activity of the 1930s might return. Captain Rice was in command of Lord Iliffe's motor yacht *Esmeralda*; there was a village crew in the fine motor-sailer *Carlina*, Walter Mussett was skippering the Class I champion offshore racer *Jocasta* owned by Essex fruit grower Geoffrey Pattinson, and others were serving as hands in yachts. But pride of them all during the late 1940s and early 1950s was the beautiful ketch yacht *Alison*, skippered and manned by Tollesbury men and laying up there each winter. Designed and built by William Fife at Fairlie in 1929, she was 84 feet long and drew 10 feet 9 inches. She was the last large Essex sailing yacht to be professionally manned and sailed in the old manner. Every summer's morning the *Alison* let go her mooring in Mersea Quarters and set her 5,700 square feet of canvas to sail out, down the Blackwater, past the Bench Head and out into the Wallet. On fine days Mr Russell sat on deck in a basket chair, talking to Captain Townsend, or the mate at the wheel. When lunch was served and eaten the *Alison* went about and headed back for the Blackwater, usually being brought up by tea time. In the evening hands were going ashore in the dinghy, rowing up the creek to the causeway and their favourite pub or a walk up the coast road to discuss oysters and the weather with their Mersea contemporaries. Now renamed, the lovely *Alison* sails out of Gibraltar with cruise charterers. Her old owner and some of her crew are dead; the others retired or maybe still working afloat.

The days of professional participation in yachting were almost ended and unlike almost every other sport, it was becoming thoroughly amateur. Tollesbury Sailing Club, established before the war, flourished again and a feature of local sailing were the fast, pram-bowed boats designed and sailed by the McMullen family and friends. This little fleet of unorthodox craft appeared at Blackwater regattas and raced in handicap events, displaying amazing speed under a variety of rigs, usually large lugsails of unique cut. The club has long since taken to established national and international dinghy classes for its sport but the handicap boats were refreshingly individual and inspiring in ingenuity of design.

Tollesbury men served as skippers and hands in several yachts of the 12-metre class in the 1920s and 30s. Here four British 12-metres are racing the American *Vim* at Harwich regatta, 1939.

Douglas Went

The 177-foot motor yacht *Alice* was the largest vessel to berth in Tollesbury Creek. She laid up there in the 1930s under Captain Drake Frost. Here she lies off Cowes in 1939.

By the late 1950s Tollesbury seemed to drowse in decline, as though exhausted by its flurry of activity forty years previously. A few motorised smacks fished from the creek and stood legged on the hard. Only a few yachts laid up and refitted there. The well maintained hulls of the old schooner yachts *Heartsease* and *Tamesis* lay in the saltings, serving out their days as houseboats; impressive in size and lending a false atmosphere of the village's earlier activity in laying up yachts. In 1958 Keith Mussett was, with Captain Stan Bishop of Brightlingsea, the professional backbone of an otherwise amateur crew of the 12-metre *Sceptre* in her challenge for the America's Cup; the first since 1937.

Tollesbury has a handsome and unique memorial to the village's seafarers in a stained glass window made for St Mary's church about 1963 at the instigation and bequest of Frederick E. Hasler, who emigrated to America in his youth. After a successful career in banking he remembered his native village and the window was conceived to depict craft typical of those which the villagers owned and sailed. One window is of working craft and shows the cutter smack *Alberta*, a boomsail barge, a spritsail stack barge and, unusually, a billyboy coaster, though it is doubtful if any of these chubby, leeboard craft usually associated with the Humber, Lincolnshire and north Norfolk, were owned in Tollesbury, though possibly one or two may have called there. The other window is of yachts; the *America* which visited England in 1851 and was awarded the cup which became the most coveted yacht racing trophy; Sir Thomas Lipton's challenger *Shamrock II* of 1901, in which five Tollesbury men served as hands, under the command of Captains Robert Wringe and Edward Sycamore, both of Brightlingsea. Of the other two yachts, *Endeavour II*, which raced for the cup in 1937, was skippered by Captain George Williams of Hamble, Hampshire, with a principally Solent crew and a better choice would have been the *Endeavour*, which in 1937 accompanied her sister, the challenger, to America, sailed by Captain Edward Heard from Tollesbury with a crew including many men from the village.

Few of those who participated in the great days remain at work afloat. Cheery Lennox Leavett, an ex-12-metre hand, carries on the old traditions in charge of the 8-metre cruiser/racer *Gi Gi*, which immaculately graces West Mersea anchorage in summer. Frost and Drake's boatyard continues to repair and occasionally build small fishing and pleasure craft and Gayle Heard, that consummate sailmaker, manufactures dinghy equipment in the village, having commenced business during the early 1960s after apprenticeship at Gowen's West Mersea loft, appropriately in the old Tollesbury loft in which Gowen worked half a century earlier.

With the growth of sailing and population drift to north east Essex, Tollesbury waterside was revived in several unexpected ways; a large yacht harbour has been excavated from the saltings and mud berths behind Drake Brothers yard; a deep pool with a cill at its entrance from the head of Woodrolfe creek, near the hard. A terrace of houses sprang up as part of the scheme and there were rumblings of disgust from some newcomers; whose ideas of parochial neatness extended to proposals to pull down the fine old storied yacht stores which have served Tollesbury so well and are part of the village landscape and history; long may they remain to dominate the saltings, refurbished and put to good use housing the gear of laid up smaller yachts which sail local waters in ever increasing numbers; a reminder of the village's proud past in yachting.

CHAPTER NINE

The Middle River

THE Blackwater above Shinglehead Point, the tip of Tollesbury Marshes, and the mouth of Bradwell Creek, leads broad and inviting to the west, where the trees of Osea Island float in the mirage haze of summer days exaggerated to mushroom-like heads on slender trunks, resembling a distant south sea atoll, apparently blocking the river's passage inland. This windswept reach has filled me with anticipation since I first turned into it in a 24-foot gaff cutter over thirty years ago, skipper of that youthful crew of three to whom its broad, green-grey, tumbling tideway promised great adventure and the anchorage of Osea might as easily have been a Pacific island, so great was its charm and satisfaction.

In those days sailing smacks still dredged the oyster grounds there in company with others with engines and rig reduced to a staysail, only set to steady them in a jobble of sea. Amongst these worked beamy, bold-bowed motor oyster skiffs with chuffing Brit engines, mostly built by Wyatts at Mersea and painted in their distinctive workboat colours of cream sides, green sheerstrakes, red bottoms, and pale grey insides. I always wanted to own one, wear thigh boots and cast a dredge like their owners, nonchalantly steadying themselves against the roll as the skiffs surged downstream at full throttle, bow waves creaming away across the choppy seas on the run home.

This reach, up to the eastern tip of Osea, is deep in places and since the mid-1920s large merchant ships have been laid up in the river during times of economic slump or the aftermath of war. These have been a varied collection, many pre-war were three-island, 10-knot cargo ships with a woodbine funnel and counter stern; the dray horses of empire, "built by the mile and cut off by the yard" in the dismal shipbuilding slums of the Tyne and Wear, ending life in rust and a last passage to the breaker's yard.

The laid-up ships made some work for watermen who moored them and unmoored them and ran the launches for maintenance personnel and the watchmen, many of whom were retired seafarers from Tollesbury and West Mersea who particularly admired the four-masted schooner yacht *Westward*, a fine 250-footer launched as the *Danefolk* at Rödby in 1920, which lay rusting in the Blackwater for many years. The ex-Dutch liner *Westernland* was another proud ship fallen on bad times and there were many others. Sometimes as many as twenty or so up to about 16,000 tons stretched from St Lawrence Stone, upstream, down to Sales Point, in the estuary, swinging to each tide with only a lonely watchman on board each, occupying the captain's cabin and walking his bridge and the boat deck in solitude for several days until his relief was put on board. Putting up the riding light at night and extinguishing it in the morning, watching the oyster dredgers and the yachts and dinghies getting becalmed under the lee of the towering steel sides and receiving staggering puffs and eddies when they emerged from the wind shadow on breezy days. He could, in fancy, be commanding a large ship; what an opportunity for a Walter Mitty!

Later there were war-shattered ships of all sorts, many of standard types with peculiar names; "Empires", "Libertys", "Forts", "Parks", "Victorys" and others. Most had strange stories behind their misfortunes, like the *Samlong*, a Liberty ship loaded with supplies which had been attacked off the beachhead at Normandy on the night of 2nd/3rd August 1944 by a German "Linse" (Lentil) explosive motor boat, which Allied sailors afterwards called a "Weasel". These 31-knot attack craft were piloted by one man and worked in threes. Two boats were steered towards the target before the pilots jumped out and they were then directed towards the ship by radio from the third, which raced off after picking up the other two pilots. The boats were filled with explosive and the *Samlong* was hit and badly damaged, along with another ship nearby. She was towed to the Blackwater soon afterwards to be laid up for deferred repairs, but the war ended before these were made.

Shooting the trawl from Major George Paget's smack yacht *Betsan*, built at Tollesbury in 1933. He was a keen sailor and wildfowler and, aged eighty-four, entered the *Betsan* in the Little Ship Club's race from Brightlingsea to Ostende. *Douglas Went*

This dismal aspect of the river's story has revived at intervals since. During the 1950s the Shaw Savill liner *Gothic*, which had carried the Queen and Duke of Edinburgh on their Commonwealth tour, returned to lay up there along with other ships, including many tankers. Many have come and gone since and a few remain as rusting reminders of the fluctuating fortunes of shipping.

In this reach, the green sea walls bordering the river become more noticeable, backed by grazing marshes and long fields of cereals, clover and maybe yellow patches of mustard. Reclamation of tidal foreshores from saltings into grazing by enclosure with sea walls was widespread in coastal Essex until the nineteenth century and the recent vast scheme to reclaim the Maplin Sands for use as an air and shipping port was the last manifestation of an old activity which led landowners and farmers to construct about 115 miles of sea wall between Maldon and Harwich, of which the Blackwater has a substantial share. There is evidence of Essex marshland being embanked by the twelfth century and wall makers were highly paid compared to agricultural workers.

Sea walls were built out over the saltings towards the lowest part of the area to be embanked, the foundations were made by digging a trench, the soft mud being removed and replaced by marsh clay which was dug from "delfs", sometimes known as fleets or borrow pits, in the marsh saltings along the inside course of the wall and about twenty feet from its foot. The clay foundations were often stiffened with brushwood and the wall above was built up with clay, chalk and stakes and was often faced with bound bundles of brushwood to protect it against erosion by wave action at high water. These facings were replaced by laid Kentish ragstone during the nineteenth century, brought in by sailing barges from Medway quarries until the 1950s. Facing a sea wall was called "close pitching"; a skilled process of fitting pieces of Kentish ragstone into a deep solid face, tamped in with a wooden mallet. This is now superseded by concrete facing blocks which have been made by the hundred thousand at Tollesbury and elsewhere. Height of the walls varies but is often about 8 feet above the marsh behind them and about 3 feet wide at the top, which is used as a footpath. Sea walls tend to settle and one of the greatest problems is the treading down of the top by cattle. Gales and freak tides sometimes breach them and repairs are not easily made even with modern earth moving equipment. In the past, scores of men sometimes spent months shovelling clay into breaches which were again washed out in a single tide down to the "toe of the wall". The work of the sea waller looks pleasant enough on a June day but is bleak and bitter in a January north-easter.

A plan proposed by civil engineer Sir John Rennie for the South Essex Estuary and Reclamation Company in 1851/52 proposed to enclose 30,420 acres on both shores of the Blackwater and on the coast of the Dengie Hundred, between Bradwell and the mouth of the Crouch. The intention was to deepen the Blackwater by confining the waters into a single channel and on the north bank marshes and mudflats which were bare at low water were to be reclaimed, from Decoy Point to Osea Island, then downstream to Tollesbury Wick, leaving narrow creeks to Goldhanger but apparently cutting off Thirslet Creek; in all a gain of 2,320 acres. On the west and south side of the river, reclamation was proposed from Northey Island to Sales Point at Bradwell, leaving channels to Mayland and Mundon and yielding 2,560 acres. Of course this project was never carried out, fortunately as it would have reduced the Blackwater to a narrow, swift flowing river with banks as featureless as those of the Crouch below Burnham.

Sea wall below Osea Island, circa 1895.   *from a painting by Ian Simpson: courtesy A. H. Purnell*

Tollesbury's railway pier projected out over the mud to low water mark on the north shore until the late 1940s. In the days when it was the terminus of the branch line from Kelvedon to Tollesbury it cost a penny to ride from the pier to Tollesbury station, but the anticipated yachts did not leave Brightlingsea to lie off Tollesbury Pier and it fell into decay. A nearby wartime defence boom almost wrecked Michael Frost's sailing smack *Boadicea* when she sailed on to its submerged top to fill and almost capsize. But with the help of friends owning the Mersea smack yachts *Snowdrop* and *Dorothy*, and Guy Harding from Clarke and Carter's yard, the owner managed to refloat this oldest of all smacks and she returned to Mersea for refitting, to continue her long life.

West Mersea smack yachts racing upriver during the 1950s. The *Boadicea* (foreground) is sailed by her owner, Michael Frost. Her transom stern contrasts with the more usual counter of the next ahead.   *The Times*

Mill Creek, beloved of wildfowlers, and Mill Point with its nearby decoy pond are by the entrance to Thirslet Creek which runs in parallel to the shore about Mill Point and reaches in to the Gore Saltings. It seems the ideal creek for smugglers and was probably much used by them to run goods ashore on moonless high waters to the farm roads running inland towards Tolleshunt D'Arcy, and the lodestone of Tiptree Heath. An oyster watch smack was stationed at the mouth of the creek until the late 1940s; a snug berth from half ebb until half flood but an uncomfortable one at high water in strong westerlies, which send a chop over the protective spit on which yachts are often to be found perched on an ebbing tide, having mistaken the broad high-water expanse for deep water.

A field at the head of Thirslet Creek is called Red Hill and was the site of ancient saltmaking, once a widespread occupation on the shores of the Blackwater. The word "saltings", describing marsh which is subject to covering by the tides, indicates the origins of the salt boilers' trade and salt pans were worked in many places beside the Blackwater. Salt water was pumped into clay-lined tanks to commence evaporation, which was completed in shallow trays of partly evaporated water, heated over fires of brushwood and later of seaborne coal. After rock salt was discovered and mined in Cheshire, about 1670, the salt makers used it to increase production by dissolving it in sea water, and the solution was then re-evaporated by boiling. Saltmaking was also carried on at Goldhanger, a small village upstream from Thirslet Creek and was transferred from there to Heybridge about 1810, probably because of the attraction of the Chelmer canal for transport. By 1894 Maldon salt works was the only one remaining in Britain. It continues to flourish and sends quality table salt to many countries.

Goldhanger village lies at the head of a shallow creek between Tollesbury and Heybridge. It does not seem to have had many maritime associations beyond occasional fishing, smuggling, the loading and unloading of barges with agricultural cargoes in the days of sail. However, it is an ancient village which for many years had a population of 500. The Will of George Osborde, a Goldhanger fisherman, dated 1575, left a "half boat", a "bream net", a "new vag net" and other gear to "my brother in law Heard". The nets' descriptions are now obscure but could have been a beam trawl and a seine net. The two surnames are interestingly local today, for Osborde must surely have been contemporary spelling of Osborne and at least one fisherman named Heard still lives in Goldhanger.

Few dramatic events took place in this peaceful place excepting the occasional smuggling run or the great tide in 1736 which burst the sea walls, drowning cattle, sheep and five men, including John Cooper, a decoy man. There were at one time four wild duck decoys at Goldhanger, typical of the many on the coasts and rivers of Essex, Suffolk and Norfolk, which were worked for gain rather than sport. A decoy pond usually had from four to eight small channels leading off it in crooked shapes; about 20 feet wide at the mouth reducing to about two feet at the ends. These were known as "pipes", being covered with tarred netting spread taut on half round wood hoops. The decoy was worked by one or more men known as a decoyman, having a thorough knowledge of the ways of wildfowl. He worked from behind a system of screens made from reeds, placed to obscure him from birds on the pond or in the pipes. Wild duck would alight on the pond to feed at dusk or dawn, which was when the decoyman made his bags. He had a number of tamed wild ducks trained to gather in the pipes and follow a routine to entice the wild ducks into the pipe which had to be one on the windward side of the pond. Whistling to his tame ducks he would throw a few handfuls of meal or other feed over the screens to fall on the surface at the mouth of the pipe. The tame ducks fed on this and the wild ones would be attracted to it also, emboldened by their actions. Then they would be enticed further up the pipe with more feed thrown over the screens. When the birds were well up the pipe the decoyman showed himself at its mouth, waving his cap, causing the wild ducks to rise and fly in panic up the narrow pipe end, where a way of escape seemed possible. The tame ducks were trained not to follow, but to swim back to the entrance calmly. How this was achieved is unknown to me. Meanwhile the decoyman seized the trapped birds at the tail of the pipe, where they were jammed in silent terror, then killed them.

By then, more ducks were attracted to the mouth of the pipe by the tame ones feeding again, assuming that the other wild ducks had merely flown off. And so the enticement was repeated. Alternatively the decoyman used a trained dog, often black and white in colour, to prance at the edges of the pipe, running behind screens and then reappearing to attract the curiosity of the wild ducks, who swam up the pipe after him until the decoyman appeared at the entrance and frightened them up to the end in terror, to be slaughtered. Many breeds of duck were taken in this way, except pochard which when alarmed, dive instead of rising. Many decoy ponds had netting screens made which were balanced with weights so that when pochard were taking off from the pond in the half light, the screens were suddenly erected and they flew into them, to be captured. Dead wildfowl were sent in hampers to Leadenhall Market, London, sometimes in vast quantities daily in the winter, which is when decoys were principally worked.

Fishermen lived at Goldhanger in the 1880s and probably kept their small smacks in the creek where cart roads from Highams and Joyces farms led to barge wharves at the sea walls of the main creek and Joyces creek, which were probably found useful by the occasional smuggler with his illicit goods bound for Tiptree heath, the local distribution centre for the trade. Four coastguards were stationed there late in the nineteenth century and had a watch post at the western end of Goldhanger Creek mouth. Their red brick cottages still stand by Church Street. Smuggled goods were reputedly sometimes hidden at the village, in the cellars of *The Chequers*, whose landlord twenty years ago was the late Jack Spitty, one-time barge skipper, a champion hand at the wheel of a barge in the revived pleasure barge races of the 1960s and 70s and the last to bear that redoubtable seafaring name on the Blackwater or Colne.

Opposite Goldhanger, Osea Island lies in mid-Blackwater, roughly diamond shaped and approached by a narrow track across extensive flats which join it to the mainland between Goldhanger Creek and Decoy Point. Thus, at high water, Osea is a true island and can only be approached by boat, and all land communication is carried on at low tide. Even the island post box deliveries

The Osea Island post box collection was "According to Tide" in 1948.

used to be delightfully stated as "According to tide". Osea is and has been for generations, an island farm; a kingdom for the happy man possessing it, particularly as some of them also owned a fine yacht which could be conveniently moored in the deep water off the island's south shore, where a beach slopes into the river, overlooked by the owner's residence which looks across the river into the entrance to Lawling Creek.

At one time years ago, the house was a home for alcoholics but its cures seem to have been delayed by the smuggling in of drink brought down by Maldon fishermen to be hidden in caches under the bushes by the shore, to the profit of the smugglers and delight of the thirsty (and often wealthy) alcoholics.

There have been few incidents in Osea's history; crops were set and harvested, barges came and went to the wharf tucked in the rill on its northern side, working in over the Stumble with the usual agricultural cargoes. I know one devoted Blackwater sailing man who reckons that the Stumble's flats covered or uncovered, all year round, contain such a wealth of marine, natural and bird life that it would take a lifetime to see and understand it all. Certainly when one stands on or sails over this lonely expanse, which few yachtsmen ever do, preferring the more certain course to the south of the Island, the sweeping skyscape above broad waters or muds and the wheeling wildfowl seem the essence of east coast space and freedom. Occasionally travellers have been caught by the tide while using the island road across the flats. A postmaster was crossing to Osea in a trap when the horse bolted and he was thrown into the water, narrowly escaping from drowning and a postman named Ruddick almost drowned there when ice on which he was crossing the Stumble gave way in the great frost of 1888.

The Blackwater participated in some of the most secret naval activity of the 1914-18 war. In the spring of 1916 the first of the Royal Navy's motor torpedo boats, or "Coastal Motor Boats" as they were called, entered service and Lieutenant Hampden, one of the originators of the type, proposed basing the first flotilla at a secret base on Osea Island. Plans for this were advanced when the Admiralty switched the venue to Queenborough, on the Swale in Kent. However, with expansion of naval activity towards the war's end, a base for coastal motor boats was established at Osea Island in 1918. Construction work soon produced jetties and berths for the motor torpedo boats and fast minelayers; also slipways, maintenance and repair shops and accommodation huts. The south shore of the island took on the appearance of a minor naval base and the Blackwater became used to the sight of these very fast coastal motor boats rushing in and out of the river on training exercises. There were three types; 40-footers armed with one torpedo; 55-footers which carried two torpedoes or four depth charges; and the giant 70-footers which arrived in 1919 and were intended for laying mines. All were designed by Thornycroft and were powered with their powerful petrol engines which gave the then amazing speeds of up to 55 knots. All were single step hydroplanes in hull form and proved themselves in many actions including the incredible heroism of the attacks on Ostend and Zeebrugge in 1918. However, perhaps the greatest exploit with which Osea base was associated was the Baltic campaign initiated by C.M.B. 4, commanded by Lieutenant Augustas Agar, V.C., and C.M.B. 7, which prepared for their stealthy mission in the Blackwater and were then shipped out to Sweden, then on to the British base at Bjorko, Finland. Operations then entered the realms of secret service, with No. 4 running at 30 knots and then sidling past Russian sea forts, before opening up to dash to the Russian coast and make contact with British agents active during the Bolshevik unrest in Russia. Agar also managed to torpedo a Russian cruiser during one of these sorties and afterwards a flotilla of C.M.Bs were sent out and made a daring and spectacular attack on the Russian naval base at Kronstadt in August 1919.

So, Osea was retained after the war to provide a peace time base for C.M.B. training, naval operations and such experimental work as might be needed for development of the light fast warship for the British navy. But the C.M.Bs were discarded from 1921 onwards and in 1926 the C.M.B. branch of the Royal Navy was paid off and Osea reverted to the quiet of farming and the anchorage of small yachts under its south shore at week-ends.

Probably few now realise this aspect of its story but having worked on some of their less speedy successors, I would like to have seen the C.M.Bs roaring and bounding over the tumbling waves of the Blackwater at full speed, leaving their characteristic twin quarter waves like rooster tails as they thundered seaward.

By the 1960s Osea was again for sale. There were rumours of it becoming a holiday camp and, later, a national sailing centre, for which the island, with the

Coastal Motor Boats hauled out at the Royal Naval Base, Osea Island, 1919. From 1918-1925 the Osea foreshore was dominated by the activities of the torpedo boats and minelayers of the Navy's fast boat service. Three types are shown—a 55-foot (foreground), a 40-foot (second), a 70-foot minelayer and two other 55-footers. These craft could achieve speeds up to 55 knots.

Imperial War Museum

deep water channel on its south side, would have been ideal. But the planners turned elsewhere and Osea remains quiet farmland, for which all must be thankful.

The south shore of the Blackwater is farmed extensively and these sweeping, backcloth acres of field and hedgerow, farms, scattered hamlets and occasional villages of the Dengie Hundred were immortalised in S. L. Bensusan's books in which the quick wits and often acid humour of characters such as Solomon Woodpecker, Mr Blite, Martha Ram and Mrs Garbole, typify the ways and outlook of many inhabitants until the late 1930s. To them the river represented another world but one road reaches the riverside at what is now called Stone or Steeple Stone, though in earlier times it was known as Ramsey Island or Ramsey Wick, though it was not an island but a broad peninsular.

In the summer of 1961 we sailed our old West Mersea oyster skiff *Oyster* about in the river, landing at the deserted foreshore of St Lawrence Stone to walk inland along a tree lined path and buy ginger beer for David, our then small son. Only a handful of sailing dinghies, mostly Snipes, lay on the beach, still scarred by the concrete hards for the ramps of the landing craft which exercised there towards the end of the 1939-45 war, when the Blackwater was watched against surprise landing by German flying boats. A thriving sailing club now occupies the spot and scores, sometimes hundreds, of dinghies are launched from the beach and the owners' cars fill a nearby meadow; the result of the sailing boom of the 1960s.

Off here, in midstream, timber-laden sailing, steam and motor ships have anchored or moored to buoys to discharge their cargoes of sweet smelling Baltic softwoods into sailing barges, to be lightered up to Maldon and Heybridge Basin. Tall-masted barquentines, barques and ships, with yards cockbilled out of the way of the tackles lowering bundles of deals down to the barges clustered alongside, have brought the flags of Sweden, Finland, Denmark, Norway and Russia to the Blackwater. The men discharging the cargoes lived in a wood hut built on deck of a pontoon which was towed down to the ship alongside a sailing barge and inevitably received the nickname of "Noah's Ark". It remained in use during the late 1920s but was superseded by daily launch transport soon after.

This Danish motor ketch was anchored below Osea Island discharging eels from tanks in her holds into a floating keep chest alongside, when the author's cutter sailed past in 1948.

The pools and fleets of Ramsey Marsh, behind the sea wall, almost bring Ramsey Island to reality and further west at Stansgate Point an ancient abbey farm hints at medieval isolation and contemplation, perhaps of the tidal narrows separating the point from the East Point of Osea Island which, with its surrounding flats, occupies the middle part of the Blackwater, narrowing its main channel to a swift flowing tide rip which can become amazingly rough when a strong wind blows against the tide. One day during the summer of 1977 a friend and I were beating his small cruiser through the narrows at half flood, against a strong westerly wind, rising to gale force. Suddenly, scores of sailing dinghies were launched off from a sailing club at Stansgate and within five minutes the whole narrows and the river to the south of Osea was covered with capsized boats, drifting to leeward, their crews clinging to them, rescue boats thrashing about in inadequate numbers and manoeuvering under the bows of sailing cruisers finding as much as they could do to keep clear of the melée. "Looks like the battle of Trafalgar," muttered my companion grimly as he put the helm down and we plunged about to avoid a capsized dinghy with her helmsman sitting on the upturned bottom, clutching the erect centreboard blowing him to leeward like a sail. Such are the modern perils of the narrows, which have been known to shake up ten tonners in a gale.

In earlier times the narrows were a critical passage for smugglers and the coastguard hulk *Richmond* was beached at Stansgate until 1870 when she was replaced by another hulk prosaically named *Watch Vessel 21*, a craft which was a feature of the narrows until the early 1920s. The men lived on board with their wives but watch vessels in which to quarter several families were not ideal as the bulkheads were so thin that conversation had to be in a whisper if it were not to be heard all over the vessel. The domestic peace of the station was not easy to maintain and the commanding officer had to use tact to preserve it. Even so, quarrelsome wives were constantly being referred to him for adjudication on some domestic matter.

Lawling Creek, once known as Lawling Fleet, and Mayland Creek which branches off it probe far inland. The entrance is shallow but the creek deepens inside. Both were frequented by barges loading stacks and unloading muck until 1914 with the 45-ton spritty *Mayland* owned by farmer James Cardnell of St Lawrence, amongst the regular traders. Many of these sailed up to load at Pidgeon Dock at the head of Mayland Creek.

Above the village of Mayland, Lawling becomes Mundon Creek. The village has the excellent yacht yard of Cardnell Brothers, who have built many yachts and before 1939 produced some fine little pointed stern shoal draught yawls. During the 1939-45 war the yard built many craft for the Admiralty including eight of the 122-feet "B" class Fairmile Motor Launches which were so useful for patrol and anti-submarine work, minelaying and light minesweeping. The commander of one of them, Arthur Bennett, who in peace time owned the yacht barges *June* and *Henry*, told me that he considered the Cardnell built M.Ls the best he had seen. The boats included Nos. 215, 285, 461 and 534. The last built was the *Clifton*, completed for use as an army hospital launch in the far east. No. 215 participated in the St Nazaire raid and returned safely. The yard recieved a letter from her skipper congratulating them on their workmanship.

As war work developed, Tom Cardnell and his brother found themselves managing 90 hands, of whom only four were boatbuilders; the remainder being carpenters, joiners, labourers and women painters, brought in for this vital war work. Even so, Cardnells completed an M.L. every eight weeks, besides several of the powerful "D" Class Fairmile 115-foot Motor Torpedo Boats and Motor Gun Boats, which had complex petrol machinery and were heavily armed. The yard also built several 45-foot Admiralty Motor Fishing Vessels and did considerable conversion work for the War Office in converting motor cruisers into army craft for inshore patrol work, carried out by the Royal Army Service Corps.

Staff of Cardnell Brothers, 1944

Building M.F.Vs at Cardnells in 1944.

In 1947 Cardnell Brothers built the 37-foot 3 inches sloop *Matawa*, designed by F. Morgan Giles and constructed almost entirely of plywood, except for the centreline structure. She was a fine yacht and it was a courageous experiment at a time when marine plywood was subject to much prejudice from yachtsmen, though the yard had considerable experience of it in their small warships.

The yard has continued to build and refit hundreds of yachts and the expansion of sailing has filled Lawling Creek, which once saw only an occasional sailing barge with scores of yacht moorings.

CHAPTER TEN

In Colliers Reach

ABOVE Osea narrows the Blackwater turns north-west and increases to a deceptive width at high water, though the deep water channel remains narrow and wanders past buoys, which were earlier beacons, having intriguing names of now forgotten origin. On the south-west shore, just above the entrance to Lawling Creek, is the Fletch Horse and over on the Osea side, the Barnacle Horse, both marking mud banks. Above the Barnacle is one quaintly named the Doctor and the Channel hereabouts is called "The Ware" as far as a mark on the south-west side named Southey Beacon, standing at the end of the Island Horse, just above the entrance to Southey Creek. This leads west around Northey Island; 330 acres of sea walled farmland, with some trees to break its bleak outline at the western end, where Southey Creek turns towards Maldon and rejoins the river almost opposite Herring Point. Shallow Southey Creek is seldom navigated and until two hours before and after high water is barred by a causeway called "the Stakes", linking Northey to the land at Mundon. The short wriggle of Limbourne Creek runs inland from its western side and was another loading berth for the stack barges.

Above Southey beacon, on each side of the river channel, are the Doubles buoys and above these was a small creek known as the Gull Fleet or the Gull Drain which led to Decoy Point, sometimes called Fauley Point, on the tip of the marshy land at the west end of the Stumble, dividing Osea Island from the mainland. A duck decoy pond gave the point its name and the fleet was used by punt gunners and an occasional barge.

Almost opposite, on the Northey shore, is Awl Creek, leading in to the green sea wall. Perhaps this was where the Viking raiders under Unlaf (Olaf) Tryggvason landed from their long boats about 993 A.D. to encamp and prepare for an assault on Maldon.

Places on the east coast of England suffered the raids of the heathen Danes and Norwegians into Saxon times. Rowing and sailing across the North Sea in lightly built open boats carrying many armed men, they sought plunder wherever it could be found near water, and often penetrated far inland up rivers to lay siege to towns which might pay a ransom or "Danegeld" to escape attack. Northey Island was the reputed scene of an encounter between them and the

Saxon English which became famous. In 993 A.D., the *Saxon Chronicle* recorded, "Came Unlaf with ninety-three ships to Folkstone, on the Kentish coast, and lad waste all around, and thence he went to Sandwich, [also on the Kentish coast], and thence to Gyswic, [Ipswich in Suffolk, to the north of the Blackwater], and harried it all, and so to Maeldune (Maldon), and there Byrhtnoth the earldorman and his force came against him and fought with him, and there they slew the earldorman and kept the battlefield."

Byrhtnoth's courageous attempt to repulse the Danes made him an east coast hero. The action almost certainly took place at Northey Island, where the Danes encamped and sent their usual demands for ransom in to Maldon. Byrhtnoth contemptuously rejected them and his forces drew up on the land around the causeway or ford connecting the island to the land. Byrhtnoth and two of his best warriors, Aelfnorth and Wulfmaer, stood on the causeway or the fording place, backed by their men, defying the massing Vikings. Battle was joined and a slaughter of the Saxons followed.

The saga of "The Battle of Maldon" tells of the rout.

> "Then hewed him (Byrhtnoth) down, the heathen men.
> And both the warriors that by him stood,
> Aelfnorth and Wulfmaer both lay there,
> Beside their lord they gave their lives.
> There were the sons of Odda, first in flight,
> Godrick from war, and the good man forsook
> Who to him many a horse oft-times had given.
> He leaped on the horse, which belonged to his lord,
> On to the housings, though it was not right,
> And his brothers with him—fled."

Despite the defeat, Byrhtnoth's courageous end inspired many in England and eventually others like him stamped out the scourge of the Danish and Norwegian pirates. As with most ancient events, there is dispute as to its site and some scholars regard the battle as having been fought at the site of Heybridge Church, for possession of the causeway which ran from there to the foot of Maldon Hill. That year the Saxon English first agreed to pay tribute to the Danes and £10,000 was paid to them to stop ravaging the coasts and country. So the practice of the "Danegeld" was established and it took many years for these dishonourable transactions to be stopped and for the scourge of the Danish pirates to be wiped out. Three years later, during a foray into southern England with Swein Forkbeard, King of Denmark, Olaf Tryggvason became a Christian at Andover, Hampshire, and departed peacefully. Afterwards he was King of Norway.

For centuries since, Northey has been quiet farmland and is now owned by the National Trust.

Northey and Osea Islands may have been those called Ruckholme and Hardholme which were given to Beeleigh Abbey, near Maldon, by Robert Martell in 1180, but in 1577 Raphael Holinshed chronicled, "In Maldon water there are in like sort three isles enverioned all with salt streams as Saint Osithes, Northeie and another (after a mershe) that beareth no name so far as I remember." This was probably Ramsey Island.

A stand of elms on Northey known as Ladies Grove was a favourite place for picnics and bathing. A duck decoy was worked at the island's eastern end where the mark above Awl Creek, on the west side of the river, is Clarke's buoy, off barely discernible Clarke's Point, above which is Hilly Pool Point, the most north-easterly part of Northey Island. Opposite this stretch is Mill Reach, filled with splashing bathers on summer high waters but backed by caravans and parked cars. The sweep of this right-angled bend in the river was known as "Blackwater Bay" and a tide mill worked in the crook of it until the late nineteenth century, its stones driven by a 16-foot diameter waterwheel served by two tidal ponds, one of which remains behind the Saltcote Sailing Club. A windmill stood close by until 1891 and the two were known as the "Barrow Hill Mills". Early in the nineteenth century the miller's tenancy required that he provide the landlord with a turkey at Christmas and keep a dog. There was a quay where sailing barges discharged and loaded grain and often also hay or straw, for which a toll was paid to the miller.

Saltcote Mill, near Heybridge Basin, in 1948. The mill barge *Saltcote Belle* is alongside the wharf.
Arthur Bennett

From the elbow bend at Hilly Pool Point, the river leads south-west as Colliers Reach, towards another angled bend at Herring's Point. Half way along the reach on the north shore is the lock entrance to Heybridge Basin, where the masts of craft afloat inside ride strangely high above the river at low water. Heybridge is nowadays noteworthy for the canal basin and the lower part of the canal joining it to Chelmsford; both of which are filled with moored yachts. The older part of Heybridge lies further inland and has been a home of seafarers for centuries; Heybridge men are recorded as fishing the Essex coast in 1377.

But it was the enterprising spirit of the late eighteenth century canal age which brought Heybridge to life, when the Chelmer and Blackwater Navigation Company commenced construction of a canal, which included widening and deepening the River Chelmer from Chelmsford to Heybridge Mill and then cutting a new final stretch through to the river wall half way along Colliers Reach, where a basin entrance and lock gave access to the River Blackwater. It was all completed in 1797 and cost £50,000 for the 14 miles of canal and eleven locks; all dug and constructed by hand labour. The canal was 30 feet wide at the surface and 20 at the bottom; suitable for its 30-ton lighters. The locks were named Beeleigh, Ricketts, Hoe Mill, Rushes, Paper Mill, Little Baddow Mill, Stonehams, Cuton, Sandford Mill, Barnes Mill and Upper Lock. Vessels up to about 300 tons could enter Heybridge Basin at high water and its depth varied from 8-12 feet.

Upstream, Maldon was naturally jealous and angered by this new outlet of trade to and from the county town of Essex, particularly as previously thousands of tons of coal and general goods were shipped annually through Maldon's quays, to be carried to Chelmsford by road transport. But this was then expensive and slow and the new canal offered cheaper rates and quicker transit.

The canal prospered and Heybridge Basin quickly supported a small community of seafarers, pilots and watermen, besides labourers to unload and load cargoes from the visiting shipping into flat-bottomed shallow draught barges which carried it to and from Chelmsford, drawn by horses and man power. Inside, the Basin was calm on even the most gale-swept day and brigs and brigantines, topsail schooners and billyboys, sailing barges and ketches, jutted bowsprits and yardarms over the quay and the tall topmasts and ensigns were visible from Maldon, whose seafarers and shippers muttered grimly against the men of ''the Basin'', who they considered had ''stolen'' a large slice of their trade.

The first part of the channel above Hilly Pool point is sometimes called ''Basin Reach'' and contained the ''ballast hole'' in mid-stream, where the deeper draught brigs and barquentines trading to Heybridge and Maldon were laid after discharge to be ballasted, before sailing, with earth and stones loaded from lighters. Without ballast these relatively sharp sectioned ships would not sail to windward at all and in most cases would have been unstable under sail. In

149

the later days of cargo by sail a cluster of barges were usually moored to a buoy in this reach, bound loaded for Maldon, or ready to slip across to the lock at the next daylight high water.

Eight timber-laden sailing barges lie to buoys in Colliers Reach, off Heybridge Basin, 1938. Considerable quantities of softwood were brought to Heybridge and Maldon by sailing barges until the 1940s, loaded from steamers in the London docks or lying anchored below Osea Island.

Douglas Went

Salt making flourished at Heybridge in a works just below the basin, extending to the Barrow Hills and operated by Bridges, Johnson and Co, who failed after the salt tax was repealed in 1825. Their warehouse was converted to maltings for Hayward Rush and later, larger maltings were built alongside it for Messrs May. These industries stood on the site of tumuli locally called Barrow Hills, which were levelled during the construction of the buildings and were of unknown origin, though several were investigated before demolition. The nearby maltings were served by sailing barges until the 1940s and the shapely little *Salcote Belle* was built by Howard at Maldon in 1895 for Frederick May, the owner, who lived at Stisted, to carry grain there, and is still sailing as a yacht barge.

The canal's transport opportunities probably encouraged the removal of Bentall's agricultural implement works to Heybridge village early in the nineteenth century. The Bentall family of agricultural implement makers originated from Goldhanger, where William Bentall, of a line of farmers, evolved his first ploughs for use on his farm. These were manufactured by the village blacksmith but after a few years local demand for them led to him building a small works in the village, and by 1805 he moved the expanding business to Heybridge to use the facilities of the Chelmer and Blackwater canal. He was followed by his son Edward Bentall, who invented the patent broadshare and subsoil plough. These products were rivalled by Joseph Warren, who later founded the Maldon Ironworks Company, not far from Bentall's Heybridge works. The Bentalls continued to expand and produced many types of agricultural machinery.

Edward Bentall had a liking for sailing and took considerable interest in the form of sailing craft and held theories for their improvement based on his experience of small yachts. In 1875 he toyed with a project to have built a large sailing yacht of novel hull form in an attempt to improve speed and windward ability over the plumb-stemmed, long keel yachts fashionable under the contemporary rating rule. Seeking the best advice and assistance in developing his concept he called in the Wivenhoe yacht designer and builder John Harvey, who was then at the peak of his notable career, ranking with William Fife, Dan Hatcher and Michael Ratsey as one of the world's leading yacht builders and designers. However, he appears to have excelled them in theoretical reasoning and scientific approach to the design of sailing craft, evolving his designs from sound mathematical principles of naval architecture with detailed design analysis, much of which was published. The principal object of the design of the new yacht for Mr Bentall was to obtain speed by reducing the area of wetted surface and its consequent friction by cutting away her ends.

W. P. Stephens, a contemporary yachting authority, wrote of her design, "Mr Bentall's part went no further than to sketch out the general dimensions and some novel features; adjustment of centres being done by Mr Harvey."

151

Thus the famous *Jullanar*, as she was named, was the joint product of John Harvey and E. H. Bentall and was recorded as such in the design credits of contemporary yacht registers. Harvey anticipated her sailing performance from his design analysis but also knew she would have been faster in lighter weather had his original and more extreme design been built. Her form had in fact been anticipated by at least two other vessels; the yacht *Australia* built at Sydney in 1858 and the fruit cutter *Margaret* designed by Tovell and built at Colchester Hythe in 1853.

John Harvey exhibited the *Jullanar* design in the Shipwrights' Exhibition of 1875, in competition with those of other yachts. The judging committee's decision was that she would be fit for neither cruising nor racing, Harvey and his partner George Pryer being the only two naval architects with complete faith in her windward ability. She was originally designed with schooner rig but this was altered to yawl during the design stage. Her mainmast was well aft and a short bowsprit complimented her clipper bow. Principal dimensions were 110 foot 6 inches overall, 90 foot waterline × 16 foot 8 inches beam × 13 foot extreme draught. The well rockered keel, vertical sternpost, comparatively small rudder tucked well under the hull and immersed canoe stern were reminiscent of trends only developed in large racing yachts twelve years later.

The *Jullanar* was commenced at Heybridge by direct labour, probably augmented by some shipwrights from Harvey's yard. She was reputedly built on the site of the present Blackwater Sailing Club but an account by A. K. Barlow, a Wivenhoe yacht owner, states that she was started in Bentall's agricultural implement factory and was constructed to just above the waterline before being launched and towed to John Harvey's yard at Wivenhoe to be completed and fitted out.

An accident with a broken chain caused her to fall over on the cradle at Wivenhoe, but she was soon afloat for cruising. Her crews and the yachting fraternity knew her as "Bentall's plough", because of her novel underwater shape. However, Bentall did not race her and in 1877 she was sold to Mr A. D. Macleay and was fitted out for racing under Captain John Downes of Brightlingsea, who sailed her to the top of the yawl class with 12 prizes and surpassed it next season by coming into Colne to lay up with prize flags almost dressed overall and with the best record of any racing yacht that year, winning £1,065 prize money. Thereafter she reverted to cruising, but at the turn of the century participated in several of the early offshore races from Dover to Heligoland for the German Emperor's Cup, skippered by Captain Turner Barnard of Rowhedge and later by Captain Turner Ennew of Wivenhoe. The *Jullanar* was broken up soon after 1900.

Soon after selling the *Jullanar*, Bentall's active fancy was ranging to a smaller but more extreme yacht and he conceived a design for a bulb-fin keel racer to sail under the Thames Tonnage rating rule of the time, which penalised beam. As a result the *Evolution*, as she was named, had in profile the characteristics of the successful light displacement "raters" of twelve years later but due to the current rating rule had very little beam. It is not known who draughted her plans but this time Bentall could not call on John Harvey for advice and assistance, as he had closed his Wivenhoe yard and emigrated to America in 1881 to set up there as a yacht designer.

The yawl *Jullanar* was designed by John Harvey of Wivenhoe and her owner, Edward Bentall of Heybridge, where she was built in 1875. Here she is sailing in the Clyde, showing her unusual canoe stern and cruising rig, with spinnaker boom topped up and down the mast.

The *Evolution* rated at 10 tons and was 51 foot overall × 10 foot draught, but had only a 6 foot 6 inches beam. Sailing trials revealed that the parallel-sided ballast keel was insufficient for stability in other than the lightest airs and lead half-bulbs were added on each side of its lower edge, but still she was overpowered in ordinary breezes. She entered at Harwich regatta without success and further experiment followed with rig and keel but eventually Mr Bentall despaired of improvement and the *Evolution* was broken up soon after.

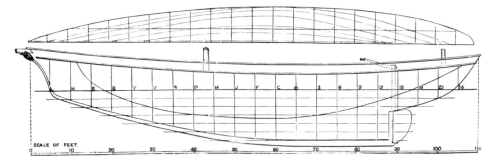

Lines of the yacht *Jullanar*, 1875, showing her then radical cut away profile and unusual stern. She was originally designed as a schooner with a plumb stem. Her form had been anticipated by the Australian yacht *Australian* of 1858.

Lines of the cutter yacht *Evolution*, built for Edward Bentall in 1882. An unsuccessful early attempt at a bulb keel racer which anticipated the form of many later yachts.

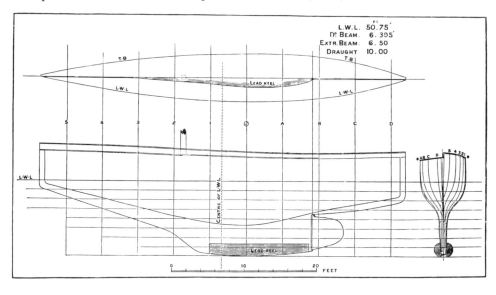

By the late nineteenth century trade to Heybridge Basin was declining, though square rigged craft still supplemented the greater numbers of ketches and spritsail barges bringing many cargoes, particularly timber, sailed round from the London Docks or lightered up from ships lying anchored below Osea Island. The lock keeper and the hufflers must have had some trying times warping unhandy brigs and brigantines into the lock entrance and out again

154

into the river, with a fresh wind ranging from north-east to south-west. Heybridge lock has 12 feet of water over the cill at high water spring tides, is 26 feet wide and will accommodate sizeable craft. The celebrated Maldon ketch barge *Record Reign* was reputedly designed to just fit in the lock chamber.

Heybridge Basin from behind the sea wall, about 1896. A huddle of houses around the lock and basin where a brigantine and a barge lie (right). A barge with sails set lies off the lock entrance (left) and a cutter beats upriver.

from a painting by Tom Simpson, in the author's possession

There was persistent and considerable rivalry between the men of Maldon and those of Heybridge Basin, whom they termed ''the cannibals'', and several affrays resulted. However, the ''Basiners'' seem to have been well able to look after themselves and many were lively characters. Alfred Clark, known to his friends as ''Tish'', was typical of the old breed of Heybridge Basin natives. Born there in 1857, he went to sea at an early age in local coasting brigs and brigantines which then traded to the Basin, Maldon and many other places. In 1888 he became licencee of *The Jolly Sailor* and was known to most east coast yachtsmen who called at Heybridge, until his death in 1933. Another was Dick Quilter who was once bet he could not jump Heybridge Lock and, getting a long pole, he vaulted over with a triumphant grin. But Heybridge Basin's most colourful character was Charlie Chaney, born there in 1858. He went to sea in small square riggers which frequented the Blackwater and became mate of a brigantine. Around 1900 he turned shipwright and joined the Heybridge firm of May and Butcher, where he worked on the repair of ships and craft and on shipbreaking, but retained a keen love of sailing, particularly racing. At Heybridge regatta he was always well in the fun. For instance, in that of 1920 he

155

sailed in the local one-design dinghies which were lent for the day by their owners to be sailed by professionals like Charlie, who came second. He won second prize in the pair-oared dinghy race, partnered by a youngster, whom he drove verbally and by example, and was second in the race for sailing gun punts and went on to another second in the single-oared dinghy race. Not content, this sixty-two-year-old then won the shovel race in duck punts and finished the day leading his own tug of war team to victory. What a splendid example of the exuberant Blackwater waterman!

Up to seven or eight gun punts raced in Heybridge regattas at that time, sailed to windward with only a paddle held over the lee side at the stern to act as rudder and leeboard. The races attracted boats from West Mersea, Tollesbury, Burnham and Brightlingsea; crowding the basin afterwards. The 1921 regatta was enlivened by the arrival from Walton of five 12 foot 6 inches one-design dinghies on the deck of a motor yacht, and others for this then popular class sailed up from Tollesbury and West Mersea. However, the dinghy which attracted most notice was a nondescript converted smack's boat rigged with a beautifully set standing lugsail, which outsailed the lot.

The canal continues in use and during the early 1950s several new wooden lighters were built for the carriage of timber cargoes along it to Chelmsford merchants. Much of this was Baltic pine in the form of ''deals'' for house-building and was brought to the Basin from ships off Osea by sailing barges, or in unrigged barges towed by a tug as lighters, to be discharged on the quay and be re-loaded into the canal lighters. At that time these were fitted with a pair of large outboard motors on the stern; useful for clearing the propellers of weeds and for removal to be used on other lighters for the return trip. Traffic so revived that the canal company ordered an icebreaker from the Rowhedge Ironworks Company; horse-drawn and worked by men standing on deck and inducing a roll, breaking the ice and allowing passage of the lighters during hard winters, when the fresh water canal froze.

Eels became another staple import to Heybridge Basin from the 1920s into the 1960s. Large quantities were brought across the North Sea in the welled holds of small wooden motor ketches, usually owned in Denmark, the eels coming from the Baltic and from Friesland, in Holland. These counter-sterned, smartly kept white-painted craft carried a stout ketch rig to steady their chubby hulls in a seaway and in a reaching breeze add a knot or so to the thumping single cylinder diesel below the wheelhouse. The Danish ketch *Karla Bjrgensen* of Kerteminde on the Store Belt, was typical; 90 feet long and 20 feet beam, drawing 11 feet when laden with 30 tons of slippery eels in her well. The passage around the Skaggerak or through the LimFjord which cuts through North Jutland from the Baltic to North Sea took eight to ten days, depending on weather, and the little ship was hard work for a skipper and two hands but was spotlessly kept with paintwork and rig as smart as a yacht.

As trade expanded, some of the ketches anchored below Osea Island to discharge the eels. Long-handled eel shears, which had blunt-ended tines like Neptune's trident, were used to bring them out into a steel pail, to be weighed on scales set up on deck. Then they were decanted via a canvas chute, into an "eel barge" floating alongside; specially built, barely floating tanks which held hundreds of thousand of eels and were towed up to Heybridge Basin to be unloaded, as required, the eels meanwhile thriving in the clean tidal water of the middle river, without the need for air to be pumped into the water to circulate oxygen as had to be done when the barges lay in the basin. One of these specialised craft was designed and built at Wivenhoe Shipyard in 1948, constructed of wood because of the embargo of steel construction at the yard; a fine piece of calculation for the designer to achieve her floating at the desired waterline with wooden hull, perforated tank holds and a live load.

Peaceful charm on the Chelmer Navigation. This fresh water canal runs from Heybridge Basin to Chelmsford, the county town of Essex. Near Heybridge it is lined with a variety of craft ranging from seagoing yachts to old "tore outs". The canal retains this calm appearance, the hulls and willows mirrored in the weedy surface.   *Douglas Went*

The principal importer at that time was Mr Kuitjen, a Dutchman, to whom the canal and the green sea walls of Colliers Reach were reminiscent of his native land. Wind whispering through the trees lining the canal made it a fascimile of a Dutch, French or Belgian waterway, rippling the weed covered surface around the motley collection of craft moored there, ranging from over-converted ship's lifeboats of the "three decks and no bottom" variety to well-found yachts fit to sail anywhere. Amongst them lay, for many years, the ex-20-rater racer *Japonica*; a yacht which fascinated. She was designed by America's most noted yacht designer, Nathaniel G. Herreshoff, for New York financier Jay Gould and was built by the Herreshoff Manufacturing Company at Bristol, Rhode Island in 1895 as the *Niagra* to race in the 20 rating class, then popular in Britain. Her captain was John Barr, a Scottish skipper who had emigrated to America, and she was successful in many races. The *Niagra* was sold and renamed *Japonica* when altered to a yawl in 1901 and in 1908 became a schooner with an auxiliary motor. After many years as a cruiser her still immaculate black hull, without its deep keel, became a houseboat at Heybridge. She left the Basin under tow in the early 1950s, bound for somewhere in the Thames area, but is believed to have been lost on passage. So ended one of Herreshoff's most successful racers.

Yachts now dominate the basin, which has become a rendezvous for several annual cruises in company by sailing clubs from the lower Blackwater and the River Colne. Members' small yachts jostle through the lock and crowd the weedy waters of the basin in a joyful annual rally such as the Wivenhoe and Rowhedge Yacht Owners' "Gooseberry Pie" event, where the cutting up and eating of a giant pie on board the largest craft is the excuse for the little cruise, which commences with a race from East Mersea Stone to Osea Island.

Sailing men fond of the Blackwater founded the Blackwater Sailing Club at Heybridge during 1899 and quickly established a tradition of cruising far afield, but never lost their love for the river. Leiutenant G. Mulhauser, the yachtsman circumnavigator of the early 1920s in his 60-foot yawl *Amaryllis*, was a member of the Blackwater Sailing Club and during his voyage described the great Trinidad pitch lake "which at first sight resembles Heybridge Basin at low water springs". The Blackwater Sailing Club's building has a tall aspect from being built on the sea wall, while the roofs of other old buildings merely peep over its top. It contains many models and pictures of the Victorian and Edwardian amateur sailors and their modest-sized but able yachts. In later years the club has also sailed one-design dinghies including the 14-foot Sprites, which were also raced by the West Mersea Yacht Club, and members continue to race and cruise far afield.

In the 1920s and 30s Heybridge had a large sawmill and the ship breaking yard of May and Baker, with skeletons of wooden ships having their bones picked on grid-irons. The foot of the wall was strewn with rusty anchors, their colour rivalling the door of the paint shop where thousands of brushes had been cleaned, caking it thick with all the colours used on yachts and barges. Amongst the craft broken up there was the large, American built, wooden four-masted schooner *Gloria*. Her last work had been as a floating cannery for sprats, lying as a hulk in the Colne. Later she was towed to Heybridge and the shipbreakers started work. Usually the principal return from dismantling a wooden ship is the copper and brass fastenings which may be in her construction, some bolts being perhaps 2 inches in diameter and many feet long. To get these out it is often necessary to burn away the surrounding timber and this was done at Heybridge, but the *Gloria* caught fire and burned with such intensity that there were fears she might set fire to Heybridge itself, but eventually she burned out. There was a resumption of this activity after 1945, when wooden minesweepers were berthed there to be scrapped. The shore is now crowded with small yachts and boats and a yard builds and repairs them. Scores of moorings along this side of the reach restrict craft beating up or down river.

Colliers Reach can be a surprising piece of water. In June 1977 my old sailing friend Phil Bollen and I were beating up the Blackwater in his little cutter *Bold Hamster*, punching a freshening gale over a flood tide all the way up from Bradwell. As we turned the buoy into Colliers Reach the *Hamster* met the full force of the south-westerly gale under a double-reefed mainsail and storm jib. She has weathered many a stormy passage and we thought little of this beat up to Maldon after the day's sailing until the first short sea crashed on board, to our surprise, though we had both often sailed through this reach. The cutter only just managed to tack when we neared those confounded moorings. After four or five boards with the astonishingly rough short seas giving us a shaking, she missed stays near the Northey Island shore and began to make a sternboard. We quickly gybed round and recommenced turning upriver, but off Heybridge lock she again missed stays on the Northey side and the anchor had to be hurriedly let go to avoid driving ashore, where lines of jagged old sea wall piles stood up from the high water waves like gaping black teeth, waiting for the cutter's bilge planks. With jib aback and mainsail down we heaved at the bar taut cable but could not bring it in more than a few fathoms before we felt she would drag and go ashore on the piles.

The mainsail was set with the third reef down, and was sheeted in hopefully to drive her ahead a little as we hauled in with much effort. The anchor broke out and we feverishly backed the jib, but she fell off on the inshore tack and it was hurriedly let go again. Fortunately it held, but the only thing to do was to gain sea room by laying out a kedge anchor in the deeper water towards the middle of the reach. We bent all the warps together—and Phil is renowned for long warps—then, waiting for a moment's smooth between waves, he jumped into the dinghy and we stowed the kedge and warp in its stern, to be rowed off and dropped as far out as possible. Phil scrambled back aboard, soaked and having been in some peril in those vicious short seas in the 8-foot pram.

Unfortunately, we could not gain anything on the kedge warp until the main anchor had been recovered and dare not let pay out any more warp to do this or we would be getting into dangerously shoal water, with risk of stranding. We laboured at the hawse and by sheering the helm and much heaving, managed to recover the main anchor and cable which smothered the foredeck, us and the jib with the black mud for which the reach is famous. We now swung to the kedge warp and the kedge was holding well. Now the real work began, the slippery kedge warp sliding through our fingers as it was hauled in foot by foot, pausing for breath in the squalls and gaining as the bow dipped to a short tumbling sea, then holding again. At last we were on a short scope, the mainsail was set and jib prepared, but we could not break that anchor out, so great a weight had been put on it. We felt we were to be cheated out of our tide up to Maldon, where friends waited, but at that moment there was a hail and a launch plunged close by with two men in it shouting and holding a towline. These good samaritans had seen our hour and a half struggle from the Blackwater Sailing Club and had put off to help with the anchor. With their aid we soon had the weight off the warp, but it took all our strength for some time to break the anchor out in the roaring, tearing wind.

Our unknown friends cheered and shouted at the final success and gave us a tow to windward, which we cast off with unintelligible thanks (which are repeated here), and surged on for Maldon just as the tide turned. As we berthed at Dan Webb and Feeseys yard, we for the first time realised our freakishly sea-worn appearance; the mainsail and jib were frosted white half way up and our clothes and faces were caked white with salt. We burst out laughing at near-shipwreck on a river well inland; salty shore indeed!

CHAPTER ELEVEN

The Haven Under The Hill

OUR first arrival at Maldon by water was in the cutter *Girl Pat* during the squally summer of 1949. We had anchored in Colliers Reach, waiting for water and did not get our anchor until a half dozen of Maldon's little cutter smacks came fetching upstream under sail, passing close by. One after another they came creaming up on the flood, gybing with a gentle thud and patter of reef points, to surge upstream around the right angle of Herring Point. We followed, observing the small can buoys and boldly berthing against the Town Quay, close astern of the sailing barge *Centaur*. Our arrival in a smart gaff cutter was watched with interest by a knot of Maldon fishermen seated on the river wall below the black tarred sheds of Walter Cook and Sons barge yard, where the hull of the big *Raybel* was repairing. One of the fishermen, Ted Pitt we afterwards learned, looked down on us from the quay and politely advised moving our berth because as he put it, "People hereabouts throw a lot of rubbish over this quay." Alas, this was true and we hurriedly shifted upstream alongside the *Centaur*, whose skipper assured us we had good soft mud under us at low water and could lie there providing we did not have a deep keel to cut up the berth and spoil it for the flat bottomed barges which sometimes laid there "two bottoms", as bargemen say when lying alongside two abreast.

We learned that Ted Pitt had a cutter-rigged smack, M.N. 17, one of the row which stretched, listed on their port bilges, bows upstream, along the stony shore of "the Hythe", that Saxon name for a landing place. Foresails were stowed on forestays and furled mainsails were swung out, with a guy to ensure a "lust in" on the ebb. 13-foot "skifts", or smacks' rowboats lay along the hard, looking strangely large compared to these small smacks, most of which had tiny, boat-shaped "keeps" of curiously Dutch appearance made fast alongside. These were full of flounders, locally termed "butts', preserved for sale to weekend summer day trippers and their delighted children who, for a few shillings, were presented with a "bend" of half a dozen still flapping flounders on a wire. Many smacks had sacks of oysters hung from their starboard sides to drench in river water as long as possible and keep fresh for despatch by rail or the merchant's lorry.

The West Mersea smack *Charlotte* prepares for the start of the smacks at the Town regatta, 1938.
Douglas Went

William Wyatt, the West Mersea boatbuilder, at the helm of the Mersea smack *Unity* before the start of the annual smack race at the Town Regatta, 1933.
Douglas Went

The Town Quay, Maldon, 1949. The author's boat lies in the foreground, ahead of the sailing barge. Fully-rigged smacks line the Hythe foreshore in the background and the sheds of Walter Cook and Sons bargeyard cluster at the end of the quay.

162

Maldon's fishing connections are ancient. Its fishermen were landing sprats at London in 1547, caught with the stall net, later to be known as the stow net, as used by fishermen from the Colne, Blackwater and elsewhere. There was no desire or need for expansion of the fisheries, the catches usually being sold locally in those days of horse-drawn transport and poor roads.

In past centuries Maldon fishermen have been adventurous. In 1581 a Trinity House return recorded that during the previous five years the fishing vessels at Maldon had increased by two craft of 25 tons; a size favoured for the North Sea fisheries or even the annual voyage to Iceland lining for cod from March until the end of summer, though it is doubtful that Maldon fishermen ever participated in this trade, which was later centred on Harwich.

In 1865 there were 30 small cutter smacks working from Maldon, trawling flat fish and eels and dredging oysters. Until the mid-nineteenth century Maldon fishermen were probably more adventurous and owned larger smacks which fished well beyond the Essex coast. In 1816 the Maldon shipwrights Williamson and Durden were advertising a 24-ton smack, ''now ready to launch, particularly calculated for the Jersey oyster fishery'', which was then worked by considerable numbers of smacks from the Colne and some from West Mersea. The Maldon men occasionally turned smugglers. In 1832 the smack *Charlotte* of Maldon was rummaged by the Customs men at Gravesend and found to have 14,402 pounds of tobacco slung around her below water in casks, ready for dropping at a rendezvous.

The small Maldon smacks generally had a transom stern, were cutter-rigged and often clinker-planked. Some were leaky and ill-found, even for their work within the river or ''on the Main'', which most regarded as ''going to sea''! One old Maldon fishermen named Taylor used to crouch over his tiller as his little craft drove down the Blackwater bound to trawl for eels on the Mersea Flats, muttering ''Blow wind, blow. A poor ole man and a poor ole boat''. Soon after, he managed to have a new carvel planked cutter built and bowled bravely down shouting to his mate ''Blow wind, blow. A brand new boat and a bloody tough ole man''!

Soon after 1900 a few Maldon smacks sailed round to the River Stour to trawl eels, working up the river almost to Manningtree, to the rage of the locals who also caught them with an eelgaw or spear, or by babbing from punts with lines, all resulting in small quantities. The Maldon men did well as the Stour was then full of eelgrass, like a green field. But the Manningtree men prevailed on the conservancy to limit all trawling to below Harkstead. Eel trawling disappeared with the eelgrass from the Mersea Flats before 1914 and the Maldon fishermen settled to the staples of trawling and peter netting for flatfish, dredging oysters, winkling and occasional wildfowling. Their modest way of life was in keeping with the usually poor returns.

During the 1920s and 30s some Maldon men bought redundant small smacks from Mersea fishermen, with whom they always had an informal working relationship, which bristled up a little in the annual tussles of the West Mersea Town Regatta smack races, which Maldon cutters sometimes won. As late as the 1950s Ernie Pitt was winning prizes there with the *Polly*. Counters do not seem to have become fashionable in Maldon smacks until after 1918 when several, such as the fast little *Polly*, had counters built on over their transoms to add deck space for oyster dredging. By then many had laid the topmast ashore but in the 1930s about a score of these little "bald-headed" cutters were still without engines, though ten years later most had a propeller under the quarter, driven by a converted car engine or a chuffing single cylinder Thornycroft.

Arthur Bennett, that consummate seafarer and shipbroker, who once owned his own floating homes in the sailing barges *June* and later the *Henry*, lay at Maldon during the summer of 1949, when he recorded something of the local waterside scene. Of the smacks he wrote of a morning high water:

". . . down below Cook's barge yard, the smacks lining the beach and the trees beyond lay mirrored in the placid waters.

They had been busy, these little Maldon smacks with their lovely flowing run, and the income tax man was said to be paying his unwelcome attentions. It was on account of oysters, though, not fish, for with the biggest fall of spat within living memory there had been much dredging for young oyster brood. The oyster companies took most of them for relaying on the beds. After four or five years of careful tending, if they survived the hazards of frosts, limpets and five-fingers, they will be ready to tickle the palate of the gourmet. The initial price of 3s. 6d. per hundred was too good to last; prices began to drop, so that some of the men were tempted to lease patches of the river bed and lay down young oysters to fatten for their own account. But human nature being what it is and with all the ingrained rivalry between the local families, perhaps it is not altogether surprising that some folk hinted of poaching and other nefarious 'goings-on'.

As I stood on deck, bucket in hand, that early morning, watching gulls lazily contending over some titbit on the river, there came the sound of a mainsail halyard block. The smacks were getting under way. One after the other, a dozen or more made sail and dropped down on the ebb. They all had a propeller tucked away under their shapely quarters, but there was no call for a motor. There was a light air westerly and the tide served. It was a sight almost unique these days."

The little fleet of sailing smacks dwindled during the late 1950s and broke up during the next ten years. There are still small motor fishing boats at Maldon, but the little cutters are nowadays used for pleasure sailing, often restored to their workaday appearance of thirty years ago.

The Maldon smack *Polly* fetches down the Blackwater in light airs on 19th March 1953 with Ernie Pitt at the tiller. The trawl head on her quarter tells she is after soles. The *Polly* is still sailed for pleasure.

Arthur Bennett

John Howard built many of the little Maldon smacks at his shipways yard, at the foot of North Street, including the *Sisters, Faith, Care, William, Rose Maud* and the slippery little *Polly*. which remains one of the fastest competitors in the Colne and Blackwater races for smack yachts. Howard also designed and built many small yachts, all of which were good sailers. Included in them were a few "gunning yachts" for gentlemen wildfowlers who liked to sail in winter as well as summer, and were off down the Blackwater or "on the main" with a punt or two on deck, to lie snug in a creek or rill, then set out with punt and shoulder guns for the evening or morning flight. Most gunning yachts were armed with a swivel gun, usually mounted on the foredeck or the coachroof amidships, when it was always fired to windward. These all-weather yachts usually cruised in search of the Brent geese, the crew keeping quiet when approaching fowl, with heads below the bulwarks. The yacht was sailed up to the geese on a reach, bringing them under the lee bow, then, as they rose, she was put about and the gun fired, the yacht beating after the flight to recover the birds and despatching the cripples with shoulder guns, recovering them with the punt always carried on the deck of these craft. The 32-foot 5 inch centreboard cutter *Scoter* launched in 1894 was typical. She was designed and built for Count de la Chappelle, a noted local wildfowling lawyer, of French extraction, who lived at Tollesbury and sailed the *Scoter* in fine weather or foul with a fisherman as hand. Later she passed to the east coast of Scotland, owned by artist Colin Grierson and the Count would hardly recognise the sturdy, bermudian rigged cutter she has become, with voyages to Sweden, Denmark and other continental countries in her log.

165

In 1894 Howard's advertisement described his business as "John T. Howard. M.I.N.A. I.M.C. Yacht designer and modeller. Building of all kinds of yachts. Barges, sailing and rowing boats. Repairs to every description of craft thoroughly executed. Designs and estimates furnished. The newly built sailing boat *Bessie*, carrying 20-30 passengers, may be engaged for Blackwater or sea trips." He was a thoroughly technical designer and an able practical builder of small craft, designing by draughting and calculations and employing good craftsmen to produce sound work.

John Sadd's cutter yacht *Ripple* fetches down the Blackwater from Maldon, her home port for more than seventy years. She was designed and built there by John Howard in 1877 as a cruising yacht of moderate draught and continued sailing into the 1950s.

The 47-foot cutter *Ripple* was amongst Howard's larger yachts, designed and built in 1877 for John P. Sadd, and launched as a yawl with the slight draught of 5 foot 6 inches for her 47 foot length. She was still sailing in the early 1950s. Elsewhere on the waterside Barr and Hockham built the smack *Joseph T*

166

and probably others, besides small yachts. In earlier times some smacks were built there by James Williamson, who launched the cutter *Boadicea* in 1808 as a clinker-planked 28-footer with a 10 foot 4 inch beam. At first she worked from Burnham then, in 1825, she was sold to John Pewter of Tollesbury, remaining owned there for almost a century, sailed by the Binks family after 1871, and then passing to E. W. French at West Mersea, from whose family she was bought by her present owner, Michael Frost, of Colchester. Michael has sailed and fished for pleasure with the *Bodie*, as she is affectionately known on the Blackwater, for over forty years and in the early 1960s commenced the task of completely rebuilding her at Tollesbury. The result is a "new" early nineteenth century small smack, with workmanship which will ensure she should sail into the twenty-second century. He has described his experiences with the *Boadicea* in his charming book of that title.

Small sailing coasters and barges for many trades were built at Maldon. In 1882 William Basham was described as a "Yacht, ship and barge builder of Bath Place". His yard may have been at the upriver side of the small creek which then ran in immediately below the salt water pool, which survives by the waterside, though the creek has long since been filled in. Wooden sheds and stores stood there in the 1880s and probably some barge blocks, and sizeable craft were brought there for repair.

From the 1870s until the early 1890s Samuel Finch built barges and boats at the Hythe, probably in the yard later occupied by Cook and Woodward and afterwards known as Walter Cook and Son.

Ben Handley's fleet of spritsail rigged pleasure boats lay below the creek in the 1890s, painted white and green. Mr Handley, senior, was a retired pilot and spent his declining years lamenting the arrival of the railway in Maldon, which reduced and finally killed the trade of the small square riggers which had been his pride.

Maldon is the only Blackwater community which gives an impression of age and its siting on a hill probably means it was inhabited by ancients seeking a defensible place close to water. The road up Maldon hill will quickly disillusion any who still regard Essex as a flat county and from the tower of St Mary's church, by the waterside, the Crouch and the North Sea can be viewed on a fine day. The course of the Blackwater at Maldon is peculiar. It flows southward below the hill of Wickham Bishops as an inland river, through Langford almost to Beeleigh Mill, which is on the River Chelmer. Then it runs parallel with the Chelmer almost to Maldon Fullbridge, where it turns northward and flows almost in a semi-circle around Potman Marsh, returning south to a confluence with the Chelmer at the mouth of Heybridge Creek, below Maldon's quays. The main stream, technically the Chelmer, is tidal to Beeleigh Mill and, as the "Blackwater", up Heybridge Creek, under the stone bridge at the north end of the causeway leading from the foot of Maldon Hill to Heybridge village.

167

Maldon Hythe on a summer's day in the early 1950s. Sailing smacks and gun punts lie on the hard and a barge is at the Town Quay. Fishermen sit on the wall and the scene breathes the peace of the river before the sailing boom.   *Douglas Went*

Craft lie snug at Maldon, no matter how hard it blows. But it can be deceptive for setting forth on a voyage without a good look at the speed of the clouds, as there is invariably more wind further downstream. We watched the clouds and stayed for two days on that first visit, fascinated by the survival of workaday sail, from the hull of Sully's black *Raybel*, refitting on the blocks at Walter Cook and Sons bargeyard, and the sturdy *Ethel Maud* and *Dawn* at the town quay, to the sail loft making canvas for the barge fleet, then still ninety strong on the coast.

At the barge yard we yarned with shipwrights fitting a new wale strake to the *Raybel*, on the blocks by the river wall and poked our heads into the shed where Alf Last built delightfully shaped clinker boats for barges and smacks. The other day I saw one left on a mooring off the Royal Yacht Squadron, her bold shape and sturdy craftsmanship looking outstandingly seaworthy against the dainty yachts nearby. The yard was then owned by Mr Cliff Cook, but in the later 1960s passed to Barry Pierce, whose shipwrights rebuild and repair most of the remaining barges now sailed for pleasure, and other craft, the yard contributing considerably to the almost unchanged appearance of Maldon from the river.

Further along the waterside a number of neat wooden sheds set by a tiny meadow held the sail loft of Arthur G. Taylor and Son. We peeped inside. Bill Raven sat sewing barge sails at his bench; a voluminous foresail, half finished, spread flax canvas over his white apron and far over the bumpy, polished floor with its chalked shapes of sails and bales of sailcloth and delightfully smelling coils of tarred hemp rope. His experience stretched back to working on the sails of the famous ketch barge *Record Reign*, in the 1890s. Fred Taylor, also in a white apron and a trilby hat, bustled about but his kindly nature took time to show us the big old books of sail plans going back to the end of the nineteenth century, holding details of sails for all sorts of craft; ketch barges, smacks, cutter yachts and luggers amongst them. In later years he was to make a suit of sails for me, and others for craft which I had designed.

The loft was established by Joseph Sadler, a sailmaker and ship chandler originally in business at Heybridge Basin before moving to Maldon about 1870, with a sail loft and wharf formerly a granary, at the Hythe, where he advertised, besides sailmaking and chandlery, "Paints, oils, leads, varnishes etc. Buntings and flags of every design. Best prices given for all kinds of second hand ships stores. Estimates given for complete outfits." In 1914 his versatile business was bought by one of his employees, Arthur Taylor, and afterwards was carried on by his son Fred, who retired in 1969 as a well liked and respected member of the waterside community. The sail loft is now owned by Gerald Dennis, who continues the traditions of his predecessors and still makes sails for barges and smacks, besides those for more modern craft. Sadler's loft was rivalled in the 1880s by sailmakers John Bruce Low, also at the Hythe, and James Heale in

Cross Road. Mrs Hannah Barbrook of Church Street hung out her sign as a marine store dealer in competition with Charles Sargeant of Wantz Road.

In earlier times Maldon had a ropewalk where men spun hemp and manilla into cordage and rope and along the Hythe, close to Cook's bargeyard, the little shed of W. Burch, "Shipsmith and block maker" stood until recent years.

Maldon was the only Blackwater port to build ships as distinct from the smacks and other small craft constructed at Tollesbury, West Mersea and Heybridge. Naval shipbuilding was giving work to Colne yards at Wivenhoe in the mid-seventeenth century and some were also built at Maldon by a Mr Starline. In 1654 the 50-gun frigate *Jersey* took the water from Starline's yard. This fine 556-tonner was 101 feet long and 32 feet beam. Captain Terry took her to sea but in 1669 Samuel Pepys was appointed her captain; though he never went on board her! Naval red tape is nothing new, as in those times only captains could attend courts martial and Pepys, who was directly concerned in one, was given "command" of a ship he never saw.

The *Jersey* served in the wars against the Dutch which followed the restoration of the monarchy to the throne. She fought in the four days battle in the North Sea in 1666 and at the battle of Solebay, off Southwold, Suffolk, six years later. A few weeks after she was commissioned the *Jersey* was dismasted in a channel gale. She also served in the West Indies and the Mediterranean but was captured by the French in home waters in 1691. They refitted her as a privateer and while cruising for prizes she met a squadron of English warships and was sunk. The site of Starline's yard is unknown but it was probably where Dan Webb and Feeseys yacht yard now stands. It must have been well established to contract for a ship of *Jersey's* size, and probably built several others.

But Maldon's greatest maritime interest was in shipping rather than shipbuilding and during the eighteenth and nineteenth centuries the port flourished and Maldon owners and seafarers speculated and voyaged in scores of brigs and brigantines, ketches and schooners, besides barges of all types and sizes. Some were built at Maldon, such as the 108-ton schooner *Wave* launched in 1848. Much of this trade was coastwise or to the North Sea coasts of the continent, but sometimes they ventured to the Baltic, Norway and the Mediterranean. In contrary winds the unhandy square riggers were backed and filled up the Blackwater's upper reaches, were sometimes kedged along in calms or in tight corners, or were towed by their boat, if the hard worked crew had sufficient strength left after all the pulley hauley of square rig. These chubby bowed, kettle-bottomed wooden worlds bred seamen used to hard times and owners who were thrifty and put much of their profit into more ships, so for years Maldon was a community with many shipmasters and seamen, and cockbilled yards and tall topmasts soared above the quays where men toiled to load and discharge the dark holds by hand.

Maldon Hythe in 1955. Fully-rigged smacks at moorings before the black sheds of Walter Cook and Sons bargeyard. The stern of one of Green's mill barges, probably the *Ethel Ada*, shows at right against the quay, where the ketch-rigged yacht *Topsy* awaits a charter party for a week's sailing.   *Douglas Went*

By the early eighteenth century and probably long before, a regular service of sailing hoys carried cargo, goods and passengers from Maldon to London, returning with similar freights and fulfilled orders for the town's shopkeepers and merchants. During the eighteenth century the malting trade to London increased and led to further growth in the Maldon fleet of coasters and sailing barges. Even during the Napoleonic wars, trade into Maldon was considerable by contemporary standards; over 6,000 tons of coal and 4,000 tons of other goods were landed there for onward transport to Chelmsford. Vessels of 200 tons drawing up to 12 feet could get up to the quays, as motor coasters still do, probably due to the River Chelmer, above the Fullbridge, having been straightened and altered in 1812 to scour the berths and bed between the bridge and the hythe.

Mid-Victorian trade led to the Maldon Harbour Act being passed in 1865 and about £10,000 was spent in widening, deepening and improving the river from the Fullbridge to about 50 yards upstream of Heybridge Basin; the rivalry with the hated ''Basiners'' still rankled! The value of this work was doubted by local seafarers who lost their free river and port. All vessels coming above Heybridge Basin had to pay a scale of tolls and to independent Essex men an even worse aspect was that their berths came under the jurisdiction of a harbour master.

By then there were six Trinity House pilots living in the town, bringing vessels up to around 300 tons to Heybridge and smaller craft up to Maldon's Fullbridge.

Maldon registered craft then included 26 schooners, 21 brigs and brigantines, 20 cutters and ketches and more than 80 sailing barges. These and many other vessels brought coal, timber, chalk, lime, manure, bricks, cement and big logs to discharge at its quays. Outward cargoes included hay and straw, corn, and root crops. Ballast was delivered to ships requiring it at the town quays and downstream at Latchingdon Hole and off Stansgate. Each week several brigs or brigantines, local or otherwise, worked up to Maldon and Heybridge with coal from the north east coast ports; some of the hundreds of colliers then laboriously working up and down the east coast; "Overloaded, undermanned, trusting to a slant". Most carried about 200 tons or just under, but the rates fell heavily when the railway was extended to Maldon and soon killed the seaborne coal trade, besides affecting the carriage of many other commodities.

Granaries and wharves for hay, straw and agricultural produce lined the river up to the Fullbridge and there was considerable trade by water for merchants including Eve, Hicks, Rutt, Warren and Humphreys, Isaac and others. There were lime kilns and railway sidings, and even a nut and bolt factory! John Gozzett, a builder and contractor, was offering "bricks, lime, cement, timber, slates, tiles etc. supplied to the trade at wharf prices". There were several sidings connecting with the Great Eastern Railway at nearby Maldon station and it was proposed to form a dock opening into Heybridge Creek, alongside the station, in what became known as Railway Pond, but this was abandoned.

Like most contemporary British maritime communities, Maldon shipowners organised their own insurance scheme in the Maldon Mutual Marine Insurance Association Ltd, with offices at Creek and Freemantle's in the town. There were also two companies specialising in the insurance of local sailing barges. Freights were fixed in Walter Locker's shipbroking office by the Fullbridge.

Maldon is noted for the production of good quality salt for table or pickling use and the Maldon Crystal Salt Company works is the survivor of the several mentioned in the Norman Domesday Book as being on the upper Blackwater. It produces salt of an unusual purity, once much in demand for pickling and now appreciated by gourmets, food manufacturers, processors and many customers abroad. During the mid-eighteenth century a Maldon Saltworks was operated by Charles Coe and a brother. At that time Charles also owned Osea Island and they were a leading business family in the area. During the 1880s Thomas Worraker was a salt and spirit merchant in Butt Lane, besides owning ships.

Maldon men were keen wildfowlers, both for a winter living and for sport. In the heyday of wildfowl punt gunning, during the mid-nineteenth century, a fowler might drop down on the ebb for a winter night's shooting and return with 80-100 fowl. The Maldon gunners made some remarkable bags. Charles Hipsey once shot 75 widgeon at one discharge and 15 more were picked up by other puntsmen. John Basham shot 288 oxbirds (Dunlin) when he fired at a flock settled on ice and Harry Handley shot 432 of these tiny birds with two successive shots off Stansgate. Basham's son John bagged 108 knots (Marle) with one firing off Bradwell but Charles Hipsey went one better, bagging 320 knots; as many birds as there were shots in his gun. However, these records were small compared with the 471 black geese shot in the river by 14 guns, or the 704 which 32 punters shot. A Maldoner named Stubbins bagged 50 at the mouth of Thirslet Creek and William Handley got 120 geese with three successive shots and also got another 24 *dozen* geese in the same week.

Like fishermen, wildfowlers are men close to natural things and the harsher the winter the more chance of good bags of fowl. They see the cold, windy dawns and paddle to a favourite creek or salting for the morning and evening flight, when most fowl are shot. Puntsmen lie in wait in the frost rimed fogs of January; cold and cramped, frozen-fingered, ears and eyes alert for sounds of feeding birds, the river full of swirling ice floes bringing an added hazard to the frail punts, faced because of the tremendous flocks winter encourages to the estuary.

Maldon was noted for its gun punts which were flat bottomed with almost vertical sides formed with two broad strakes. The usual length was 16 foot 6 inches to 17 foot and the beam 2 foot 8 inches to 2 foot 10 inches. John Howard was the noted local builder and the type was handy for "setting to fowl" as the narrow beam enabled the puntsmen to use his arms to best effect at the paddles or with push sticks in shallow water. However, this also made them easily upset. The Maldon punts were often sailed, using a single spritsail set on a short mast stepped to one side of the gunstock, through a thwart. The rig was usually used to ease the labour of rowing up and down river over long distances but the punts were keenly raced in regattas at Maldon and Heybridge, when larger spritsails were set and the puntsmen steered with an oar over the lee quarter, balanced against a foot, with the body weight to windward in a breeze. The punts went to windward surprisingly well in smooth water. There were also rowing races for punts and in 1950 Maldon's Ernie Pitt was still winning at the age of seventy-six.

Maldon always seems to have attracted more than its share of characters. During the 1890s the versatile H. Bate of 11 Market Hill was in business as a "Gun and bicycle maker, cutler and optician". He advertised "Guns and revolvers of every description. Cartridges and ammunition for muzzle loaders.

Agent for Singers Coventry Machinist Co. and 'Star' cycles. Bicycles, tricycles and perambulators for sale. Every description of best Sheffield cutlery at moderate prices. Sole agent for Henry Laurance's spectacles. Repairs of all kinds at shortest notice. Guns, bicycles, etc. for hire". Contemporarily the *Ship and Anchor Hotel* at 188 High Street was presided over by Samuel Shawyer (late sergeant-major 7th Hussars). In contrast Henry Handley, who kept *The Welcome Home* in North Street also described himself as a "yacht owner" with forty years experience of the River Blackwater. "The commodious yacht *Lark* (18 tons) is available for tidal and sea trips and may be hired by day, week or longer periods. Special arrangements for shooting parties during the winter season. Punt guns of 120 lbs and 90 lbs."

A view of Maldon regatta, taken from the church tower in 1896. A sailing race for gun punts is in progress at centre, between the barges anchored as spectator craft and the white yacht at anchor off the bathing machines along the beach. Smacks are anchored in the mouth of the shallow creek which ran behind the enclosed bathing place. In the foreground the sailing barge *Dawn* is in frame at Cook and Woodward's bargeyard.

During the 1890s Maldon was attempting to become something of a resort for day visitors, encouraged by its rail link with the main line to London. Benjamin T. Handley of the Bath House, the Hythe, Maldon was offering "safe rowing boats on hire. Sailing boats manned by competent men.

Bathing machines with the best of attention. Rowing on lake at any state of the tide. Established 54 years (1840), never an accident.'' Competitive rowing was then a popular sport amongst working people in waterside communities and the Reverend Edward Horwood was president of the Maldon Rowing Club with headquarters at the *Kings Head Hotel* and a boathouse at the Hythe. The thirty members rowed in colours of dark blue and primrose.

At the end of the nineteenth century many at Maldon wished the town to develop facilities for yachts and yachtsmen and reap something from the sports expansion, as for instance Tollesbury was doing. However, all the foreshore from the lane below St Mary's church to the end of the path which served the town as a promenade was owned by one aged mariner, who refused to sell to Maldon Corporation. But yachting in the grand style did not become established at Maldon, very few of whose seafarers served as professional yacht hands and none so far as I know as skippers of yachts of any size. The late Ted Pitt, smack owner and fisherman, told me he was one season in John R. Pyanes 12-metre racing yacht *Vanity* during the early 1930s but, as he said, after six months of yacht racing he felt ''tore out'' and never repeated the experience. In 1927 local members of the London-based Little Ship Club established the ''Maldon Little Ship Club'', and their monthly half crown dinners at the *Rose and Crown* were the meeting place of many east coast and London cruising men. The club has continued to flourish and its members are amongst the most active sailing from the river.

During the 1940s the green-hulled yawl *Topsy* often lay at the town quay. She sailed out of Maldon with paying guests who were usually treated to a sail to West Mersea, Bradwell and Brightlingsea, where various pubs were visited and a cheerful time was had. It was reputed that, one tide, the *Topsy* lifted from her berth at Maldon quay and her keelbolts could stand the strain no longer, leaving her iron keel struck fast in the mud. She was built at Brightlingsea by Robert Aldous as a smack yacht for Mr Lidell, for whom he had also built the 114-ton steam yacht *Anemone V* in 1906. Later the *Topsy* returned to the yard to be lengthened and re-rigged as a yawl. Below the Fullbridge, at the foot of Maldon's steep hill, was a pool of deep water. In this lay the red-hulled cutter *Molly*; the pride of her young crew who sailed her hard and appeared bravely at the Blackwater regattas, complete with jackyard topsail and, whenever possible, a mastheadsman aloft.

The earliest known regatta held at Maldon was in 1783, and probably included races for fishing smacks, the few pleasure boats then owned in the area, rowing and sculling races and watersports.

The yachtbuilding tradition was carried on at Maldon by Dan Webb who, after John Howard's business closed, reopened the Shipways yard in 1921 to build small yachts and lay-up and repair others. Like his contemporary David Hillyard of Littlehampton, Dan had worked in the Colne shipyards and both realised the need for small, modestly priced craft suitable for coastal cruising and built to a standard design and specification to reduce costs. His 18 and 20 foot "Blackwater Sloops" have been popular since the early 1930s and although the standard 27 foot motor cruiser he introduced in 1930 never achieved a following, he was anticipating a since lucrative market. After his retirement the yard was continued as Dan Webb and Feesey and since the tragic death afloat of Jack Feesey, has been ably carried on by the Swinton family.

Further upstream along the riverside known as "The Downs", Dixon Kerley developed to build and repair yachts on the site of older premises. During the 1930s these were owned by Charles Barker and in his black tarred shed was built one of Maldon's larger and most interesting yachts. Walter Stewart was a canoeist, a lifelong devotee of paddle and sail who in 1886 and 1888 won the Challenge Cup of the New York Canoe Club in sailing races on Lake George, New York. His love of sailing and modest means to indulge it led to the designing and building of several small cruising yachts all having shoal draught, pointed sterns and light displacement, from his canoeing experience. This series culminated in the *Escapade*, on which he lived for long periods, often mooring in Heybridge Basin. In 1937 his son, Tony, designed a 45-foot bermudian cutter with small displacement, long ends, a true canoe stern and wineglass sections. In the blaze of development of small seagoing yachts during the late 1930s this design was conceived as a fast cruiser with a chance in offshore racing. Her mast was stepped almost amidships. She was two years building, with every frame selected by the designer before cutting.

Maldon Hythe on regatta day, 1896. Smacks and barges predominate as there were then few yachts at Maldon. It appears a smack race has just finished, with many competitors anchored at the right. Twenty smacks are visible in this photograph.

The 127-ton brigantine *Emma Eden* was owned by R. Eden of Maldon, who was also her master. She was typical of the many small square-rigged vessels owned at and trading to Maldon until the late nineteenth century in the coastal and European trades. Some ventured to the Baltic and the Mediterranean. The *Emma Eden* was built at Sunderland in 1840 as a "Snow"; a type of brig having a secondary mast abaft the mainmast, to which the luff of the spanker was bent.

Netherlands Historical Museum, Amsterdam

Unfortunately war commenced before she was completed and the hull stood in Charlie Barker's yard until she was bought and completed by John Sadd in 1947 and was launched as the *Amione*. My first sight of her was when sailing up the Wallet one day in our little cutter and watching with fascination the leaning sails of a yacht coming up rapidly astern and pointing unusually high. Soon she overhauled us and slashed past with an easy, pitching motion. There was a wave from her helmsman and she left us with a view of her cheekily lifting stern.

A century after the brigs and brigantines crowded Maldon's quays, its river remains filled with activity. Scores of small yachts, old and new, conventional and very unorthodox, lie on moorings and in mud berths wherever there is room. Week-end sailors crowd the clubs and pubs and as one local put it, "Blast mate, yew need sea boots to stand in them bars when that sailin' lot run on about gales in the Swin and carryin' away sails"! Yachts, sailing barges and an occasional coaster come and go on the tide and the lure of the first of the morning ebb running in sun glitter seaward remains as strong as ever to those who take their pleasure afloat.

CHAPTER TWELVE

The Maldon Barges

SAILING barges have probably been owned and sailed from Maldon since the type was first used on the east coast. The town's barge trade was principally the carriage of hay and straw to London from farms by the Blackwater, but quantities of oilcake, lime, coal and chalk were shipping in, along with cargoes of manure from London stables. There was also a large trade in grain and timber, much of which came to John Sadd's timber wharf. The older Maldon "stackies" included the *James and Harriet, Friends Goodwill, Good Intent, New Hope* and the ancient and quaintly named *Honest Miller* and *Rouge in Grain*. Owners included Smee, Eve, Sadd, Gutteridge, Piggott, Seex, Keeble and Murrell.

During the mid-nineteenth century many Maldon barges were built on the Thames or in Kent; strongly constructed but usually full-bowed and with tucked-up quarters which did not encourage speed. Taylor's yard at Murston built the *Keeble* and *Diligent* in the 1870s and these were still in use as lighters at Heybridge Basin eighty years later. Ebenezer Keeble ordered several barges from Robert Shrubsall of Milton, Kent. The *New Hope*, owned by Eve, a miller, was built at Whitstable in Kent in 1872. She was tiller-steered, as was then normal; a flat-sheered stack barge with a long sprit and a short topmast setting an almost horizontally headed topsail.

The local barge trade was at its peak between about 1870-1914 and during that time and possibly earlier, barges were insured by the Maldon Barge Insurance Club, with offices in London Road. Their insurance limits were set between Orfordness in Suffolk and the North Foreland in Kent; the Maldoner's usual trading area, though occasionally a barge would voyage to the Humber for coal or venture down Channel with a freight.

During the 1880s there were about 65 Maldon registered barges and local owners seemed to buy and sell craft frequently, leading to change in the town's fleet. There were many owners. Eve the miller had the *City of London* and *New Hope* and Howard built the *Jess* for him; an unlucky barge, run down and sunk during fog by a railway steamer in Harwich harbour. Henry Stevens had the *Albion, Burnham* and *Eva Annia*. Samuel Thompson owned the *William and Elizabeth, Diligent* and the *Ann Elizabeth* and James and

Ebenezer Keeble owned at various times the barges *Eva Annie, Sunbeam, Emily, Keeble, Burnham* and *Diligent.* George Batt contented himself with the sturdy *Sunbeam.*

Like the Rivers Crouch and Roach, Stour and Orwell, the Blackwater had its solitary little river barge; the Brightlingsea-built 18-tonner *Energy,* launched in 1866 and usually carrying cargoes between Bradwell and Maldon as a feeder service to the town's hay and straw merchants. Before 1914 there were still about 45 sailing barges owned at Maldon. A couple of stack barges left each week for London and half a dozen men found a living "huffling".

Sailing barges were built and repaired at Maldon during the period 1870-18195 by Samuel Finch, William Basham and Cook and Woodward. By 1879 John Howard, noted as Maldon's leading builder of yachts, smacks and barges, commenced designing and building barges at his yard at the foot of North Street, where the premises of Dan Webb and Feesey now stand. His first barge was the 44-ton *Surprise,* launched in 1879 for William Strutt, Maldon hay and straw merchant who also owned the same sized barge *Two Friends.* The 42-ton *Rose* followed in 1880 for Samuel Thompson, another hay and straw merchant in the town, and next year the round-sterned *Oak* slid down the ways for John Sadd, the Maldon timber merchant, who also ordered the *Cypress* in 1887 and owned the *Falcon,* built at Paglesham, on the River Roach, in 1868 and the Maldon built *James and Harriet.* The *Surprise* ended her working life in Kent, owned by Burley in the brick trade at Sittingbourne and finished as a hulk at Queenborough. The *Rose* was finally cut down as a lighter for the Heybridge Basin timber trade.

In 1883 John Howard designed and built his largest trading barge, the 113-ton ketch *Malvoisin*, for Burnham owners; a giant amongst the stackies of Maldon. Later she was owned at Whitstable by Anderson and was typical of these bold "boomies", as these barges were known from the boom and gaff mainsail and mizzen. These carried cargoes to many ports on the east and south coasts of England and frequently to and from Germany, Holland, Belgium and France as well. These leeboard ketches had a crew of four and even then were hard work and sometimes unprofitable. They were uncomfortable on passage in a Channel sea, as the flat bottom pounded when light, but the ability to sail without the expense and loss of time of ballasting was their principal advantage over the earlier round-bottomed ketches and schooners whose work they frequently displaced in many trades.

Charles Gutteridge of Maldon owned the spritsail barges *Ready* and the *Morning Star*, winner of one of the early Maldon barge races. In 1888 he ordered the *Mermaid* from John Howard and in the early 1890s matched her reputation for speed against the Howard built *Hyacinth*, launched in 1889 and owned by Edward Bentall of Heybridge. The course was a real test, much longer than those sailed in other barge races; starting from Maldon, then rounding the Cork Light vessel off Felixstowe, Suffolk, and returning to Maldon; about 75 miles. The *Mermaid* won the wager and was probably the fastest barge owned at Maldon. For 28 years she was skippered by that shrewd little bargeman Billy Austin, frequently trading between Maldon and the Medway. She finished her days as a yacht barge. She was involved in an unusual mishap in the late 1920s when her chine stranded on the edge of Maldon Town Quay. Fortunately timbers were able to be slipped under the chine amidships and as the tide fell these bore the weight of the barge safely back into the river until the next tide floated and righted her.

Mayland was launched in 1888 for farmer James Cardnell of St Lawrence, downstream, and survived in trade in the ownership of Reg Prior, the Burnham yachtbuilder, into the 1950s. Howard built the 45-ton *Violet* in 1889 for Bentall. The 49-ton *Ready* was built in 1892 for William Walter Keeble for his stack trade. She was only 5 foot 8 inches deep yet carried a large rig when completed, the sprit being 63 feet long and the topmast 44 feet. John Howard accompanied the Keeble family on her first trip and took the wheel as she turned to windward up Swin. She was not sailing well, as he pinched her, and old Jim Keeble at last turned to him saying, "Yew built a good barge, but yew can't sail her, that yew can't. Let my nevvy take her, he'll make her goo." But her large sail area was too much for her and she returned to Maldon to have 7 feet removed from the sprit end. She was a fast barge and about 1900 raced against Seabrook's *D'Arcy* and *Defender* and Marriage's Colchester *Fleur de Lys* at Brightlingsea regatta, which that year unusually featured a barge race. The *D'Arcy* went so far as to have her bottom

The Maldon stack barge *Unity* in the lower Pool of London with a deck stack of hay during 1884. The skipper stands on top of the stack and she has the smaller "stack foresail" bent and the mainsail is temporarily reduced by reefing to set above the deck load.

blackleaded for speed but the *Ready* was busy unloading a freight of London muck up the Blackwater and had only time for a quick tar round before entering, to beat the lot. Later, she too passed to Francis and Guilders, was renamed *Mirosa*, and for many years was sailed by Billy Austin and his mate Jack; a pair of the most competent bargemen one could meet, each knowing exactly what the other would do or wish to do in all circumstances, handling the *Mirosa* like a racing dinghy and always keeping her smart.

By 1894 they were getting larger; *D'Arcy* was 56 tons, built for Richard Seabrook of Tolleshunt D'Arcy who also owned the tiller-steered stack barge *Pride of Essex*, launched at Limehouse on the Thames in 1857, and who later ordered the 63-ton *Defender*, launched in 1900, which cost £2,150 compared with the then usual £1,250 for a similar craft built elsewhere. But owners were willing to pay Howard's prices for he had a great flair for designing a fast barge and certainly the surviving craft from his yard are all shapely enough, even in old age. Always he designed in detail by draughting and calculation, as befitted a qualified naval architect who was constantly striving for refinement and seldom built two craft alike, though often there were four barges laid down at once in his yard.

The *Saltcote Belle* was perhaps the prettiest of all Howard's shapely barges, launched in 1895 for Frederick May of Stisted but working to Saltcote Maltings, below Heybridge. Later she passed to Colchester barge owners Francis and Guilders' fleet and was still working under sail without an engine in the early 1950s with a young skipper and mate of eighteen and sixteen years of age respectively. She was in collision with a steamer in the Thames estuary,

The *Ready* working up to Maldon with a deck stack of timber in 1936. She was renamed *Mirosa* in 1945 and is still sailing as a yacht.

Arthur Bennett

which almost brought down her mast and sprit and ran back to Hole Haven for temporary repairs, then put to sea again but got into trouble in the Spitway, that treacherous shallow gutway between the hard Buxey and Gunfleet sands, off Clacton. The *Saltcote Belle* dragged over the sands with two anchors down, making water until there was 18 inches over the cabin floor. The crew burned flares and the lifeboat arrived to take them off but the barge remained afloat and was eventually brought in by two fishing smacks to have her cargo of maize discharged and the bilges cleaned. Soon after she was sold for a yacht.

The 64-ton *Emma* came out in 1897, owned by Simeon Stanes of Maldon and was reckoned by many to be the fastest barge out of the Blackwater. She was lost during the 1939-45 war when a mine exploded as she was unloading from a steamer at Rotherhithe, blowing off her stern. The skipper and mate escaped unhurt. The *Emma* was often in the coastal trade to Newcastle and sometimes down Channel, once rounding Dungeness in a gale, deep loaded with 140 tons of stone from Portland for London, surviving though the Rye lifeboat was lost nearby. Her mate was washed overboard but saved himself by grabbing the lee vang falls.

Howard built several coasters, larger barges with bolder sheer and deeper hull for work "down the north", to the Humber or beyond and down Channel or across to the Continent, as trade demanded. The 70-ton *Jachin* was a typical example launched in 1893 with proper coasting bulwarks and a 7 feet depth of hold. Howard maintained the fine entry and run which characterised his smaller barges and she would tramp to windward in a seaway with her long bowsprit down and the big jib set. In 1907 she was owned at Southampton by James Frost. On one passage the *Jachin* was abandoned by her crew in the Channel and was found and boarded by French fishermen, who towed her into Boulogne.

During the 1914-18 war, with freights sky high, she was driven ashore on the beach at Newhaven, Sussex, stranding across a groyne and sustaining severe damage. She was brought by Shrubshall, on the Thames and was "doubled", the term for nailing another skin of planking on to a barge's hull, and her name was changed to *Venta* to confirm with his other craft whose names began with the letter V. Miss Elsie Shrubshall was her managing owner; one of the few ladies to be so registered. The *Venta* subsequently continued her coasting and short sea trading, visiting many ports on both sides of the English Channel. For instance, in twelve months from March 1927 she made 26 consecutive passages with stone from Cherbourg to Hayling Island and Bosham in Sussex. As Channel work fell off during the 1930s the *Venta* entered the usual barge trades to East Anglian and Kentish ports, and to the Thames, under the "bob" of Francis and Guilders of Colchester. After the 1939-1945 war she was sold to Judge Blagden who had her converted as a yacht barge.

A Maldon mishap. The result of a spring high water when the barge *Mermaid* stranded her chine on the edge of Maldon's Town Quay. Fortunately timbers were able to be slipped under the chine towards amidships and as the tide fell these bore the barge safely back into the river until the next tide floated and righted her.

Howard's best remembered commercial barge was the clipper-bowed ketch *Record Reign*, launched in 1897, the year of Queen Victoria's Jubilee and a whopping 153 tons. She was 112 foot 3 inches between stem and sternpost, 24 foot 2 inches beam and drew 10 feet loaded and 7 feet light. She once loaded 282 tons of stone in the Channel trade but was designed to just fit the dimensions of Heybridge lock, to discharge timber in the basin. However, when she first entered the lock they found no allowance had been made for the rake of her graceful counter when she was deep loaded, and she could only bring in a full cargo on spring tides, at some risk to her figurehead of Queen Victoria.

She was weatherly and fast and carried a squaresail, square topsail and a topgallant; the braces for the yards leading to the mizzen rigging. Later she was fitted with "double topsails". The gaff topsails were jib-headed and the luffs set on a wire jackstay, known to bargemen as a "switching line". The tall mizzen was stepped well forward and a mizzen topsail could be set. Although a ketch, her rig was sometimes called a "Jackass schooner", because of her square canvas. With pale grey sides, black rails and white canvas she was a picture to delight a sailor's heart. Those who sailed in the *Record Reign* said that despite her flat bottom and shallow draught she was amongst the best sea boats in the coasting trade and could weather a gale comfortably. She was also handy in narrow waters and could turn away down the Blackwater from Maldon Quay, but her splendid rig needed five hands, which made her expensive to run.

184

Sadd's used her in the timber trade and she often carried big logs, besides sawn timber. She frequently voyaged to the north-east coast, returning with coal for Maldon and elsewhere. By 1907 she was owned by Joseph Sadler, the Maldon sailmaker, probably as a speculation.

Her skippers included N. Handley and Simeon Stanes of Maldon, and J. D. Sullivan who was her skipper before she was taken over by the Admiralty in 1915 to be converted to an anti-submarine decoy ship. Two 40-horse-power Bolinder engines and twin screws were installed and the exhausts were led up a tubular steel mizzen mast, to preserve her appearance as a sailing vessel. She and the similar ketch barge *Sarah Colebrooke*, were selected as anti-submarine decoys because their shallow draught was not apparent and a torpedo fired at them would pass harmlessly underneath without exploding, allowing the concealed guns to open fire on the attacking submarine. Several sailing schooners and ketches were similarly disguised as "Q" ships, as these craft became popularly known. They were manned by Naval crews dressed as merchant seamen and were commanded by Naval officers. The white ensign was broken out before they opened fire and these decoys became the terror of submarines operating around the British coast. The *Record Reign* was heavily armed; a large gun was mounted in the main hatch amidships, disguised by an imitation ship's boat which slid apart when the gun was to come into action. There were four smaller guns, probably 12-pounders, one at each bow and quarter, hidden behind false bulwarks. Despite her armament, she was never in action with a German submarine and spent much of the war in dockyards being repaired and altered.

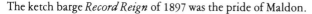

The ketch barge *Record Reign* of 1897 was the pride of Maldon.

After 1919 the *Record Reign* resumed trading for John Sadd and Son with Captain Sullivan again in command. She retained her twin screws and the fore and aft canvas, working in the coasting and short sea trades, once getting ashore on the Dutch coast and, later, was reputedly smuggling spirits into Norway. She went ashore just west of Beer, on the Devon coast, in February 1935 and was holed on rocks. She broke up there soon after.

John Howard prepared the plans for several barge yachts, which were even more shapely than his stack barges. In 1909 he launched the large yacht barge *Thoma II* for Frank Callingham of Great Baddow. She was larger than an ordinary working barge; 100 foot overall, 80 foot waterline × 18 foot 6 inches beam and drew 4 foot 6 inches with the leeboards raised. She was yachtlike, having a clipper stem, ample freeboard and fine ends, and with a counter stern the *Thoma II* resembled the earlier *Record Reign*, but was smaller. The timber for her construction cost £345 and was brought in by Jack Keeble in his barge *Emma* earning him £9 freight. The oak had been five years seasoning and was so hard that holes had to be drilled before each fastening could be driven.

The *Thoma II* was the pride of Maldon as she lay at the Town Quay ready for sea. The noted Mistley barge skipper Jim Stone was her first skipper, with a crew of three. One of them, Lewis Wakeling of Rowhedge, a yacht hand, remembered how with the owner and his family on board, a brimming high water and a brand new big barge, Jim Stone merely ordered them to single up on the moorings, set the topsail and let go, then took the wheel as she glided out from the quay on her maiden passage down the Blackwater, with half Maldon looking on. She cruised extensively from the Blackwater and on passage from Maldon to Guernsey, in the Channel Islands, in 1912, her rudder broke off Portland Bill. The owner immediately suggested a tug but Jim Stone managed to work her in to Weymouth harbour with the sails; a smart piece of seamanship. Her large sprit was a familiar sight on the east coast and when the wind failed an auxiliary motor brought her qhickly home. The start of war in 1914 found her at Oban, in the west coast of Scotland where she laid up, sailing home through the Caledonian Canal in 1919.

In 1919 Mr Callingham commissioned naval architect James A. Smith to design a mule rig for the *Thoma II*, with a sprit mainsail and gaff mizzen, but the owner died before the work was finished. The sails were made by Gowen and Mr Callingham's sons had the rigging completed. Under this rig the *Thoma II* could work along in heavy weather with the mainsail brailed up, leaving only the topsail and foresail set. Afterwards she was sold to Christopher Turnor, a member of the Royal Yacht Squadron, who thought the *Thoma II* should be rigged as a boomsail barge and had a complete alternative rig made for her. She crossed the Bay of Biscay four times under his ownership, visiting the French and Spanish coasts and later the Mediterranean, making in 1926 an eight-day passage to Gibraltar. Her hull form, rig and leeboards caused astonishment at

Riviera ports and she was remembered for years afterwards by the fishermen of St Tropez as "the yacht with wings". In 1928 she had two auxiliary engines installed but remained fully rigged and sailed from Brightlingsea in the ownership of Sir Matthew Thompson. The *Thoma II* was refitted after the 1939-45 war and raced in the 1950 Medway barge race, besides cruising the east coast. Some years later she was unrigged and converted to a motor yacht with twin screws and a large deckhouse. Since this transition she has voyaged extensively between the Mediterranean and Norway, and continues to be a useful and seaworthy yacht.

The Maldon-built barge yacht *Thoma II* in the Medway, 1948. Her clipper bow and counter stern were reminiscent of the larger trading barge *Record Reign*, also designed and built by John Howard. The *Thoma II* is still sailing as a motor yacht. *Arthur Bennett*

The ketch-rigged 97-foot barge yacht *Mamgu* was a feature of the Blackwater during the 1930s and 40s, owned by R. de B. Crawshay, who lived on board. She was built as the *Cawana* by Gill and Sons at Rochester in 1904 for marine artist W. L. Wyllie and for some years cruised on the east and south coasts rigged with a standing gaff mainsail.

187

By the 1890s Maldon regatta included a barge race and was won one year, possibly in 1890, by Gutteridge's *Morning Star*, beating the Maldon *Surprise* and *Sisters* and the *Minerva* from Southend, at the mouth of the Thames, as these races were open to outside competition. However, the last series of Maldon barge races, from 1921-1936, were restricted to local craft which raced for a challenge cup given by John Sadd and Son, Maldon timber merchants and barge owners. A short course of about 9 miles was sailed, starting off Heybridge Basin, to give room for starting over the flood tide. Later the start was moved downstream off Hilly Pool, near Mill Beach. The course was downriver to turn a buoy at the mouth of Goldhanger Creek, to the east of Osea Island, then back upriver to finish off the promenade at Maldon, sometimes several together, probably surging up the narrow river amongst the finish of a smack's race and small yachts, with cool heads needed all round.

Skipper Billy Austin at the wheel of the barge *Mirosa* in 1947.   *Arthur Bennett*

Skipper "Hobby" Keeble of Maldon at the wheel of the *Dawn* in the 1940s. *Arthur Bennett*

The barges raced in working trim, though bottoms had usually been scrubbed. They started from anchor with the mainsail brailed, but the topsail sheet was allowed to be pulled out in readiness. Unlimited crew were allowed and there was frenzied activity on board the usual three or four entries. The

Ethel Maud, owned by Greens, the Maldon millers, won the first race in 1921, sailed by George Hales, and the second in 1922. The fast *Mermaid* won in 1923, sailed by Billy Austin, who skippered her for about thirty years, and the Maldon-built *Dawn* sailed by "Hobby" Keeble won the following year, the only barge not built by John Howard to do so, having been built by Walter Cook and Son. The fast *Saltcote Belle* won the cup outright by being first in 1925-1926 and 1927, sailed by E. J. Keeble who then presented the "Ebenezer Keeble Cup" for challenge under the same rules. It was won by the *Mermaid* in 1929. The next race was in 1931, when she again won. The *Edith Maud*, sailed by Maldon's R. Hedgecock, won in 1934 and the *Emma*, sailed by Russell Dent, in 1936; the last event. By then few owners could spare a barge for the several days needed to prepare for the race, still less the expense incurred.

By 1950 Green Brothers' mill barge *Ethel Maud* was the sole survivor of the many barges once owned at Maldon, but many others traded there with cargoes of grain, timber and occasionally sand. Maldon should be seen through the masts and yards of sailing vessels and although the square riggers of its eighteenth and nineteenth century heyday are gone and cargo by sail ended during the 1950s, the resurgence of refitting yacht and charter barges which moor to its quays has revived much of its waterside atmosphere.

However, the sailing of barges for pleasure would have sorely puzzled the workaday skippers and crews of the old Maldon fleet.

Maldon waterside about 1895. The still tree-filled town clusters by the river where barges lie at Cook and Woodward's yard, below the church, with small smacks and other craft at the Town Quay beyond. Bathing machines stand on the beach and a barge drives down with the ebb.

GLOSSARY

An explanation of some of the terms used in this book. The definitions are not exhaustive and have been restricted to clarification of terms in the sense and period covered by this history.

Barge . . . . In this book the term generally refers to the spritsail, cargo carrying barges of the east coast.

Barque . . . . A three- or four-masted cargoe vessel carrying square sails on the fore and main masts and fore and off sails on the mizzen. Any barques visiting the Blackwater would be of the smaller, three-masted, type.

Bated . . . . Overhauling or examining and repairing nets. A term common in fisheries for sprats, herring and mackerel.

Belay . . . . To make a rope fast to a cleat, pin, bollard, cavil, etc. An order; ''Belay the jib sheets''.

Bermudian . . . . Bermudian rig. A main or mizzen sail, or the foresail of a schooner; of triangular shape set from the mast by slides running on a track, or by the luff rope fitting in a mast groove. Bermudian rig was revived for small racing yachts about 1911 and spread to the large racing yachts after 1919. The rig has since become predominant in sailing yachts, which were previously principally gaff rigged. Bermudian rig was commonly used by sailing craft in the West Indies at least 170 years ago. The rig as set by modern yachts is very efficient to windward and in large racers enabled the number of crew to be reduced.

Berth . . . . In shipbuilding a place on which a ship is built. ''Building berth''. A vessel is said to be ''berthed'' when she is moored alongside a quay or in a dock, i.e. ''In her berth''. To sailors, ''getting a berth'' meant obtaining a place in the crew of a vessel. In accommodation on board ship a berth meant a sleeping place for one man.

Board . . . . Making a tack to windward. ''Making a board'' (to windward). A term widely used but of obscure origin. The term may have been a survival from use of the ''Traverse Board'' for course plotting in seagoing ships.

Bobstay . . . . The chain or wire staying the end of the bowsprit to the stem.

Brig . . . . A small, square rigged cargo vessel or sailing warship. Brigs were much used on the east coast, particularly in the coal trade from the north-east coast to London.

Brigantine . . . . A three-masted cargo vessel carrying all square sails on the foremast and fore and aft sails (gaff) on the main and mizzen masts.

Bumkin . . . . A 15-18 foot clinker-planked open sailing boat used principally by winklers from West Mersea: sometimes also used for oyster dredging. Now sometimes referred to as ''winkle brigs''.

Cable . . . . The anchor cable. Substantial chain or rope attached to an anchor and from which a vessel ''rides'' or lies at anchor.

Capstan . . . . A mechanical device for hauling ropes or tackles. A cylindrical barrel mounted on a spindle is turned by capstan bars thrust into slots in its top, which are pushed round by men. Alternatively, it may be turned by one or two handles, via gearing to the capstan barrel.

Cheesecutter . . . . A peaked, close fitting seafaring cap worn by captains, mates and others in yachts and smacks during the period covered by this book.

Clipper bow . . . . A form of stem which rises from the water in a graceful, forward curving line; in yachts usually ending with a small decorative emblem at deck level. The bowsprit protruded forward extending the outreach of this stem. The mid-19th century clipper ships generally had this type of bow.

Colours . . . . An old term for an ensign and probably also a burgee (Flags).

Counter . . . . A counter stern. A usually graceful shape. In profile the under part of the vessel's stern rises at a gentle angle from the water and ends in a shapely and short, upward raking line. Counter sterns were used in most types of craft mentioned in this book.

Culch . . . . The clean shell, often oyster shell, laid broadcast over oyster layings before spring "spatfall"; the period of birth for young oysters which cling to the clean culch to commence their life cycle. Culch was often dredged from the sea bottom by sailing smacks who sold it to owners of layings. Also rubbish.

Cutter . . . . A single masted sailing craft usually setting a gaff mainsail, staysail (or foresail), jib and a topsail set above the mainsail. A jib topsail is also often set above the jib. This is a most speedy, seaworthy rig and was usual for the Essex fishing smacks and for racing yachts. Yacht's cutter; the principal small sailing boat carried by a large yacht as one of her tenders.

Draughting . . . . Drawing. Usually refers to drawing plans. Draughtsman.

Dredging . . . . Oyster dredging. A form of fishing by smacks towing oyster dredges along the sea bottom by dredge warps to gather oysters.

Fetch . . . . To sail towards and arrive at a certain position despite the wind and weather, e.g. "to fetch a mark", "to fetch a port".

Fish . . . . To catch fish. Quantity of fish. Alternatively, to repair a broken spar or mast by supporting it with spare spars or other improvised items such as hand-spikes, etc., which are bound to it with rope, like splints.

Fo'c'sle, or forecastle . . . . The forward compartment of a sailing vessel's hull. In yachts, small smacks and traditional merchant ships this was the space where the crew lived. In large smacks the crew usually lived aft and the fo'c'sle was used as a store.

Foresail . . . . More fully: "Forestaysail". An alternative term commonly used for the "staysail" in sailing vessels (see staysail). In a schooner the large fore and aft sail set on the foremast is termed the foresail.

Gaff . . . . The spar supporting the head of a gaff sail. Hoisted and lowered by the throat and peak halyards.

Gig . . . . A long, clencher built rowing boat pulled by four to eight men and usually between 22-32 feet in length. Carried by large yachts for the owner's use before small steam and later motor launches became common.

Gun punt . . . . A small, low, pointed stern boat used by wildfowlers and generally mounting a long barrelled, fixed gun.

Headsails . . . . Staysails, jibs and jib-topsails are frequently referred to as "Headsails", i.e. sails at the "head" or forward end of a vessel.

Jackyard topsail . . . . A large topsail in gaff rigged craft, principally used by racing yachts. The luff (forward end) was extended above the masthead by the topsail yard and the clew (after, upper corner) was extended beyond the end of the gaff by a "jackyard". Jackyard topsails were also sometimes set in light weather by working craft.

Jib topsail . . . . A triangular sail set from the topmast head, down the fore topmast stay above the jib. Racing yachts usually set three types of jib topsail; the "Long roper" (large), the "Baby" (small) and the "Yankee".

Ketch . . . . A two masted sailing vessel with gaff or bermudian sails on each mast. The after or mizzen mast is shorter than the mainmast (the forward mast) and is stepped forward of the vessel's sternpost or rudder stock.

GLOSSARY

Lift . . . . More correctly "Topping lift". The item of running rigging used to raise or "top" (lift) a boom. In small craft a single rope. In smacks and yachts usually also fitted with a purchase to give adequate power.

Luff . . . . The forward edge of a sail. In a gaff or bermudian sail the edge abaft the mast. To luff; the act of steering a craft closer or into the wind.

Mastheadsman . . . . A sailor with special duties aloft, particularly in a racing yacht. Large yachts had a first and second mastheadsman; positions of extra pay and advancement.

Mingle . . . . A wooden or iron instrument used to discharge sprats from a stowboat net. Mingles were placed under the after end of a net and parted off the desired amount of its contents for discharge on deck or down the fish hatch. This quantity was termed a "cod" (about four bushels).

Mizzen . . . . The after mast or sail set on the after mast, in a ketch or yawl rigged vessel. The after mast of a square rigged vessel, other than a brig or brigantine.

Moused . . . . Bound around with spunyarn.

"One-design" . . . . When all the craft of a racing class are built and equipped exactly alike to ensure that skill in handling decides the result of a race they are termed "One-design". Originally more fully: "One class—one design".

Oyster Dredge . . . . A triangular shaped iron frame with a cross bar and hoeing edge, having a rectangular shaped net with an iron mesh bottom and fibre net upper part or back, and tapering sides. The net is held parallel to the hoeing edge at its rear end by a cross stick laced to it. Dredges were generally of two sizes; small ones about three feet across the hoe and large or deep sea dredges often six feet or rather more, across the hoe or "scythe". Dredges were towed by bass rope warps from the smack, in varying numbers depending on the work.

Oyster dredgers . . . . Fishermen cultivating or gathering oysters with dredges towed by smacks or oyster skiffs. Alternatively, smacks engaged in an oyster fishery.

Oyster layings . . . . Areas of a river or creek noted for the good growth of oysters. Usually clearly marked by withies (saplings driven into the bottom with their heads above water). Layings were frequently owned by individuals; oyster dredgers and merchants.

Oyster skiff . . . . A beamy, shallow draught, clench-built open boat about 18-25 feet in length, used for transporting oysters from smacks to shore, or to oyster layings. Usually rowed or sculled by an oar over the stern.

Peter Boat . . . . Term used by Essex fishermen for a pointed stern sloop- or cutter-rigged fishing boat of the Thames.

Prize money . . . . Paid to crews of racing yachts, or smacks racing in regattas, from the money given as a prize. In racing yachts prize money formed a substantial supplement to the crew's wages, which for a hand in a fast yacht might almost be doubled thereby. Racing yachts' captains and mates received a larger proportion of the prize money than the hands.

Quarter . . . . The sides of a vessel's stern, i.e. the port and starboard quarters.

Raking . . . . Rake. As applied to a vessel's rig this means at an angle to the vertical, e.g. "raking masts"; masts sloping aft. "Rakish"; with much rake or speedy looking.

Ratlines . . . . Ropes secured at vertical intervals between the shrouds supporting a mast to provide a "ladder" for climbing the shrouds to the mast heads.

Reef . . . . To reduce the area of a sail by reefing. The position line of a reef across a sail. To reef; act of reefing. Reefed. Reef points; short lengths of rope sewn to a sail at the line of a reef. The sail below the reef points is bunched up after the reef pendants have been hauled taut (see reef pendants) and the points tied under the sail in a knot, reducing the sail area.

Reef pendants . . . . Stout ropes which are rove through "cringles" (reinforced holes) at the luff and leech (forward and after edges) of a sail and which are hauled down taut to the boom before tying the reef points, e.g. "Hauling down a reef". "Shake out a reef"; to untie the reef points and release the pendants to restore sail area.

192

Rigger . . . . A skilled man usually employed by a shipyard or yachtyard to make and overhaul rigging. Often an ex-seaman with exceptional skill in working with fibre or steel rope.

Ruck, rucked . . . . When the peak or upper end of a gaff sail is lowered by its halyard to swing freely, while the luff remained set up taut, the peak is said to be "rucked", rendering the sail less powerful in driving effect. A manoeuvre much used to regulate a vessel's speed when fishing, coming to anchor or moorings, or to ease her in bad weather. An alternative term for ruck is to "scandalise" a gaff sail.

"Runners" or running backstays . . . . Stays supporting a mast at the "hounds" and leading aft. These were usually of wire (the runner pendant), the windward of which was set up by a tackle (the runner tackle).

Salvager . . . . A seaman or a smack engaged in giving assistance to a stranded or wrecked vessel, particularly in winter: helping to save life or remove cargo and equipment from wrecks.

Schooner . . . . A two or more masted sailing vessel with the masts of equal, or almost equal, height and fore and aft sails, either gaff or bermudian, set on each mast, also having headsails forward of the foremast. Schooners fitted with square topsails were termed "topsail schooners".

Scope . . . . The amount of cable let out and to which a vessel lays at anchor, e.g. "Give her more scope; pay out more cable.

Set . . . . A fore and aft sail is set when it is hoisted. A square sail may be set when it is loosed from the yard and sheeted.

Sheer . . . . The line of a vessel's profile at deck or the top of the bulwarks; usually a gentle curve. "A sweeping sheer". Alternatively, sheer; to move obliquely through the water, commonly against the tide: "to take a sheer".

"Shifters" or shifting backstays . . . . Stays supporting a topmast head and leading aft. These were usually of wire (the shifter pendant) which was set up by a tackle (the shifter tackle). They were called "Shifters" because, unlike the runners, they had to be "shifted", i.e. slacked right off and the windward one set up, at each tack the vessel made.

Shrouds . . . . Wire rope rigging transversely supporting a mast and set taut with rigging screws or "deadeyes and lanyards". Before c. 1870 shrouds were usually of hemp rope, which stretched badly.

Smack . . . . A cutter or ketch rigged sailing vessel used for fishing. These craft were developed to near perfection by the Essex fishermen and shipbuilders.

Spit . . . . The point of a shoal.

Spitfire . . . . A small storm jib.

Spreaders . . . . A pair of struts supporting topmast shrouds on a mast. An earlier term was "Crosstrees".

Stack barge . . . . A spritsail barge built for or adpated to the carriage of hay and straw in bulk, including the building of a stack on deck.

Staysail . . . . The triangular sail immediately forward of the mainmast or foremast in fore and aft rigged craft. More fully, forestaysail (see foresail).

Stem . . . . The forward member or edge of a vessel's bow.

Stowboat net. (Stow net) . . . . The large, close-meshed, funnel-shaped sprat net of the Essex and Hampshire fisheries. It is now obsolete. Dating from the Middle Ages this was earlier known as the "stall net" from the smack setting it lying at anchor with the net beneath her, when fishing.

Tingle . . . . A marine borer which feeds on oysters.

Topmast . . . . An addition to the head of the lowermast usually attached to its forward side and arranged to "house" or lower when required either for relieving strain on the vessel in bad weather or for repair. Most of the Essex smacks and the gaff rigged yachts were fitted with topmasts which could be housed.

Topsail . . . . The sail set from a topmast above a gaff main or mizzen sail, or above the gaff foresail in a schooner. Also a "square topsail" in square rigged vessels such as brigs, barques, etc., or in a topsail schooner.

Trawl . . . . A fishing net and associated gear for catching bottom-swimming fish and shrimps. The "beam trawl" was the type used by the sailing smacks. A triangular shaped net spread behind a wooden beam which might be 25-35 feet long. This was towed astern of the smack, along the sea bottom, by a rope warp whcih passed through a large block attached to the trawl heads at each end of the beam by a rope bridle. The net was attached at the upper forward edge to the beam by lacings, and at the bottom forward edge to a ground rope between the heads, which might be weighted to seek out fish lying close to the bottom. At each end of the beam an iron trawl head carried it above the bottom in a sledge-like manner. The trawl nets mesh varied with the type of fish to be caught. The smallest mesh being used for shrimps. When trawling, fish entered the net's mouth and were trapped in its apex called the "cod end". Those attempting to escape back towards the mouth along the net were caught in pockets in the wings or sides. The trawl was hauled up by the trawl warp by hand, or with the aid of a hand capstan in the Essex smacks.

Trim . . . . The adjustment of a vessel's floating disposition longitudinally or transversely, e.g. "Trimmed by the stern"; a vessel drawing more water aft than forward. To trim sheets (of sails); to adjust the sheets. To trim cargo; to level or adjust it for the best seaworthiness.

Truss, trice-up . . . . When the tack of a gaff sail is lifted part way up the mast by a tricing line (truss) or tackle, the tack is said to be "triced up".

Trysail . . . . A sail of moderate area usually set as a substitute for the mainsail in storms, or in case of accident to the mainsail. Large racing yachts set a trysail for passagemaking to preserve the set of the racing mainsail. A storm trysail was of much smaller area than a mainsail and was made of stouter sailcloth. Until about 1914 trysails were usually quadrilateral and were set by a trysail gaff. In later years they were increasingly triangular.

Ways . . . . Long wooden timbers of rectangular section placed under a vessel to be launched. There were two sets; the fixed or "ground ways" and the upper or "sliding ways". The surface between them was well greased to permit easy movement when the time came for the launch. Similar ways were sometimes used in small yards to haul vessels out of the water. They were also commonly used to "strike over" craft of all sizes and types which needed to be moved about in a ship or yacht yard.

Wending . . . . A term for staying round or coming about when sailing to windward. To wend.

Windlass . . . . The mechanism for raising an anchor. The Essex smacks were fitted with a primitive wooden windlass, the barrel of which was rotated by two handspikes fitting into slots and turned by one or more men. Several turns of the chain cable were taken round the barrel which could be retained by a ratchet pawl. After about 1850 most yachts had a compact iron windlass of patent design, or an iron capstan.

Yawl . . . . A two masted sailing vessel with gaff or bermudian sails on each mast. The after or mizzen mast is considerably shorter than the mainmast and is stepped aft of the sternpost or rudder stock. Also, a fishing vessel, often cutter-rigged, of the Blackwater or from Whitstable.

Index

About the Author

BORN into a Liverpool family of seafaring, shipbuilding and marine engineering background, the author moved as a boy, with his parents, to north-east Essex where his mother's family had long been prominent in fishing and yachting.

John Leather is by profession a Naval Architect and was involved with the design, construction and survey of ships of many sizes and types throughout his career. He is a Fellow of The Royal Institution of Naval Architects and a Chartered Engineer.

Since 1945 he has owned a succession of small sailing, motor and rowing craft in which he has explored east and south coast waters. His first book, GAFF RIG, won the Daily Express 'Best Book of the Sea' award in 1970 and his second, THE NORTHSEAMAN, won second prize in 1971. He is author of thirteen other maritime books.